Reverse Engineering Deals on Wall Street with Microsoft Excel

Founded in 1807, John Wiley & Sons is the oldest independent publish company in the United States. With offices in North America, Europe, Austra, and Asia, Wiley is globally committed to developing and marketing print and etronic products and services for our customers' professional and personal knowle and understanding.

The Wiley Trading series features books by traders who have survived market's ever-changing temperament and have prospered—some by reinventing stems, others by getting back to basics. Whether a novice trader, professional, or sowhere in-between, these books will provide the advice and strategies needed to proer today and well into the future.

For a list of available titles, visit our web site at www.WileyFinance.co

Reverse Engineering Deals on Wall Street with Microsoft Excel

A Step-by-Step Guide

KEITH A. ALLMAN

John Wiley & Sons, Inc.

Published by John Wiley & Sons, Inc., Hoboken, New Jersey.
Published simultaneously in Canada.

For general information on our other products and services or for technical support, please contact our Customer Care Department within the United States at (800) 762-2974, outside the United States at (317) 572-3993 or fax (317) 572-4002.

Wiley also publishes its books in a variety of electronic formats. Some content that appears in print may not be available in electronic books. For more information about Wiley products, visit our web site at www.wiley.com.

Library of Congress Cataloging-in-Publication Data:

Allman, Keith A., 1977–
   Reverse engineering deals on Wall Street with Microsoft Excel : a step-by-step guide / Keith A. Allman.
      p. cm. — (Wiley finance series)
   Includes index.
   ISBN 978-0-470-24205-6 (paper/cd-rom)
   1. Financial engineering—Mathematical models.   2. Investments—Mathematical models.
3. Deals—Mathematical models.   4. Microsoft Excel (Computer file)   I. Title.
   HG176.7.A45 2009
   338.8′30285554–dc22

                                                                                    2008025012

Printed in the United States of America.

10 9 8 7 6 5 4 3 2 1

Contents

Preface

Years after starting my career in financial modeling at a bond insurer, I decided it was time to move on to Citigroup's conduit to advance my knowledge of the securitization industry. I was no longer a newbie analyst with the lurking fear of not knowing enough about modeling or structured finance to justify my employment. Instead, I joined as a semiseasoned associate, questioning if the skills and knowledge I had thus far accumulated justified the lateral hiring. Luckily I was presented with a task my first week of work at Citigroup that would provide the answer to such a question, and given my place on the corporate food chain at the time, I would have to accept that answer whether I liked it or not.

The task at hand was to validate the conduit's mortgage model to ensure that all calculation processes were correct and that the model essentially returned accurate durations, yields, and, ultimately, rating assessments of a transaction. "No problem," I thought. "Enter data, push a few buttons, determine some durations and yields, and I complete my first task." Like any great underestimation in life those were the thoughts of grandeur prior to the fall. I quickly learned that the process was going to be much more intense.

To validate the model I had to have one of the top four auditing firms provide a letter stating that the conduit's model returned the same results as the auditing firm's model. To obtain such a letter I had to select a deal with the auditor that was publicly rated and would cover many mortgage modeling concepts. The auditor and I would have to model the deals on our systems and tie durations and yields to the fifth decimal place. Still, it was my first week and I thought, "Well, that's a bit more complicated than I thought, but they have a mortgage model, so how difficult could it be?"

Let's just say, it was difficult. Opening the existing mortgage model, I found that it was a standard amortization engine. For those new to structured finance, this means that only the asset amortization was mostly done. There was essentially no liability structure in place and the deal we selected had nine tranches of debt, ratio-stripped classes, prepayment lockouts, and a host of other complexities. At this realization I took a breath, peered above my cube to see if somehow my boss had sensed the fear emanating from outside his office, and sat down again to refocus. How would I accomplish this task in a relatively short period of time? I stared at the 273-page document on my desk that would be my savior: the deal prospectus.

I got to know the deal prospectus for that transaction very well. I took it with me everywhere. I read it at home, on the subway, in my cube, on planes, and any other imaginable place. I realized that the prospectus was a very large map to proving my competence. I navigated through dates, timing issues, special amortization assumptions, complex liabilities, and advanced structuring concepts. Each page represented a section in my model. After a few weeks, I transformed legal jargon into functions, formulas, and code. The end result was, in my mind, a beautiful, harmonic merger of words and numbers. I use the words "in my mind" because as readers of finance material, you probably know the looks you get when trying to convey any excitement about this topic. Regardless of my enthusiasm level, I did tie to the fifth decimal place with the auditor's output sheets and successfully completed my first task.

I often compare that model audit experience to when I first started in the finance industry and had to build a more basic model from scratch. I was overwhelmed by the task and worked incredibly hard to get a simple senior subordinated structure to work correctly. Similarly, reverse engineering the prospectus to be able to tie to the auditor's model took hours of reading and rereading lawyers' prose. Testing amortization scenarios and checking the resulting yields and durations consumed entire days. I had to constantly flip between reading sections of the prospectus to understand the details, working on my model to implement them, and then jumping back to the prospectus and the auditor's printouts to check if I was correct.

Luckily, I already had a background in understanding deal documentation from my prior work in the financial guarantee business. As a third party to transactions providing financial guarantees, the company I worked for rarely wrote the bulk of the documents. Instead, we had to adapt a large amount of other bankers' and lawyers' writing into our analyses. Reading literally hundreds of term sheets and indentures made me relatively fluent in legal terminology and conventions.

Even with my prior experience, the task of reverse engineering a deal was not simple. It required many hours spent coming to a solution that could have easily been explained to me by a more senior professional. Unfortunately, given division budgets, such a senior professional on hand to answer modeling questions is a fantasy. Obtaining that knowledge in a text is much more of a reality, which was the logic for writing my first book on building a basic structured finance model from a blank spreadsheet.

However, reverse engineering a complete Wall Street transaction is much more complicated than just building a basic model. These complications have been highlighted by the subprime crisis that started in mid-2007. Some investors, risk managers, and many financial professionals responsible for structuring, purchasing, and trading Wall Street products only took rudimentary approaches to analyzing these complex securities, often relying on credit ratings alone. Whereas the collateral posed a major problem, with underwriters offering risky products to poor credit quality borrowers, the structures of these transactions became so complicated that, as the markets deteriorated, people with exposure became unsure of how the transactions would perform. Ultimately, investors were not clear if the deteriorated assets would produce enough cash to pay their tranches of debt. Complicated triggers and alterations in cash priority further exacerbated the problem. With sometimes hundreds of securities having similar collateral and virtually meaningless ratings, investors did not know how to price their securities, and chaos reigned in the market.

A properly trained staff of reverse engineers can solve this problem for any company. Most of the information required to model individual deals is available from multiple public sources. Understanding how to translate that information into an intelligible form is a challenge that this book addresses. I firmly believe that whether you are an investor, banker, auditor, or a student learning the business, thoroughly understanding the documentation and how it is translated into a computer-based model ultimately provides a complete understanding of deal mechanics and gives you the power to make confident, well-informed decisions.

KEITH A. ALLMAN

New York, New York
October 2008

Acknowledgments

The idea for this book started right after a training session I facilitated through my financial training company Enstruct. It was a three-day course on financial modeling for a large bank that wanted to focus on understanding the calculations behind the complex terminology in deal documentation. I cannot divulge the bank's name, but I thank them for helping stimulate the idea. From that point on, a number of people have helped me along the way. Primarily, Ralph Armenta provided a great recommendation in using the example deal that is reversed in this book and assisted with materials collection. Another excellent resource was Permjit Singh, who reviewed material that I sent and offered corrections and detail verification. Permjit is extremely detail oriented and incredible at finding even the smallest discrepancy. Finally, I would like to thank all of the staff at John Wiley & Sons who work on my books: Emilie Herman, Laura Walsh, Mary Daniello, and Bill Falloon.

K. A. A.

About the Author

Keith Allman is the founder and principal trainer of Enstruct, a financial training company that specializes in quantitative finance and modeling instruction. He began Enstruct as a structured finance-focused training company, but has expanded the core curriculum to cover other topics such as corporate modeling, valuation, programming for finance, and using applications outside of Excel for more robust financial analysis. Mr. Allman also leads the consultancy work that Enstruct has been engaged in, which has largely been structured finance–related, such as mortgage and auto securitizations. His particular area of expertise is international in scope, with training and transaction work in most of Latin America, the Caribbean, the Middle East, South East Asia, Australia, Russia, and parts of Southern and Western Africa.

Prior to his current position, he was a Vice President in the Global Special Situations Group at Citigroup, where he focused on principal finance in emerging markets. Previously, he worked in Citigroup's Global Securitized Markets division modeling conduit transactions and in MBIA Corporation's Quantitative Analytics group. Mr. Allman is also the author of *Modeling Structured Finance Cash Flows with Excel: A Step-by-Step Guide* (Wiley & Sons 2007). His education includes a master's degree in international affairs with a concentration in finance and banking from Columbia University and dual bachelor degrees from UCLA.

Reverse Engineering Deals on Wall Street with Microsoft Excel

CHAPTER 1

Introduction

In my first book, *Modeling Structured Finance Cash Flows with Microsoft Excel: A Step-by-Step Guide*, I took readers through building a basic structured finance model from a blank worksheet. The text is a practical guide to transforming the concepts of a structured finance deal into an Excel-based model. However, in the finance industry, few people rely on a concept to close a deal. Instead, they rely on strict legal documentation that dictates the precise mechanics of the transaction. The difference between a deal based on general concepts and one based on well-defined rules can be substantial. This is why documentation exists for every concept in a deal. Attorneys spend hours writing terms sheets and indentures, banking associates review every word and integrate documents into a deal prospectus, and finally junior analysts lose sleep formatting and making charts to enhance the final prospectus.

Unfortunately, even with all this effort, reading through deal documentation can be arduous and difficult to interpret. However, well-written documentation provides a wealth of valuable information for those who want to know exactly how the deal works. Parties to the deal want to make sure every part of the transaction is well defined and published for understanding. Investors are the primary third-party readers who need to understand all the risks and rewards prior to investing in the deal. Savvy financial institutions read their competition's prospectuses to keep track of developments in structures. Auditors can use a public prospectus as a basis for evaluating a client's model. In general, anyone interested in understanding industries, asset classes, or even specific deals can gain valuable insights from deal documentation.

Reading through documentation allows for a strong understanding of the details, but the real value of documentation is that a reader can actually use the documents to reverse engineer a computer-based model of the transaction. Public prospectuses alone provide all or nearly all the information necessary to build a model that is representative of the deal. The resulting model will allow investors to see precise investment returns and the scenarios where their yields or durations are stressed. Financial institutions can model transactions to see the quantitative results of certain structures under differing stresses. They can also select a prospectus, use an internal model to reverse engineer the prospectus, hire an auditor to reverse engineer the same deal, and check both models' outputs to calibrate and audit the financial institution's model.

THE TRANSACTION

Many types of Wall Street deals can be reverse engineered. No doubt my background in structured finance influenced my decision to choose a mortgage-backed security as the example that will run through this book. However, structured finance transactions are ideal examples for reverse engineers to learn from because they are heavily documented. The deal chosen for this book is the Citigroup Mortgage Loan Trust 2006-WF2, serviced by Wells Fargo.

You do not need to be a structured finance professional to gain knowledge from this book. The focus will be on how legal documentation transforms into modeling. For those unfamiliar with structured finance transactions, specifically mortgage-backed securities, entire books are available that can help explain the concepts. For those who have an understanding of structured finance transactions, this book will reveal the inner workings of all the complex challenges presented in understanding and modeling a modern mortgage-backed security. For the benefit of the unfamiliar reader, and as a basic review for the seasoned professional, I will briefly explain the basics of this type of transaction.

Citigroup Mortgage Loan Trust 2006-WF2 is a mortgage-backed security issuance with seven senior tranches and five mezzanine tranches of debt. In general, a mortgage-backed transaction is composed of these *tranches* or "slices" of debt, which have each been funded by investors. The investors receive principal and interest that are primarily generated from assets. In this case, the assets are thousands of mortgages that have been pooled together. The interest and principal that mortgage obligors are paying are aggregated and passed through to the transaction. Depending on the tranche invested in, investors will receive certain allocations of this interest and principal. The basic transaction structure is shown in Figure 1.1.

THE DOCUMENTS

So where do you begin? First we should clarify what each document is, what it does, and what information we can procure from it. For this review, we turn to the Securities Act of 1933, the origin of securities registration. This act requires issuers to provide information about their transaction in the form of a registration statement. The exact information required by the Securities Act is detailed in Schedules A and B of the act. Other key documents that will be reviewed are shown in Figure 1.2.

Prospectus

The Securities Act requires a prospectus that discloses important facts regarding the company and the proposed transaction. The prospectus must provide full

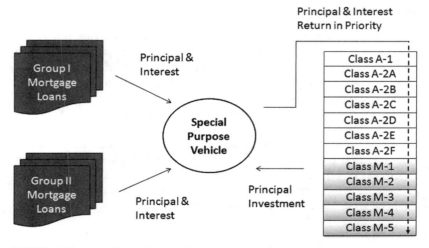

FIGURE 1.1 The flow of a standard structured finance transaction.

disclosure of all relevant facts about the securities being issued. The most important information includes:

- Information about the parties to the transaction such as the issuer, underwriter, and any entity owning greater than a 10% share.
- The amount of the issuer's securities owned by the parties to the transaction.
- The amount of debt created by the offered security, along with descriptions of the debt in terms of date, maturity, character, rate of interest, amortization style, and any terms of substitution.
- A balance sheet of the issuer.
- A profit-and-loss statement of the issuer.

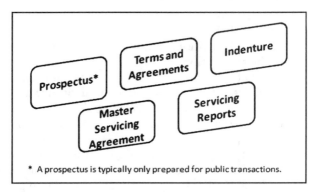

FIGURE 1.2 The core documents of a transaction.

Terms and Agreements Sheet

Prior to the creation of a prospectus, documentation begins with a terms and agreements sheet (*terms sheet* for short). Besides a few preliminary legal agreements such as confidentiality agreements, a terms sheet is one of the first major documents created for a transaction. As the name suggests, the terms sheet defines key terms for the transaction and is a precursor to a prospectus. Often a prospectus will even have a section called "Terms Sheet," which provides important, selected information regarding the transaction.

For private transactions that are not sold into the public capital markets and therefore do not require a prospectus, a terms sheet is often the central document of the deal. Regardless of public or private intent, the terms sheet is often the document that is passed between parties and marked up as they come to agreement. A standard terms sheet for an asset-backed transaction includes:

Transaction Overview: A description of the deal, program, or facility.

Parties: The parties involved in the transaction including, but not limited to the borrower, seller, lender, servicer, trustee, collateral agent, custodian, liquidity provider, swap counterparties, rating agencies, and any other key parties to the transaction.

Program: A more detailed description of each aspect of the program that can be broken down into the following components:

- Fees: The percentage of variable and fixed fee amounts due to parties in the transaction.
- Debt Description: Important information regarding the debt size, pricing, tenor, call terms, and dates.
- Collateral: Eligibility criteria, concentration limits, and collateral definitions (e.g., default vs. delinquency).
- Priority of Payments: A description of all allocations of money during a collection period, which often changes depending on triggered events, such as an event of default.
- Credit Enhancement: Details of any reserve accounts or overcollateralization mechanisms/calculations.
- Hedges: Description of any derivatives or hedging mechanisms and parties in the transaction.
- Events of Default: Definitions for when the transaction is considered to be in default. These can be both qualitative and quantitative.
- Representations and Warranties: A detailed section that make a number of important items clear between parties, such as the financial soundness of the parties, authority to enter into the transaction, no conflicts of interest, no pending litigation, enforceability of documents, accuracy of information, government regulations, margin regulations, taxes, solvency, and many other statements that prevent ambiguities about each party and their role in the transaction.

Indenture

An *indenture* is essentially a contract between bondholders and a bond issuer. The indenture details the specifics of the bond issuance including rate, term, priority of payments, and so on. Its relation to structured finance is that an indenture exists between the trust, which is technically issuing the bonds, and the investors who are purchasing a share of the trust.

Master Servicing Agreement

A master servicing agreement (MSA) explains and defines the role of the servicer and how they will service the assets. This agreement should detail specifically how the servicer defines assets into certain states such as delinquent or defaulted. The MSA should also explain conditions for advancing missed interest or principal.

Servicing Reports

Most deals that require monthly servicing of assets are required to have some type of monthly report. This report often contains valuable data for reverse engineering, such as current asset characteristics. This is important because it allows the reverse engineer to see the current state of the assets with regard to balance, rates, periods, and so on. A reverse engineer can use this data to create expected cash flow into a transaction.

Limited performance data can also be obtained by carefully analyzing a series of servicing reports. Usually information on delinquent, defaulted, and prepaid assets is available. This information allows a reverse engineer to piece together transition rates and possibly default and prepayment curves depending how the data is reported. You should be very careful about the rates that are used in servicing reports. For instance, defaulted assets are often reported as a percentage of current balance, which is not the ideal way to capture and use default data.

Liability data is also usually included in servicing reports. The important data includes the current balance of the liabilities, the rates they are paying at, and maturity dates. This is information that a reverse engineer can use to get a current picture of the liability exposures and enhancement percentages (liability data shows the balances, so one can make a general guess on the liability priority to estimate credit enhancement).

A servicing report also shows the current status of tests and triggers. This will be seen in detail later in the text, but understanding the trigger and test calculations is important to engineering a model that correctly captures actual cash flow. Note though that a servicing report usually does not provide enough information to completely show the liability structure, namely the priority of payments.

Information Availability

One of the challenges that a reverse engineer has is obtaining information. If the reverse engineer is reversing a deal with the cooperation of the originator or a party close to the transaction, then obtaining many deal documents may be relatively easy. He or she may be able to access loan level data tapes, loss curves, or granular recovery information. However, the more distant the reverse engineer is from the source of the deal, the more difficult it will be to obtain such information. This is where the reverse engineer's ingenuity and analytical ability come into play.

THE PROCESS

Given the vast quantities of information available from documents, there needs to be a systematic approach to reverse engineering a transaction. The process can be generally encompassed by following these four steps:

1. Read
2. Conceptualize
3. Transform
4. Verify

The process, as a whole, is similar to creating a map of a hiking trail. The cartographer should first have a general idea of the area that he or she wants to map. This is akin to taking a survey of the area from above or from a vantage point that helps show a majority of the project area. Once the area is surveyed, the cartographer then begins the process of determining the relevant items on the landscape to incorporate on the map: the trail path, bodies of water, elevations, dangerous areas, roads, rails, and so on. He or she must conceptualize what objects to represent on the final map. Next the cartographer goes through the tedious process of transforming those objects to paper and digital media. Finally, the cartographer will want to test out the accuracy of the map, perhaps by trying to use it to navigate the trail.

My construction process is conceptually very similar in many respects. Let's take a look at each step in more detail.

1. Read

It may sound simple, but for first-time reverse engineers I suggest a page-through of the prospectus. A question I normally get at this point is: "Do I have to read the whole prospectus cover to cover?" I usually answer "Yes" to this question, because if a person is new enough to the process to ask the question, then they should probably read every page. As one's skill and experience increases over time, there will be sections that the reverse engineer can skip or pass through quickly. However, a new reverse engineer might skip over important sections such as footnotes that directly contribute to a section of the complete model.

Eventually, as you get more familiar with documentation, you'll tend to jump to specific sections of the prospectus to be able to pull the necessary data. Although this may be appropriate in many situations, a quick scan of the entire document is preferable, as new deals are constantly evolving with subtle differences that have profound impacts on transactions.

2. Conceptualize

The conceptualization part of reverse engineering seems ambiguous, but one of the goals of this book is to develop a system for breaking down the information in the documentation so it can be applied to an Excel-based model. Conceptualization is the process of grouping related data points so they can be applied to all necessary sections of the model. The primary groups of data that are necessary to reverse engineer a deal include:

- Dates and Timing
- Asset Performance
- Asset Amortization
- Liabilities
- Structural Components
- Metrics

As you progress through the documentation you should take notes of each data point that can be grouped into one of these cohorts. This prepares the reverse engineer for the next step, transformation.

3. Transform

With all the data grouped accordingly, the next step is to transform the data into a working Excel model. This is done by incorporating each data point in its relevant group into a fully dynamic model. Each group on its own is of little value, but combined, they produce a working model where the deal is clearly visible and assumptions can be changed to see the impact on the transaction. Every conceptual section needs to be transformed.

Dates and Timing   Dates and timing need to be incorporated as scalar and vector inputs. These will create the framework for the model, upon which all other sections are predicated. The date and timing inputs must be set up in a dynamic framework because of the unique timing challenges that reverse engineering presents. A deal can be reversed at any time after closure and can either be completely paid off, where the dates and timing are all historical or the deal can be in progress and the timing will be a combination of historical and projected. Also, the reverse engineer has the option to model the deal from closure as a new transaction, where all the dates and timing are projected.

For the most part, the dates and timing used will be tied to the deal documentation, but if the reverse engineer envisions running any scenarios that require altering the dates or timing, then the computer setup must be done so that the user can quickly alter any of the inputs and have the resulting change flow through the model.

Asset Performance   The next concept, Asset Performance, is incredibly important because the assumptions related to asset performance have the most profound impact on transaction performance. The two main performance factors for asset-backed securities are loss and prepayment. How loss and prepayments are modeled in a transaction can vary widely between deals, and also between the deal and how it is presented in the final documentation. Between deals, the loss calculations may use different bases such as defaults based off original balance or defaults based off current balance. Prepayments might be expressed as conditional prepayment rate (CPR), absolute prepayment speed (ABS), or a number of other prepayment methodologies.

Standardized rates for certain asset classes may also be used. For example, in mortgage modeling, the final prospectus might show the results of using various standard default assumption (SDA) curves in combination with various Public Securities Association prepayment (PSA) curves. Whereas these curves might be shown in the public prospectus, the originator or banker may have performed a more granular analysis on the historical loan level data.

With such variability of information, the best practice would be to first reverse the deal with available information that can be checked against outputs in the model. I discuss this process in the "Verify" section of this chapter. After the model is verified, the reverse engineer can try other performance assumptions that might not be explicitly stated in the available documentation, such as using a custom loss curve that might be more representative of the assets instead of an SDA assumption. Because this situation is similar to Dates and Timing, where there may be a number of possible performance inputs, flexibility should be kept in mind while building the model.

Asset Amortization   Asset amortization itself is a straightforward process, however, it can get complicated when having to reverse engineer a deal. The complications arise because a number of methods can be employed for amortization. For term deals, where the assets that were sold into the deal are the only assets that will ever exist in the transaction, loan level amortization is often done by the original structurer. However, loan level information is never incorporated directly into the prospectus and it may not be readily available. In the prospectus, though, there is often data on loan groups, known as representative lines (*rep lines* for short) that "represent" all the assets in the deal. To initially verify a deal the rep lines can be used for reverse engineering.

Many private deals done in conduits or other financing vehicles are set to revolve where, as assets pay off or default, new ones can be added. This presents a challenge for amortization that is overcome by instituting rigorous eligibility criteria. As mentioned earlier, eligibility criteria are typically detailed in the deal documentation. Original deal structurers usually create rep lines for the assets based on the most adverse limits of the eligibility criteria. For instance, imagine an agricultural equipment deal where the eligibility criteria allowed for concentrations of no more than 40% cranes, 40% harvesters, 5% pivots, 10% dusters, and 5% tractors. Now from a static loss analysis the structurer sees that pivots have the worst loss rates. Even if the originator only plans on selling 1% of total assets as pivots into the pool, the structurer must assume that 5% of the assets are pivots. There is no guarantee except for the eligibility criteria on the concentration of assets.

This is important because when it is time to amortize the assets, the structurer should create a separate rep line for pivots and use the default rate for pivots to amortize the assets out. Likewise, unless the amortization assumptions are explicitly stated, the reverse engineer will want to amortize the assets using rep lines that represent the most adverse possible pool.

Amortizing loans or rep lines can be a challenge for a reverse engineer because there can be many, many amortization schedules to create and aggregate. Solutions do exist in Excel, but a powerful option is to use Visual Basic Applications (VBA) code to transform the amortization concept into the computer model. This book covers the code necessary to amortize a loan in VBA.

One additional complexity in reverse engineering a deal occurs if the assets pay interest on a floating-rate basis. This requires the reverse engineer to find the proper rates at the time of the deal. Also, depending on when the analysis is being completed vis-à-vis the inception of the deal, a combination of actual and expected rates might be necessary.

Liabilities The bonds, notes, or certificates that fund the deal are the easiest to reverse engineer because the Securities Act requires their characteristics and terms to be precisely laid out in the documentation. The two main types of data necessary to reverse engineer the liabilities can be grouped into loan characteristic data and deal level liability data. Loan characteristic data includes items such as original balance, current balance, fixed rate, index, margin, original term, remaining term, or any other data necessary to correctly amortize the loan. Deal level liability data is information pertaining to the ordering and style of liability payment.

Note that the style of liability payment classified as deal level liability data can be confusing to differentiate from the loan amortization created from loan characteristic data. The difference is caused by the potential of the transaction structure to alter the standard amortization of the liability. The loan characteristic data instructs the reverse engineer on how to amortize the loan as a separate entity, however, the deal level liability data refines the amortization by giving instructions on how the liability is paid when it's incorporated into the deal.

Structural Components   I touched on structural components when I described deal level liability data, but given the number of possible structural features, they can be classified as a group of their own. Structural components include features such as triggers, swaps, reserve accounts, wraps, credit guarantees, and any other mechanisms that direct the flow of payments or attempt to mitigate the cash flow divergences or shortfalls caused by prepayment, default, and other risks, such as interest rate mismatches or foreign exchange rates.

Reverse engineering structural components can vary in difficulty. Reserve accounts, wraps, and credit guarantees are relatively easy to incorporate into a model. They are all mechanisms to cover shortfalls of cash. Each has inputs to determine how much loss the mechanism will cover, if and how the mechanism gets reimbursed, how much the mechanism costs, and a detailed description of which liabilities can use the mechanism and the ordering for all the fees and reimbursements resulting from the mechanism.

Triggers are tests in a deal that, if failed, can cause the liability structure to change. Quantitative triggers are easy to model because they are just conditional statements based on a test involving numeric comparisons. However, qualitative triggers exist in transactions that are sometimes accounted for during the original sizing, making it difficult for the reverse engineer to model. For example, in a private transaction, a structurer might run a scenario where they test for an event of default based on the bankruptcy of the originator a year from the start of the transaction. The structurer notices that the current structure would sustain a slight loss in such a case and suggests advancing the originator a smaller amount to mitigate against such a scenario. Without the knowledge of such steps, a reverse engineer would not know why the advance rate was set slightly lower than quantitatively necessary.

A more difficult component to reverse engineer can be derivatives in a transaction, such as a swap. Although swap rates can be assumed as the liability rates, a more precise model would want to use the swap rates in combination with market rates and the notional schedule to determine how much cash was flowing in and out of the transaction because of the derivative. For a reverse engineer this can require some research to transform a swap into a working model. The reverse engineer will have to find historic market rates and try to see how the swaps paid or took in money based on the prevailing rates.

Finally, there are a number of structural components that structurers create on their own. These are structures such as yield supplement over collateralization accounts (YSOA), net weighted average coupon (WAC) carryover, cross collateralization, and so on. Each of these changes the cash flow in very specific ways to parse and mitigate loss. For instance, YSOA accounts are typically used in auto transactions when there are auto loans in the pool that are under the deal funding rate. The extreme example is when an auto lender offers zero percent financing. The obligor is not paying any interest, but is making up for the difference in their principal amount. However, this would be a problem for a structured transaction that is a true pass-through security because there are fees and interest to be paid to debt holders. In a pass-through, the entire principal would be passed through to the debt holders and there would be nothing for transaction fees and interest. Structurers have created methods for discounting the principal of the assets so that they create an implied interest amount to be used in the waterfall. Most structurers that create YSOA accounts include a schedule of the YSOA balance, however, newer structurers have been using dynamic accounts, which are difficult to reverse engineer.

The same is true of other substructures that are very complex in nature, but only vaguely described in the deal documentation. This forces the reverse engineer to look for auxiliary data that can allow him or her to back into the correct calculations. These substructures are usually transformed last as they can be the most difficult to verify the model with when incorporated.

Metrics   Beyond analytical purposes, metrics such as yield, duration, and weighted average life allow reverse engineers to verify that their model is correct. Before we discuss verification as the final step, the transformation of metrics from a concept is very important. First, each metric needs to be calculated correctly with the right formula. This is the easiest part of transforming it from a concept to a workable system because the mathematical formulas translate easily into Excel formulas, often with preexisting functions.

Setting up a system to calculate the metrics for scenario combinations is the second step. This is an important part of the transformation, particularly for verification purposes, because a model may produce the correct results for one set of assumptions, but when the assumptions are switched there is a chance that a structural concept was transformed improperly. These errors can be detected by running combinations of different scenarios and checking the results. Often, prospectuses provide output tables for a given set of assumptions, such as prepayment and default.

4. Verify

Verifying that the model is correct is the final step of reverse engineering a transaction. This is largely an extension of the "Metrics" section where the reverse engineer verifies that the model produces results that can be matched up against the documentation. To do this, the reverse engineer needs documentation with results. Two excellent sets of documents and the results they contain include:

Prospectus: Typically contains yield and duration tables for different prepayment and default scenarios. Also includes decrement (often referred to as *dec*) tables, which provide the periodic balances as a percentage of original balance for the assets and all liabilities. Dec tables are usually created for various prepayment and default scenarios.

Servicer Report: Historic servicer reports include information regarding balances, prepayments, defaults, interest rates, and so on. A reverse engineer can piece together historic servicer reports and check if their model produces the same balances.

When should a reverse engineer use either set of documents? This goes back to the question of availability and purpose. With prospectuses, the precision of verification

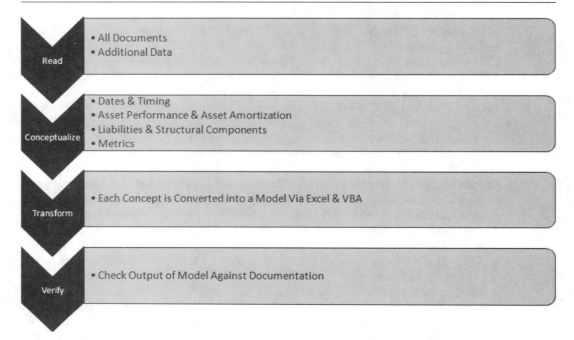

FIGURE 1.3   The general reverse engineering process should follow these four steps.

or "tying the model" to the documentation should be very good. This is because the outputs are based on a set of assumptions that are decided during the structuring. The prepayment and default curves used are either standard curves such as PSA or SDA or they are curves that have a specific assumption each period. Therefore, if the prospectus is available and the purpose is to calibrate a model, then this document should be used.

Servicer reports are based on actual performance and will have prepayment and default figures that can vary significantly from month to month. These can also be used to reverse engineer the deal with the goal of producing the most current results. Basic information about the assets though can also be garnered from servicer reports. More importantly, they are the best way to try to back into a deal's current state. The general reverse engineering process is summarized in Figure 1.3.

HOW THIS BOOK WORKS

This is a complicated book. Although I always strive toward transparency and simple explanations and demonstrations in Excel, there are topics inherent in the complexity of the deal structure that will require complex formulas and the implementation of VBA coding at an intermediate level.

The chapters take you through each concept of the transaction by discussing the concept, showing how it is captured in written documentation, and then explaining and demonstrating how it is converted to an Excel-based model. To keep the conversion process as straightforward as possible, the model will be built off one primary document: the Citigroup Mortgage Loan Trust 2006-WF2 prospectus supplement. As I mentioned previously, this is a modern mortgage-backed security deal with seven senior tranches and five mezzanine tranches of debt. As excerpts from the prospectus supplement are examined, corresponding Model Builder sections will follow, that work through the conversion in a step-by-step format. All the information in the prospectus and referenced in the book is publicly available on the SEC Edgar web site, but a PDF version of the prospectus supplement has been provided on the CD-ROM. Readers will find the PDF version much easier to use as it has page numbers, whereas the HTML version from SEC Edgar does not. Also included on the CD-ROM is the completed model that corresponds to the final work from all the Model Builder exercises.

The Model Builder sections instruct you in a step-by-step format on how to reverse engineer the transaction and construct the model. You may notice some cosmetic differences between your final model and the example model included on the CD-ROM. This is largely because formatting instructions have not been included. You may want to use the same formatting style as the example model, but you have the option to implement your own formatting as it will have no effect on the model calculation. In addition, some unnecessary summary cells (cells that total up columns) have been left in the example model, but not instructed in the text. The ones that have not been detailed are useful to you as a reader, but not critical to the model calculation.

There is also an appendix for some VBA functionality that is not critical to the model, but greatly enhances the builder's ability to create and audit a model. This appendix provides explanation of the functionality in a method similar to the Model Builder exercises.

Finally, you will notice that from the screen shots, exercises, and model, everything was created in Excel 2007. There are many major differences between Excel 1997–2003 and Excel 2007 with regard to memory allocation and some VBA libraries; however, none of these differences should matter for this book. There are, however, some minor differences such as cell naming conventions and function problems that I will highlight in a section at the end of this book.

CHAPTER 2

Determining Dates and Setting Up Timing

All financial projects are bound by dates and timing. The parsing of amounts into defined periods allows for the application of statistics and uniform measurement. Knowing when a transaction begins, the units of time in which amounts are paid or unpaid, and when the transaction ends is imperative to understanding the risk embedded in the transaction.

Reverse engineering a transaction, at first glance, may seem easy in respect to dates and timing, as from a time perspective the transaction is completed and all dates and timing have been set. Although it is true that most timing information is already defined and usually available, the act of piecing it together is not so simple. Legal wording can be complex and scattered throughout documentation. This chapter shows you how to navigate documentation to find relevant dates and timing indicators. Once found and understood, those indicators will be used in the Model Builder section that contributes to the final complete model.

DIFFERENCES IN TIMING APPROACHES

Prior to jumping right into dates and timing, we should take a step back to think about our overall goal. In the example model, we are reverse engineering the deal to create a model that starts from the transaction closing date to maturity. This is called the *Origination Method*. For many people who seek to understand how the structure works or who are auditing models, this will be the method of choice. The assets cash flow and deal liabilities will be recreated as if the transaction were being issued on the closing date. All funding amounts and balances for the first period will be as stated in the prospectus. Actual performance will be assumed to be unknown and any delinquency, default, or prepayment will be based on either the prospectus or from a separate analysis.

The other option, called the *Current Method*, is to reverse engineer the deal focusing on the current period and actual transaction history that has taken place thus far. This method requires the use of documentation such as servicer reports to piece together the history that has taken place since the transaction closed. The

Origination Method	Current Method
• Model Begins from Closing Date	• Model Begins from Current Date
• Balances Reflect Those in Prospectus	• Balances Reflect Those From Most Recent Servicing Report
• Cash Flow Completely Projected Using Prospectus Assumptions. May include Prospectus Generated Prepayment and Default Curves	• Cash Flow That Actually Transpired is Used, Up to Current Date. From Current Date on, Cash Flow is Projected

FIGURE 2.1   The differences between the two methods are easy to understand, but have a profound impact on the reverse engineering results.

model would still begin at closing date, but actual numbers could be populated up to the most recent period in the life of the transaction. Careful attention must be paid to the differences between original and current balances, original and current terms, and existing and projected interest rate assumptions. The differences between the Current Method and the Origination Method are highlighted in Figure 2.1.

Going forth using the Origination Method, here are a number of general questions you should ask yourself on any deal you seek to reverse:

- When did the transaction close?
- When is the legal final maturity date?
- What periodicity should be used in creating the model?
- What is the age of the assets?
- Are there any specific dates or timing issues that I need to model?

As we progress through this chapter, each one of these questions will be answered.

A FIRST LOOK AT THE PROSPECTUS

At this point it is worth opening the Prospectus from the CD-ROM for the first time. Before we get to specific dates and timing sections, take a moment to read the Table of Contents on the second page of the document (page S-2). Start to think about which sections will provide the most useful data and which may just take up time.

Table of Contents

Prospectus Supplement

SUMMARY OF PROSPECTUS SUPPLEMENT	S-4
RISK FACTORS	S-12
AFFILIATIONS AND RELATED TRANSACTIONS	S-21
USE OF PROCEEDS	S-21
THE MORTGAGE POOL	S-22
STATIC POOL INFORMATION	S-54
THE ORIGINATOR	S-54
THE SERVICER	S-64
THE TRUSTEE	S-66
THE TRUST ADMINISTRATOR	S-67
THE SPONSOR	S-68
THE DEPOSITOR	S-68
THE ISSUING ENTITY	S-69
YIELD ON THE CERTIFICATES	S-69
DESCRIPTION OF THE CERTIFICATES	S-80
POOLING AND SERVICING AGREEMENT	S-107
FEDERAL INCOME TAX CONSEQUENCES	S-113
METHOD OF DISTRIBUTION	S-116
SECONDARY MARKET	S-116
LEGAL OPINIONS	S-116
RATINGS	S-116
LEGAL INVESTMENT	S-117
CONSIDERATIONS FOR BENEFIT PLAN INVESTORS	S-117
ANNEX I	I-1
ANNEX II	II-1

FIGURE 2.2 The highlighted chapters will be the most often used section of the prospectus supplement.

One of the challenges in reverse engineering a transaction is the volume of data that may exist. Sifting through the data and determining what is relevant is a skill that will be built over time. For now, take a look at Figure 2.2 and notice the sections that have been highlighted.

Also note that although we will mainly concern ourselves with the final prospectus supplement, the prospectus itself is located after Annexes I and II. Occasionally a reverse engineer may have to refer to the prospectus for definitions and rules that are referred to in the prospectus supplement.

IMPORTANT DATES

Cut-Off Date

The two best dates to start with, the cut-off date and the closing date are the easiest to find. Look on page S-4 of the prospectus supplement and you will see a section called the, "Summary of Prospectus Supplement." Partway down you will see both the cut-off date and the closing date, as shown in the excerpt here:

Cut-off Date .... *May 1, 2006.*
Closing Date .... *On or about May 31, 2006.*

The first date, the cut-off date, is the day all the mortgage loan information is reported by. Any information regarding the characteristics of the mortgages is current as of the cut-off date. In this case it is May 1, 2006. The cut-off date for the mortgages is very important because this is when payments made by mortgage obligors in the pool are captured for use for the transaction. This date can be thought of as the first point indicating the start of the transaction, as it is the basis for other dates. Look to page 60 of the prospectus (the prospectus comes after the prospectus supplement and does not have an "S" in front of the page number). On this page there is a section on Distributions that is captured in the excerpt:

Distributions

Distributions allocable to principal and interest on the securities of each series will be made by or on behalf of the trustee each month on each date as specified in the related prospectus supplement and referred to as a distribution date, commencing with the month following the month in which the applicable cut-off date occurs. Distributions will be made to the persons in whose names the securities . . .

This section informs the reader that the first day on which the transaction pays any money, the first distribution date, occurs in the month after the cut-off date. In the example, the month after the cut-off date is June. This begins the framework for reconstructing the beginning of the transaction and its timing.

Closing Date

The closing date is the date that the transaction closes and technically speaking, funds. There are many uses for the closing date, several of which are not related to reverse engineering a model. One particularly important use is a date that determines if reps and warrants are breached. Typically if items that would have breached a rep or warrant occur after the closing date, then there is no breach.

The closing date signifies the official start of the transaction. Because this is the day the transaction is funded by investors, it is also the day that certificate interest starts accruing. A very important point is that the closing date usually does not correspond to the periodic distribution date, or the date on which principal and interest distributions to the certificates occur.

Distribution Date

As mentioned, the distribution date is when principal and interest amounts are distributed to certificate holders. There is no single distribution date, as it is a date that occurs every month after the cut-off date. There are two sections in the prospectus supplement that make this date obvious. The first is shown in the excerpt here from page S-5, where the distribution date is defined.

> *Distribution Dates .... Distributions on the certificates will be made on the 25th day of each month, or, if that day is not a business day, on the next succeeding business day, beginning in June 2006.*

You can also see that the distribution date will fall on the 25th of each month when you look at the decrement tables (tables that show periodic balances as a percentage of original balance). Figure 2.3 shows an excerpt from the decrement tables.

The distribution date is referenced throughout the prospectus supplement, as it is the date that most events are initiated off each month. We will encounter this date as we progress to other sections, but the most important thing you should understand is that the frequency of the distribution date sets the periodicity for the model. Notice from definition excerpted previously that the distribution date occurs "each month." Given that most of the cash flows on the distribution date and it occurs each month, the model created should show monthly cash flows.

The first distribution date is often known as the first payment date. As mentioned earlier, it is important to note the first payment date because it can often come at an interval different than those between the distribution dates. For instance, note that the closing date in our example is set to May 31, 2006, whereas the first distribution date is June 25, 2006. This means that the payments for the first distribution will be based on a partial month. However, for modeling purposes occasionally you will see the assumption that there is a complete month between closing and the first distribution date.

Percentage of Initial Certificate Principal Balance Outstanding							
	Class A-1				Class A-2A		
Distribution Date	I	II	III	IV	I	II	III	IV
Initial Percentage	100%	100%	100%	100%	100%	100%	100%	100%
May 25, 2007	89	80	70	60	70	45	18	0
May 25, 2008	76	58	42	27	37	0	0	0
May 25, 2009	66	42	23	10	9	0	0	0
May 25, 2010	56	32	18	9	0	0	0	0

FIGURE 2.3 There are often multiple indicators of the date and timing structure of the transaction.

Day Count Conventions

The final piece of information we need to completely capture the correct timing convention is how much time is assumed to elapse in a month. For those unfamiliar with day count conventions, this point may seem ridiculous, but the financial markets have created multiple ways of counting the number of days in a month as a fraction of a year.

For the most part many different types of securities typically use a standard day count convention, such as 30/360 for mortgage-backed securities. 30/360 meaning the assumption that each month has 30 days in a year consisting of 360 days. Reverse engineering a deal is made easier by the prospectus supplement, which typically defines the day count system. The excerpt from page S-86 of the prospectus supplement shows the day count convention for this transaction:

> *Interest will accrue on each class of Fixed Rate Certificates on the basis of a 360 day year consisting of twelve 30-day Interest Accrual Periods.*

Maximum Number of Periods

A concept often thought about late in the model building process is how many periods the model should encompass. You might be quick to jump to the Final Scheduled Distribution Date as seen on page S-5 of the prospectus supplement and excerpted here:

> *Final Scheduled Distribution Dates .... The final scheduled distribution date for the certificates will be the distribution date in May 2036. The final scheduled distribution date for the certificates is calculated as the month after the maturity of the latest maturing loan in the pool. The actual final distribution date for each class of certificates may be earlier, and could be substantially earlier, than the applicable final scheduled distribution date.*

Here the wording suggests that the last possible distribution date is May 2036, but it could be much earlier. The reason it could be earlier is because of the clean-up call feature that we will discuss later, but the question remains: how many periods should the model encompass? The simple answer is we should set it up with the maximum number of periods we would expect to see in any stress scenario that we run. You would expect this to be the Final Scheduled Distribution Date, however, we do not want to use that date in case we get late-stage recoveries. Specifically, if a loan defaults very close to May 2036 the trust is typically allowed the recovery on that asset. This means our model will extend beyond May 2036 in case we want to capture those recoveries. For this reason, the maximum number of periods should be a reasonable number of recovery periods beyond the Final Distribution Date. In our example model, we will use 500, as it would be odd to expect anywhere close to a 140-month lag between default and liquidation.

TRANSFORMING DATES AND TIMING FROM WORDS TO A MODEL

Now that you understand what the relevant dates and timing concepts are, it is time to implement them in a computer-based model. Because this is the first chapter that deals with model construction, there are a few general points to discuss regarding the model building and the Model Builder exercises.

First, the Model Builder exercises will work from a blank spreadsheet. They will be step-by-step instructions that you should follow exactly to produce the complete Model Builder exercise and eventually the complete reverse engineered model. Failing to complete one section means that the model as a whole will not work correctly. If at any time a section goes uncompleted or you are lost, it is recommended you review the final complete model, as this is the version you are trying to achieve.

Also, there may be noticeable visual differences between your model and the completed exercises and final model. Although there will be details for labeling, there is no instruction on color schemes, gridlines, or fonts. The formatting seen in the exercises and model is suggested for readability and there are no instructions to create this format.

For readers of *Modeling Structured Finance Cash Flows with Excel: A Step-by-Step Guide* the first Model Builder section on dates and timing will have many similar instructions, as dates and timing are fundamental basics to a transaction. Those readers can implement their previously created sections or work through this Model Builder section. Note though that there are differences between this "Dates and Timing" section and those in the other book.

Finally, as a reminder, if you are using versions of Excel prior to 2007, there are noticeable visual difference between the screenshots in this book and your program. Also, the instructions in Model Builder are designed for the Excel 2007 ribbon system and will not completely make sense for readers using earlier versions. Please see the appendix for more details.

With these considerations in mind, we truly begin reverse engineering the deal with Model Builder 2.1.

MODEL BUILDER 2.1: REVERSING DATES AND TIMING

1. Open Excel. The default setup should include three blank sheets labeled Sheet1, Sheet2, and Sheet3. Rename Sheet1 **Inputs** and Sheet3 **Hidden**. The Inputs sheet will contain many of the scalar inputs required for the model. As a modeling convention, inputs that are variables are usually created in a bold blue font. The Hidden sheet will contain ranges of list data that are referenced throughout the model.

2. Enter the text **Project Name** in cell B1. Name this cell **gbl_ProjName**. If naming cells is unclear consult the Help menu or reference an Excel operations book. Notice that a convention is being used for the name, where the first three letters

are *gbl* followed by an underscore and then a description of the cell. The *gbl* stands for global in this case because it is a global input that can be used all throughout the model. The project name should be replaced by the transaction name under consideration.

3. Enter the text **GLOBAL INPUTS** in cell B3. This is merely a label for the first section of inputs. In cell B4, enter the text **Cut-Off Date**. To the right in cell C4, enter the cut-off date that is found in the prospectus as mentioned before: **May 1, 2006**. Because this is an input variable, we should format the value as blue and bold. Going forward it will be assumed that you will know when to format the input variables. Name cell C4 **gbl_OrigDate**.

4. In cell B5, enter the text **Closing Date**. To the right in cell C5, enter the closing date of **May 31, 2006**. Name cell C5 **gbl_ClosingDate**.

5. Enter the text **First Payment Date** in cell B6. This is the first distribution date that was discussed earlier. In cell C6, enter the date of **June 25, 2006**. Name cell C6 **gbl_FirstPayDate**.

6. In Cell B7, enter the text **Day Count System**. Cell C7 will contain a data validation list for three of the most popular types of day count systems: 30 / 360, Actual / 360, and Actual / 365. Instead of storing data validation lists throughout the model, it is convenient to have them all on one sheet. For this reason, we have created the Hidden sheet, where we will create and name all of the necessary lists for use in the model.

   Go to the Hidden sheet. Label cell A1 on the Hidden sheet **Hidden**. Enter the text **DayCountSys**. Enter the following text in the respectively referenced cells:

   A4: **30 / 360**
   A5: **Actual / 360**
   A6: **Actual / 365**

   Name the range A4:A6 **lst_DayCountSys**. Note that there are spaces before and after the forward slash in the day counts. This is important because later a formula will reference these values and for the function to work correctly the values must be entered exactly as stated.

7. We are only going to implement the model on a monthly basis, so we are going to create a drop-down to display the payment frequency for user knowledge. The model can be altered later to create a dynamic payment frequency system. Still on the Hidden sheet, enter the text **PMTFreq** in cell A8. Enter the following text in the respectively referenced cells:

   A9: **Monthly**
   A10: **Quarterly**
   A11: **Semi-Annual**
   A12: **Annual**

   Name the range cell A9:A12 **lst_PMTFreq**.

FIGURE 2.4 The Dates and Timing section is the top left section of the Inputs sheet.

8. Go back to the Inputs sheet. In cell C7, create a data validation list referencing the named range lst_DayCountSys. Name this cell **gbl_DayCountSys**.
9. In cell C8 create a data validation list referencing the named range lst_PMTFreq. Name this cell **gbl_PMTFreq**. So far the sheet should look like Figure 2.4.
10. We will put the Maximum Periods in a separate section below the Global Inputs, as it is highly related to the securitization amortization. Go to cell B10 and enter the text **SECURITIZATION INPUTS**. In cell B12, enter the text **Maximum Periods**. Cell C12 will contain the maximum number of periods that the model should extend out. As mentioned earlier, enter the numeric value **500**. Name this cell **gbl_TotalPeriods**.
11. Dates and timing will permeate throughout many sheets in similar ways. Primarily, we need to create numerical period references, deal dates, collateral dates, and day-count factors. The first sheet that these sections will be seen on is the Vectors sheet. Name Sheet2 **Vectors**. On the Vectors sheet, enter the text **Vectors** in cell A1. Enter the following text in the respectively referenced cells:

A7: **Deal Period**
B7: **Deal Date**
C7: **Left Blank Intentionally**
D7: **Collateral Date**
E7: **Collateral Day Factor**

12. Still on the Vectors sheet, start in cell A8, enter 0, and in each cell below, enter a number that increases by one each time. For example, cell A9 should have the numerical value of 1, cell A10 should have the value of 2, and so on. Continue this until you reach 500. Now this section could be set up to be dynamically tied to the Maximum Periods on the Inputs sheet, but rarely will a user exceed 500 periods so the functionality adds unnecessary complexity.
13. The next section to work on is the Deal Date column. The Deal Date corresponds to the transaction relevant dates. Typically this will start with the closing date and increase, falling on the distribution dates. On the Vectors sheet in cell B8, enter the following formula:

=IF(A8=0,gbl_ClosingDate,IF(A8=1,gbl_FirstPayDate,EDATE(B7,1)))

Copy this formula from cell B8 down through cell B508. This formula checks the period first to see if it is the zero period, which is the Closing Date. If it's not the 0 period, but the first period, then it should be the First Payment Date, and finally if it is neither, then the date should increase monthly. It is within the EDATE formula that the dates can be made dynamic by putting a cell reference that changes as the user selects different periodicities instead of an increase by 1.

Be careful using the EDATE function in Excel 2007. Early versions of Excel 2007 have bugs that cause cells with the EDATE function to generate a *Data Lost Error*. Following this error, the cells referencing the EDATE function convert to *N/A#* errors and the original formulas are lost.

14. The next section is for the Collateral Date. Recall that the collateral is based off the cut-off date, which starts earlier than the closing date. For this reason, we need a separate vector for the collateral. On the Vectors sheet, enter the following formula in cell D8:

=IF(A8=0,gbl_OrigDate,EDATE(D7,1))

This formula checks to see if the period is 0, and then initiates the collateral cut-off date. If not it uses the EDATE function to increase the date for each period. Copy this cell down to cell D508.

15. After finishing the collateral dates we should create the Collateral Day Factor. This is a fraction that represents the time between two dates in a decimal format. Because there can be no day factor for period 0, enter the following formula in cell E9:

=IF(gbl_DayCountSys="30 / 360",DAYS360(D8,D9)/360,
**　　IF(gbl_DayCountSys="Actual / 360",(D9-D8)/360,(D9-D8)/365))**

This formula checks the day count system selected on the Inputs sheet and calculates the correct day factor. Notice the use of DAYS360 for the 30 / 360 day count system. Initially, a user may wonder why not to just divide 30 into 360 for the day count factor. DAYS360 is used because if a partial month were to elapse between the cut-off date and the first period, then the value would be calculated correctly. Copy this cell down to cell E508. The Vectors sheet should look similar to Figure 2.5, which shows a cut-out section of the area just completed.

16. There is an important step for you to complete to use the collateral day-count factor for asset amortization. Name cell E8, **strt_DayFactor**. The reason for this will be more apparent in the next chapter.

17. The dates and timing section is nearly complete. There are a few more sections that you will complete now and come back to later. The reason we do it now is that it relates to the timing, but as it isn't utilized until the Liabilities and Analytics sections, we will not explain the functionality until those chapters.

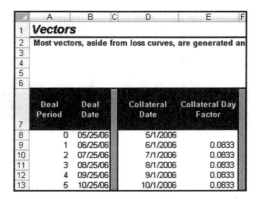

FIGURE 2.5 The Dates and Timing are converted from input entries to vectors in the Vectors sheet.

There are three main sheets that you will need for the liability waterfalls. Insert three sheets and name them:

Group 1 – Waterfall
Group 2 – Waterfall
Mezzanine – Waterfall

Starting with the Group 1 – Waterfall sheet enter the text **Group 1 – Waterfall**. Enter the text **Dates & Timing** in cell A6 and **Day Count Systems** in cell C6. Enter the following text in the corresponding cell references:

A7: **Period**
B7: **Date**
C7: **30 / 360**
D7: **Actual / 360**
E7: **Actual / 365**

This prepares us for entering-in values beneath each label.

18. Underneath cell A7, in cell A9 (leave row 8 blank for this section) enter the value 0. Increase this value by one in each row beneath cell A9 until you reach cell A509 and there is a column of 500 periods.

19. Underneath cell B7, in cell B9 enter the following formula:

=**Vectors!B8**

Copy this down to cell B509.

	A	B	C	D	E
1	**Group 1 - Waterfall**				
2	Asset cash flows generated from the Asset Amortizer ar				
3					
4					
5					
6	*Dates & Timing*		*Day Count Systems*		
7	Period	Date	30 / 360	Actual / 360	Actual / 365
8					
9	0	05/25/06			
10	1	06/25/06	0.083	0.086	0.085
11	2	07/25/06	0.083	0.083	0.082
12	3	08/25/06	0.083	0.086	0.085
13	4	09/25/06	0.083	0.086	0.085
14	5	10/25/06	0.083	0.083	0.082

FIGURE 2.6 Dates and timing are very important for the waterfall sheets as certain liabilities may pay using different day count systems.

20. Underneath cell C7, in cell C10 (notice that we cannot have a day-count for the initial period so cell C9 is left blank) we will create the day-count system for 30 / 360. Enter the following formula:

=DAYS360($B9,$B10)/360

Copy this down to cell C509.

21. Underneath cell D7, in cell D10 we will create the day-count system for Actual / 360. Enter the following formula:

=ABS($B9-$B10)/360

Copy this down to cell D509.

22. Underneath cell E7, in cell E10 we will create the day-count system for Actual / 365. Enter the following formula:

=ABS($B9-$B10)/365

Copy this down to cell E509. The area should look like Figure 2.6.

23. We now need to do the same process for the other two sheets that were just created: Group 2 – Waterfall and Mezzanine – Waterfall. Repeat Steps 17 through 22 for both sheets so they are identical, except their labels in cell A1 (these should correspond to the sheet name).

24. Finally, there is one more sheet that we need to create and add dates and timing. Insert a sheet and name it **Analytics**. This is where we will create relevant metrics for the collateral and liabilities. However, prior to getting to that section, we should implement the dates and timing.

25. On the Analytics sheet, enter the text **Analytics** in cell A1. Label the following cells with the corresponding cell references:

A18: **Period**
B18: **Date**
C18: **Day Factor**

We are going to reference the Group 1 – Waterfall in the same way we did before. It's a bit arbitrary for this sheet as to which sheet and day-count system we reference, because we will have the possibility to have unique ones for the collateral and each liability. However, the most important column here is the "Period" column because it will be used in calculations on this sheet later. For now complete the following:

A20: =‘Group 1 – Waterfall’!A9
B20: =‘Group 1 – Waterfall’!B9
C21: =‘Group 1 – Waterfall’!C10

Copy and paste all three cells down to row 509 in their respective columns.

CONCLUSION OF DATES AND TIMING

We will no doubt implement items related to dates and timing throughout the model, but the main concepts have been covered. In particular, in Chapter 3 we will make use of the day-count system and the periods to create the asset amortization. Creating such amortization would be inaccurate and inefficient to implement without first creating the dates and timing.

Creating Asset Cash Flow from Prospectus Data

Once we have established a timing framework and date boundaries, we are ready to reverse engineer the first major part of the transaction. For a mortgage-backed security, half the work goes into selecting an appropriate pool of assets. Reverse engineers have it easy in that the pool is already selected and they must only be able to recreate the cash flows from data that already exists.

This is not to say that this is an entirely unsophisticated process. In fact, to model a deal correctly the cash flow coming into the model should be created by amortizing each asset exactly as its terms state. Most free public information does not provide loan level detail to the asset pools, but prospectuses typically have multiple cohorts of loans organized by loan characteristics (otherwise known as rep lines) that approximate the underlying pool. Although third-party sources such as Loan Performance are available to determine underlying asset information, they may not be necessary depending on the level of detail you want to put into reversing a transaction. These private sources of data are expensive and should only be implemented if the results of the reversed transaction are business critical.

Regardless of loan level data or rep lines, this section will show a reader how to create asset cash flow using an unlimited number of assets. Whether you are loading up the rep lines from the prospectus supplement or loan level data from Loan Performance, the methods and code from this section allows you to build a powerful amortization engine.

IT'S ALL IN THE PROSPECTUS SUPPLEMENT

We will assume that you do not have access to Intex or Loan Performance and will only rely on the prospectus supplement for asset data. There is actually a considerable amount of asset data contained in the prospectus supplement. However, the subprime credit crisis that started in 2007 focused criticism on prospectus supplements for not disclosing enough information about the underlying assets. Most likely future prospectuses will include more asset-related information. For now, we will work with the data contained in the prospectus supplement.

The first indication of what the asset pool contains is on page S-6. The excerpt here depicts the overview that is provided in the prospectus supplement.

The trust will contain 6,358 conventional, one- to four-family, fixed-rate mortgage loans secured by first liens on residential real properties. The mortgage loans have an aggregate principal balance of approximately $1,131,286,782 as of the cut-off date, after application of scheduled payments due on or before the cut-off date whether or not received and subject to a permitted variance of plus or minus 5%.

This information is only useful in describing the assets that will create the cash flow for the transaction. The most important piece of information here is that we see the total size of the asset pool at $1,131,286,782.

As we read further down page S-6, we see that the asset pool is actually divided into two separate pools. The excerpt here shows this distinction.

The mortgage loans will be divided into two loan groups, loan group I and loan group II.

An initial question may be, "Does it really matter whether we treat the assets as a single large pool or two different pools?" The answer to this question is "yes, it does matter." The reason for this is that the pools are separated based on whether the mortgages conform or do not conform to Fannie Mae limits; however, the more important implication is that loan groups support specific tranches of debt. When we get to the liabilities section, we will see exactly how tranches are supported by loan groups and how the tranches interact. For now we must understand that we will have to create two separate aggregate amortization schedules, one for loan group I and one for loan group II.

The next item to notice on page S-6 is further detail regarding the loan groups. Figure 3.1 shows this detail.

Although this is useful for garnering a brief description of the loans and could technically be used to create an approximate cash flow, there are better sections from which to derive cash flow generation. The one statement of interest in Figure 3.1 is "The mortgage loans have the following approximate characteristics as of the cut-off date." Notice that this reinforces the information date for the assets and is the date that we will begin loan amortization.

The next section where we see asset data is on S-23, entitled "Mortgage Loan Statistics for the Mortgage Loans." This section is important for understanding characteristics about the collateral. This data will not be directly used for the asset amortization, but the characteristics of the mortgages that are described in this section help reverse engineers gauge a number of very important factors relating to performance.

Most importantly, the propensity and ability of obligors to pay can be determined from key characteristics such as credit score, loan-to-value ratio,

> **The mortgage loans have the following approximate characteristics as of the cut-off date:**
>
> | | |
> |---|---|
> | Interest only mortgage loans: | 11.23% |
> | Range of mortgage rates: | 5.500% - 10.250% |
> | Weighted average mortgage rate: | 7.777% |
> | Weighted average remaining term to stated maturity: | 353 months |
> | Range of principal balances: | $13,473 - $999,276 |
> | Average principal balance: | $177,931 |
> | Range of loan-to-value ratios: | 12.50% - 95.00% |
> | Weighted average loan-to-value ratio: | 82.09% |
> | Geographic concentrations in excess of 5%: | |
> | California: | 16.03% |
> | Florida: | 13.83% |
> | New Jersey: | 6.51% |
> | New York: | 5.96% |

FIGURE 3.1 Asset pool characteristics as depicted in the prospectus supplement.

documentation level, property type, and so on. Reverse engineers should be careful though because the data stratifications can only clue them in on generalized pictures of the pool. If the results of the modeling are to be used for critical decisions, then estimating the probability of payment should be attempted as rigorously as possible. This would include trying to create a historical static loss analysis or projecting future delinquency and loss by creating transition matrices and simulating loans' performance.

In addition, the characteristics can help determine appropriate prepayment assumptions. We will discuss the generalized prepayment assumption the prospectus provides later in the chapter. What we should focus on in the characteristics section are factors that may affect the tendency of loans to prepay. This would include data describing prepayment penalties, interest rates, spreads, and items that help determine property value. By putting this data into a prepayment model we might have a better indication of how the assets may prepay.

Recovery rates are another performance factor that can be partially assessed through the mortgage characteristics. For mortgages, geographic distributions should be analyzed based on home price appreciation (HPA), property types, and so on.

Note that this section exists in most financial transactions that are supported by collateral. If this were an auto loan transaction there would be data on credit scores, debt-to-income, vehicle make, model type, and so on. Or on more esoteric deals such as insurance you would have descriptions of a pool of insured individuals with relevant statistics about age, gender, health, and so on.

Regardless of the type of transaction, if the deal is collateralized, there should always be a section describing the collateral in detail. This aids the reader of the documentation in assessing the performance risk of the pool. If there are large concentrations in risky areas, then as the deal is reverse engineered these risks should come out. For example, if studies show a high default rate for multifamily housing in the state of Nevada, a reverse engineer can apply that high default rate to the deal-specific concentration of Nevada multifamily home loans when it comes time to amortize the loans.

THE BASICS OF AMORTIZATION

If assets paid strictly according to their terms, calculating cash flow would be very simple; it would be a quick exercise in math taking the balance, term, and rate of each loan to determine a payment and then breaking that payment down into principal and interest. Loans may have more complications such as variable rates, rate caps, rate floors, interest-only periods, balloon payments, and custom payment structures, but once all the terms are known the cash flow is a standard calculation. Unfortunately, it is not this easy because economies and humans are fallible and may be forced to or choose to alter the terms of payment. For assets that pay over time, such alterations in payment take the form of delinquency, possible default, or prepayment.

If these behavioral factors occurred at random it would be impossible to create a reasonable expectation of cash flow. However, when one analyzes historical payment data through the lens of loan and obligor characteristics, quantifiable patterns emerge. These loan and obligor characteristics can be classified into two categories:

1. Performance Groups
2. Rational Metrics

Performance groups are descriptive characteristics of a loan or obligor that, when analyzed, exhibit patterns in performance. More specifically, they are characteristics that define variations in payment between loan obligors. For instance, credit scores are the ultimate performance group. A credit score is a number that primarily represents how one has paid their obligations over time. Other performance groups would include property type, loan type, and so on. Performance groups are more relevant to assess delinquency and default.

Rational Metrics are loan characteristics that directly determine the performance of the loan. A perfect example of a rational metric is a loan-to-value ratio. Obligors will behave rationally in regards to loan-to-value because it represents how much equity obligors have in their assets. If the loan-to-value is very high an obligor most likely will have a higher propensity to default than a person with a lower loan-to-value. Rational metrics are particularly relevant for prepayment behavior. It is a rational decision to refinance to a lower interest rate, a lower spread, a lower fee type mortgage, and so on.

Performance characteristics should be analyzed against all possible loans that fit into mixtures of the cohorts previously described. For instance, to analyze loss we may want to perform a loss analysis for loans that are for single-family homes, for credit scores between 600 to 625, and loan-to-values of 75% to 80%. The goal of grouping the historic loans in cohorts is to be able to get a reliable indication of performance. If we use too many characteristics to make up a cohort we will not have enough historic loans to analyze and our results will be volatile and statistically insignificant.

Once historical performance is determined it can be applied directly to the loans. This can be implemented using two different methods: deterministic and/or stochastic. A *deterministic* model is the one that is described in this book, where loss and prepayment assumptions are applied against all loans in the pool using curves. Fractions of loans are assumed to default and prepay. In reality, a fraction of a loan never defaults and partial prepayments typically make up very small parts of actual prepayment. The alternative methodology is a *stochastic* methodology, where each loan is simulated for delinquency, default, or prepayment. Transition matrices can be calibrated based on the historical loan performance, and Monte Carlo simulations implemented to simulate whether a loan is delinquent, defaulted, or prepaid.

As we will be using a deterministic model as the example, we will move forward discussing the integration of that type of historical analysis into loan amortization. The results of a deterministic analysis will be performance curves that were created by multiple cohorts. Any pool of loans under analysis can now be mapped to these curves. Figure 3.2 represents this process.

After assigning a curve to each loan, the loan can then be amortized as its specific terms state, with the performance assumptions.

PERFORMANCE AND THE PROSPECTUS SUPPLEMENT

Rarely do prospectuses themselves provide full historical performance data. In fact, many only indicate current delinquency percentages and offer no estimate of loss for the pool of mortgages. For prepayments, there is usually a range of general assumptions, but rarely does the prospectus tailor the prepayment assumption for the pool of assets at hand. However, this is not to say that this information is not available.

On page S-54 of the prospectus supplement there is a note about static pool information. The prospectus directs us to a Web link where we can download static pool information regarding the originator. This data goes back to 2001 and includes delinquency, loss, and prepayment data, which would certainly provide an excellent

Loss Curve Mapping

Historically Generated Default Rates				
LTV		FICO		Generated Default Rates
Lower Bound	Upper Bound	Lower Bound	Upper Bound	
95%	100%	500	600	35%
90%	95%	500	600	27%
85%	90%	600	700	18%

Pool Characterisitics			
Rep Line #	WA LTV	WA FICO	Assigned Default Rate
1	92%	527	27%
2	98%	558	35%
3	87%	601	18%
4	91%	590	27%
5	99%	501	35%

FIGURE 3.2 Loss curve mapping involves first performing historical analyses on cohorts of assets. Once performance is understood for a specific cohort, the performance factor can be applied to a pool of loans under analysis by mapping similar characteristics based on the cohorts from the historical study and the pool cohorts.

amount of data to analyze and create performance assumptions. The wording is captured in the excerpt here:

> *The Depositor has made available, on its internet website located at https://www2.citimortgage.com/Remic/securitydata.do?DATA_SELECTION= abReportsShelf, static pool information about previously originated mortgage loans of the originator beginning in 2001, which information is incorporated by reference into this prospectus supplement. The static pool information includes (i) information about the characteristics of the previously originated mortgage loans and (ii) delinquency, loss and prepayment information about such mortgage loans in quarterly increments through March 2006.*

DELINQUENCY

Delinquency is discussed because it is a precursor to default, however it is often skipped in the modeling process. Prospectuses usually give an indication of the current state of delinquency for a pool, but given a low-seasoned pool this does not mean much. Rough estimates could be created from loss curves, but the best way to determine delinquency curves is through a Monte Carlo roll rate analysis as discussed previously.

Delinquency can have a profound impact on a deal. Most deals have a delinquency trigger that directs cash in a sequential manner rather than pro rata. The excerpt here from page S-94 describes a trigger event based on delinquency.

"Trigger Event": With respect to any distribution date, a Trigger Event is in effect if:

(i) (A) the percentage obtained by dividing the aggregate principal balance of mortgage loans delinquent 60 days or more (including mortgage loans delinquent 60 days or more and in foreclosure, in bankruptcy or REO properties) by the aggregate principal balance of all of the mortgage loans, in each case, as of the last day of the previous calendar month, exceeds (B) 36.00% of the Senior Enhancement Percentage for the prior distribution date; or ...

In our example model, we will implement the trigger test and use a proxy delinquency curve.

LOSS

Prospectuses often use the Public Securities Association's standard curves to incorporate performance related attributes into amortization. For loss, this takes the form of the SDA. The standard SDA curve is 100% SDA, which assumes an increase of 0.02% annual default in the first 29 months (starting with 0.02%), a level 0.60% annual default for months 30 to 60, and then a decrease of 0.0095% annual default for months 61 to 120, and finally a level 0.03% for months 121 through 360. The SDA curve takes on various stressed instantiations by multiplying the annual default rates by a multiple and naming the curve in a percentage format. For example, 200% SDA multiplies all annual default rates by a factor of two. When graphed, the 100% SDA curve should look like Figure 3.3.

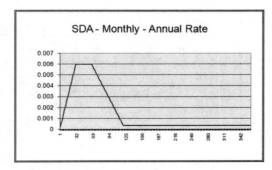

FIGURE 3.3 100% SDA as created by the Public Securities Association.

This single default curve is built off data on U.S. thirty-year mortgages. It is crafted with annual default rates that are applied against current balance. If the deal is being modeled monthly, then these rates must be converted to monthly rates. Only in very rare circumstances should a transaction be completely analyzed only off this curve. Even if the collateral is all U.S. thirty-year mortgages, a comprehensive default analysis should be done to create curves for relevant cohorts. In particular, most modern mortgage transactions have a floating rate collateral, which will exhibit different loss patterns than a fixed rate collateral.

Why are SDAs even used? Prospectuses use them to give readers an understanding of how loss would have an impact on the deal if it occurred. It's more focused on how the debt that is offered by the prospectus would perform under loss situations. An important value for reverse engineers is having the prospectus include liability performance under standard loss assumptions, which allows the reverse engineer to calibrate their model to make sure it is correct. This is a topic we will focus on in Chapter 6.

In the example transaction we are reverse engineering there is no loss assumption. In the absence of such an assumption we will create one in this chapter and build the functionality into the amortization engine to test the flow of funds later.

PREPAYMENT

As with loss, many prospectuses rely on the Public Securities Association for prepayment assumptions. The Public Securities Association created a standard prepayment curve called the PSA curve. One-hundred percent PSA assumes prepayment rates of 0.2% CPR in the first month following origination of the mortgage loans (not the pool) and an additional 0.2% CPR in each succeeding month until the 30th month.

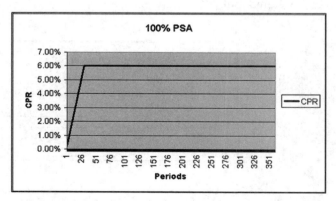

FIGURE 3.4 100% PSA as created by the Public Securities Association.

In the 30th month and beyond, 100% PSA assumes a fixed annual prepayment rate of 6.0% CPR. Figure 3.4 depicts the standard 100% PSA curve.

Similar to SDA, PSA can be stressed by multiples and is referred to in percentages depending on the stress. For example, 200% PSA doubles the CPR at every month.

In general, prospectuses take a similar approach to prepayment as they do with loss. A reader will often see PSA used even though it may not have any relevance to the current or expected prepayment environment. The PSA curves are implemented to demonstrate the debt's sensitivity to prepayments. This is particularly obvious in agency deals from entities like Freddie Mac, where planned amortization class (PAC) and targeted amortization class (TAC) bonds are sold with duration as a primary motivator.

In our example transaction, the deal structurer created a custom prepayment curve. The curve is described on page S-72 with an excerpt of the relevant text here:

> *The model used in this prospectus supplement (referred to as the Prepayment Assumption in this prospectus supplement) assumes 100% of the Fixed-Rate Prepayment Vector. The "Fixed-Rate Prepayment Vector" assumes a constant prepayment rate, or CPR, of 4% per annum in the first month of the life of such mortgage loans and an additional approximately 1.727% per annum (precisely 19%/11) in each month thereafter until the 11th month. Beginning in the 12th month and in each month thereafter during the life of such mortgage loans, the Fixed-Rate Prepayment Vector assumes a CPR of 23%.*

As one can see this curve has a similar "ramp" as PSA, but it is much faster with a steeper slope. See Figure 3.5 for a graphical representation.

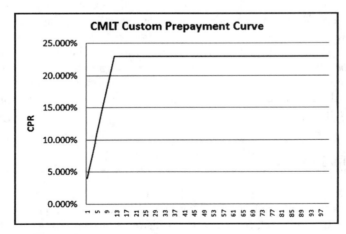

FIGURE 3.5 A graphical representation of the prepayment curves used by the CMLT example deal.

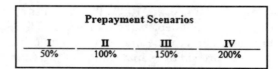

FIGURE 3.6 The prospectus supplement tests various prepayment scenarios from 50% to 200% of the CMLT curve.

This prepayment curve is also given possible stress scenarios where the "Fixed-Rate Prepayment Vector" is reduced or increased by a percentage. We will want to test each of the prepayment scenarios seen in Figure 3.6.

RECOVERY

Nearly every collateralized transaction on Wall Street demands a perfection of interest in the collateral. With such legal rights, assets can be seized if the obligor defaults on payment and the asset sold to recover any remaining balance. These recovered amounts are transmitted to the trusts and can be used in multiple ways depending on the exact wording of the documentation. Some documentation directs the recoveries as excess yield, whereas others direct it as principal.

We will see in the example transaction that there are detailed directions for recovered monies, but no indication of how much can be recovered from defaulted mortgages or how long it may take to receive the recovery. The preferred method of determining these rates and lags is if the originator can provide data specific to their historic recoveries. Like loss and prepayment data, recovery data should be analyzed in cohorts. Logical cohorts for recovery include geographic region and property type. Without such data, a reverse engineer can still try to estimate recoveries based on appraisal values if known, home price appreciation/depreciation studies (such as those produced by Office of Federal Housing Enterprise Oversight [OFHEO]), and rating agency market value decline rates. Regional analysis can be done to determine the time it takes to foreclose and whether there is a judicial process or a fast track system.

CREATING CASH FLOW

With a conceptual understanding of what must be done, we can now move on towards implementation. The first step is determining what level of data to use: rep lines or loan level. Although the decision is more complicated if the deal is revolving in nature, the example transaction is a term deal, meaning that the asset pool we

			Remaining Amortization		Remaining Interest Only
		Gross	Term to		
	Aggregate Principal	Mortgage	Maturity	Age	Term
Group	Balance ($)	Rate (%)	(months)	(months)	(months)
I	16,106.83	8.87500	179	1	N/A
I	995,326.97	7.56453	353	3	N/A
I	1,516,153.73	7.87381	358	2	N/A
I	778,494.94	7.22902	177	2	N/A
I	504,731.45	7.07003	177	2	N/A
I	12,087,186.37	7.90269	357	3	N/A
I	11,304,638.36	7.98362	357	2	N/A

ANNEX II
ASSUMED MORTGAGE LOAN CHARACTERISTICS

FIGURE 3.7 The prospectus supplement provides numerous rep lines that allow the reverse engineer to create asset amortization.

start with cannot be added to after closing. For this we will want to do a loan level amortization if we have such data from a source like Loan Performance. However, most individuals do not have the luxury of such a database and are forced to use rep lines.

Most prospectus supplements have some representation of the pool. In our example transaction this is in the Annex on page II-1. Figure 3.7 depicts a snapshot of the rep lines. Note the column on the left that denotes the loan group. Each loan group has rep lines that summarize the loans. A rep line is an aggregation of similar loans into one loan. Our approach to reverse engineering the collateral cash flows will be to amortize each rep line to produce an amortization schedule and then aggregate all the rep loans' amortization schedules. At the same time, we will incorporate prepayment, default, and recovery functionality.

A COMPLEX IMPLEMENTATION

This will be a complex section to those unfamiliar with VBA. There were multiple considerations that went into the design of this chapter. I wanted to provide you with a method more powerful than amortizing a single rep line, yet I did not want to deter those of you without programming backgrounds.

The end result is a chapter that is heavily in favor of readers with basic VBA programming skills, but straightforward enough for a nonprogramming reader to implement without completely understanding the code. My personal philosophy with VBA is to only use it when it is absolutely necessary. To be able to amortize an unlimited number of loans, it is necessary. However, it is taught with a limited number of programming concepts to not overwhelm the reader. For a thorough understanding of VBA and code writing, I recommend purchasing a separate book that is dedicated to teaching this topic. Otherwise, the final code at the end of the chapter can simply be copied into the Visual Basic Editor (VBE) with the provided instructions and used without complete understanding.

For those with beginning-to-intermediate VBA knowledge, this chapter will show you a system of using VBA that is powerful and flexible. The approach is straightforward and relies on large subroutines to handle loan amortization. It is certainly not as efficient or as elegant as implementing a methodology where a loan class is created, but it is easy to understand and nonetheless very powerful. Advanced VBA programmers may choose an alternative implementation, but the one provided is the balance struck between having the ability to implement a loan level methodology and appealing to a diverse range of readers' skills.

MODEL BUILDER 3.1: ENTERING IN THE RAW ASSET INFORMATION

1. The first step to implement the asset amortization is to prepare the area for entering asset data. Create two new sheets and name one **Group 1 – Assets** and the other **Group 2 – Assets**.
2. On the Group 1 – Assets sheet insert the following text in the respectively labeled cells:

A1: **Loan Number**		M1: **Introductory Interest Rate**	
B1: **Group I**		N1: **Reset Frequency**	
C1: **Original Balance**		O1: **Initial Cap**	
D1: **Current Balance**		P1: **Subsequent Cap**	
E1: **Original Term**		Q1: **Ceiling**	
F1: **Remaining Term**		R1: **IO Expiration Date**	
G1: **Seasoning**		S1: **Per to IO Expiration**	
H1: **Provided Payment**		T1: **Prepay Flag**	
I1: **Fixed Rate**		U1: **Default Flag**	
J1: **Index Description**		V1: **Recovery Rate**	
K1: **Index Flag**		W1: **Recovery Lag**	
L1: **Margin**			

3. Column A contains a number count of the representative assets. Start by entering **1** in cell A2 and continue growing by one for each asset. There are 55 assets in Group 1.
4. Column B contains a marker for noting whether the representative asset is part of Group 1 or Group 2. Enter a 1 for Group 1 and copy it down for all 55 assets.

5. Column C contains the Original Balance of the assets. Notice that the Original Balance is not available, but instead we have the Aggregate Principal Balance. We will assume that the Aggregate Principal Balance is both the Original Balance and the Current Balance. Copy the Aggregate Principal Balances for each asset for Group 1 from the Prospectus Supplement and paste the values starting in cell C2 and going down each row. Make sure to only copy the first 55 assets because Group 1 and Group 2 are combined in the prospectus supplement. Column D contains the Current Balance, which is the same as the Original Balance in this case. Copy the Original Balance data and paste the values into cells D2:D56.

6. Because we are assuming that each asset has the same balance for Original and Current Balance, the original and remaining term will also be the same. Copy the Remaining Amortization Term to Maturity (in Months) from the prospectus supplement and paste the values starting in cell E2 and going down each row. Copy the Original Term data and paste the values into cells F2:F56.

7. Note that although we are assuming the same Original and Current Balance and original and current term, the assets are not new. The seasoning of the assets will be required to determine each asset's interest, default, and prepay rate. Copy the Age (in Months) from the prospectus and paste the values starting in cell G2 and going down each row.

8. In cells H2:H56, enter a 0. There is no provided payment. If there were a payment that was already provided for each asset we would enter it here. The code we will implement will pick up any value greater than 0 to use as the payment. If 0 is entered then it will calculate a payment.

9. In cells I2:I56, paste the values from the Gross Mortgage Rate (%) section of the prospectus supplement. Make sure the values are in percentage format otherwise later calculations will be very wrong.

10. The example transaction has all fixed rate products, which simplifies the explanation. However, we will still build in the necessary functionality to accept variable rate products. For now enter **N/A** for all cells in the range J2:J56. In all cells for the range K2:M56, enter 0. You may want to format the Margin and Introductory interest rates as percentages now.

11. For cells N2:Q56, enter the value of 1. Because the assets are all fixed rate none of these assumptions will be used, but it is better to make sure that there are no caps (1 essentially means the cap is 100%) rather than keeping the default value at 0 where no interest is charged.

12. Column R contains the Interest Only (IO) Date if there is one. In our deal, we have a few Group 2 loans that have IO terms, but no exact dates. For this reason we will rely on a different column of data to determine IO parameters. Enter 0 for cells R2:R56. This can be formatted as a short date now for future use.

13. Column S contains the Periods to IO Expiration, which are the number of months an interest-only asset has until it begins to pay principal. As there are no IO loans in Group 1, as can be seen from the Remaining IO Term (months) on the prospectus supplement, a 0 should be entered in cells S2:S56. Do not

enter **N/A** if there is no IO period (as the prospectus shows); the code we will implement will not understand text in this column.

14. Columns T, U, V, and W are where the performance assumptions are integrated. We will discuss this functionality more later, but for now we have to understand that we will be entering reference flags for default and prepayment assumptions and actual recovery rates and lags for each asset. A reference flag is a number that refers to the curve that will be used for the specific asset or rep line. For instance, entering a 1 for the default flag for an asset indicates that the asset will be run using the first lost curve. In cells T2:T56, enter **2** in each cell. In cells U2:U56, enter **1** in each cell. In cells V2:V56, enter an initial recovery assumption of **30%** in each cell. And finally, in cells W2:56, enter a recovery lag of **12** for each cell. We will definitely come back to how these are used later as these settings are incredibly important for proper amortization. So far the Group 1 – Assets sheet should look similar to the cut-out portion shown in Figure 3.8. Note that this figure only shows 8 lines of the full sheet. Make sure there are exactly 55 assets for Group 1 that come from Annex II in the prospectus supplement.

15. The final step is to name cells in row 1 for selected fields. This is critical for the code that will be written later. Name the following cells with the corresponding name:

A1: **strt_gp1_Data**	M1: **strt_gp1_OrgRate**
C1: **strt_gp1_OrgBal**	N1: **strt_gp1_ResetFreq**
D1: **strt_gp1_CurBal**	O1: **strt_gp1_PCap**
E1: **strt_gp1_OrgTerm**	P1: **strt_gp1_SubsCap**
F1: **strt_gp1_RTerm**	Q1: **strt_gp1_Ceiling**
G1: **strt_gp1_Season**	S1: **strt_gp1_IO**
H1: **strt_gp1_ProvPMT**	T1: **strt_gp1_PPayFlag**
I1: **strt_gp1_IR**	U1: **strt_gp1_DefFlag**
K1: **strt_gp1_Index**	V1: **strt_gp1_RcvyRate**
L1: **strt_gp1_Margins**	W1: **strt_gp1_RcvyLag**

	Loan Number	Group I	Original Balance	Current Balance	Original Term	Remaining Term	Seasoning
1							
2	1	I	16,106.83	16,106.83	179	179	1
3	2	I	995,326.97	995,326.97	353	353	3
4	3	I	1,516,153.73	1,516,153.73	358	358	2
5	4	I	778,494.94	778,494.94	177	177	2
6	5	I	504,731.45	504,731.45	177	177	2
7	6	I	12,087,186.37	12,087,186.37	357	357	3
8	7	I	11,304,638.36	11,304,638.36	357	357	2
9	8	I	612,419.80	612,419.80	358	358	2

FIGURE 3.8 The prospectus supplement asset information is transferred directly to the example model.

16. This process must be repeated for the Group II loans on the sheet Group 2 – Assets. Copy the information for all Group II loans starting with the last rep line from page II-1. The process will be identical as for Group 1, but there is one nuance. There are loans with active IO periods in Group II. For the loans that have remaining IO periods, enter the values as they are in the prospectus supplement. Also, make sure to name the first row of cells similarly, except changing the convention *gp1* to **gp2**.

So far all we have done was enter the raw data for each loan with references to default and prepayment assumptions. The next step is to actually create the default and prepayment assumptions. These will be done on separate sheets and are described in the next Model Builder section, 3.2

MODEL BUILDER 3.2: ENTERING IN THE DEFAULT AND PREPAYMENT ASSUMPTIONS

1. Deterministic models, such as the one we are building, use default curves to estimate default amounts. We have discussed that there can be multiple loss curves depending on different criteria. We now need to set up a system for managing an unlimited number of loss curves. Create a new worksheet and name it **Loss Curves**. Enter the text **Loss Curves** in cell A1.
2. Enter the text **Period** in cell A7. Below, in cell A8, enter **0** and continue to grow this value by one in each cell a row below. Cell A9 should contain **1**, cell A10 **2**, and so on. Continue this process for 500 rows until you reach cell A508.
3. In cell C5 enter a **1** and continue entering growing integers by increments of one across the sheet. Cell D5 should contain a **2**, cell E5 a **3**, and so on. This process can go on to the limits of the sheet, but for the purposes of the example model continue this until column L so there is the option for ten possible loss curves.
4. Cell C7 holds a designation of the interval for the loss curve. For the most part this is usually done on a monthly basis, but we should have an area to denote if it is on a different interval. Enter the text **Monthly** in each cell of the range C7:L7.
5. What we have set up so far are the boundaries for a matrix of loss curves. We can insert ten possible loss curves that each go out 500 periods. For now we are going to leave the loss assumption empty so enter a **0** for the range of cells C9:L508. Note that there is no loss assumption for period 0.
6. The default curves that should be entered here must be on a monthly, non-cumulative basis. Advanced functionality could be built in to handle various default curves, but for now the code that will be created accepts curves that are noncumulative. To be able to quickly compare two curves we should sum up each loss curve in row 6. In cell C6 enter the following formula:

=SUM(C9:C500)

Copy and paste this formula into the range of cells C6:L6. This completes the Loss Curves sheet. You may want to format the sheet with borders and fill in as I have done in the completed model.

7. There are a few cells we will have to name for use in the upcoming amortization code. Name cell B9 **strt_Default** and the range of cells C9:L508 **rng_DefaultCurveTable**.

8. The next step is to enter prepayment curves. Theoretically you can have an unlimited number of prepayment assumptions, but as we have seen from the prospectus supplement there are only four prepayment assumptions assumed. These prepayment assumptions can fit on the Vectors sheet we created earlier. Go to the Vectors sheet and label the following cells with the corresponding text:

V6: **Prepayments**
V7: **SMM 1**
W7: **SMM 2**
X7: **SMM 3**
Y7: **SMM 4**
Z6: **Prepay in CPR Form**
Z7: **CPR 1**
AA7: **CPR 2**
AB7: **CPR 3**
AC7: **CPR 4**

9. Prior to entering any values for the prepayment curves, we have to create a number of items on the Inputs page to simplify model use later. Go to the Inputs sheet and enter the following text in the corresponding cells:

G21: **Fixed Prepayment Curve**
G22: **Initial**
G24: **Period 12 and After**

10. Notice that cell G23 was not addressed in Step 9. This is because we will have some special functionality with this cell. Enter the value **11** in cell G23. Now right click and select **Format Cells**. On the Number tab select **Custom** for Category. Type the following for the Type (make sure to include the quote marks):

"Up to Period (Incremental)"

Click **OK**. Cell G23 should now read "Up to Period 11 (Incremental), however, when the cell is active the value in the formula bar should be 11. Name cell G23 **struc_PpayIncPd**. This is a trick that many financial modelers use to be able to reference a number, but have more description in the cell.

Fixed Prepayment Curve	
Initial	**4.00%**
Up to Period 11 (Incremental)	**1.73%**
Period 12 and After	**23.00%**

FIGURE 3.9 The prepayment vector parameters are entered into the Inputs sheet.

11. We know the values to create the prepayment curve from page S-72 (refer to Figure 35). From the prospectus wording, we can calculate that the 100% Fixed-Prepayment Vector begins with 4.0% CPR in the first month. Enter the value **4.0%** in cell H22. Name this cell **struc_PpayInit**. After the first month the prospectus states that an additional 1.727% or precisely 19%/11 should be added to the previous month up to month 11. Enter the formula **=0.19/11** in cell H23. Name this cell **struc_PpayInc**. Finally, for month 12 and beyond, the prospectus states that the 100% Fixed-Prepayment Vector should assume 23%. Enter **23.0%** in Cell H24. Name this cell **struc_PpayFinal**. So far this section should look like Figure 3.9.

    You should be very aware of a few phrases and concepts in this paragraph. The first two phrases are "in the first month of the life" and "in each month thereafter." The most obvious point that this phrase makes is that the prepayment vector is a monthly assumption. If we switch the periodicity of this model, we must be cognizant that this prepayment vector is created monthly. Second, the term "of the life" is important because this prepayment vector is created for every period of a loan. If a loan is brand new it will start in month 1, however, a seasoned loan must start on its appropriate point on the curve. Recall that we have seasoned loans and must make sure the correct prepayment rate is applied to them. The next phrase that is important is "per annum." The assumptions provided are in CPR form, which is an annual representation, and must be converted to a monthly representation, or SMM, for a monthly model. Keep this in mind when we return to the Vectors sheet.

12. Prior to going back to the Vectors sheet, we must add inputs for the possible prepayment stress cases that the prospectus assumes. Enter the following labels in the corresponding cells:

    I19: **Prepayment Scenarios**
    I20: **I**
    I21: **II**
    I22: **III**
    I23: **IV**

13. The prospectus supplement assumes three other prepayment scenarios: 50%, 150%, and 200%. These scenarios are based on multiplying the monthly CPR

values of the 100% curve, created using the parameters in Step 9, by the prepayment scenario values. To prepare for this enter the following values in the corresponding cells:

J20: **50%**
J21: **100%**
J22: **150%**
J23: **200%**

Name cell J20 **scen_PrepayOne**, J21 **scen_PrepayTwo**, J22 **scen_PrepayThree**, and J23 **scen_PrepayFour**.

14. Now go back to the Vectors sheet so we can actually start creating the prepayment curves. In cell AA9, enter the following formula:

**=IF(A9=1,struc_PpayInit,IF(A9<=struc_PpayIncPd,
    AA8+struc_PpayInc,struc_PpayFinal))**

This formula first checks to see if the period is the first period. If it is the first period, then first month prepayment assumption should be used. If the period is past the first period, then the formula checks to see if the period is less than or equal to 11 periods. If this is the case, it adds the incremental increase to the previous period's rate. If the period is anything else (essentially period 12 and beyond) the formula uses the fixed final prepayment assumption. Copy and paste this formula over the range of cells AA9:AA508.

15. In cell Z9, enter the following formula:

=AA9*scen_PrepayOne

This cell will stress the 100% case by the first prepayment scenario on the Inputs sheet. Copy and paste this formula over the range of cells Z9:Z508.

16. Step 14 should be repeated for the other two remaining prepayment scenarios: 150% and 200%. Enter the following formulas in the corresponding cells:

AB9: **=AA9*scen_PrepayThree**
AC9: **=AA9*scen_PrepayFour**

Copy and paste these formulas over the range of cells AB9:AB508 and cells AC9:AC508, appropriately.

17. As mentioned earlier we must make sure to convert the CPR rates to SMM. Enter the following formula in V9:

=1-(1-Z9)^(1/12)

Prepayments				Prepay in CPR Form			
SMM 1	SMM 2	SMM 3	SMM 4	CPR 1	CPR 2	CPR 3	CPR 4
0.168%	0.340%	0.514%	0.692%	2.00%	4.000%	6.000%	8.000%
0.242%	0.490%	0.746%	1.009%	2.86%	5.727%	8.591%	11.455%
0.316%	0.644%	0.983%	1.336%	3.73%	7.455%	11.182%	14.909%
0.391%	0.799%	1.227%	1.677%	4.59%	9.182%	13.773%	18.364%
0.466%	0.958%	1.478%	2.030%	5.45%	10.909%	16.364%	21.818%
0.542%	1.119%	1.736%	2.398%	6.32%	12.636%	18.955%	25.273%
0.619%	1.284%	2.002%	2.783%	7.18%	14.364%	21.545%	28.727%
0.697%	1.451%	2.276%	3.184%	8.05%	16.091%	24.136%	32.182%
0.775%	1.622%	2.558%	3.605%	8.91%	17.818%	26.727%	35.636%

FIGURE 3.10 The prepayment vectors are created in the example model on the Vectors sheet.

Copy and paste this formula over the range of cells V9:Y508. For code functionality later name cell U9 **strt_Prepay** and cells V9:Y508 **ppay_Table**. Thus far the prepayment area on the Vectors sheet should look like Figure 3.10.

18. The default and prepayment assumptions are nearly complete, but we would like a quick way to further stress the curves, perhaps by a multiple. On the Inputs sheet enter the following text in the corresponding cells:

D11: **Default Multiple**
D12: **Prepayment Multiple**

In cells E11 and E12, enter **1.0** for now, which is a base unstressed assumption. Name cell E11 **loss_Mult** and cell E12 **ppay_Mult**. The cells may need to be formatted as in the example model.

MODEL BUILDER 3.3: INTEREST RATES AND ADDITIONAL ASSET AMORTIZATION INPUTS

1. A number of items remain to prepare for the amortization code. One consideration we have allowed is variable rate loans. Although we do not have any variable rate loans in the prospectus supplement, many transactions require this functionality. Interest rate assumptions should be stored on the Vectors sheet. Enter the text **Interest Rates** in cell G6 and enter **1M Libor** in cell G7. The range of cells G9:G508 requires an interest rate assumption. For now copy and

paste the values from the example model into this range. Finally name cell G8 **strt_AssetFloat1** for code use later.

2. Another standard assumption that is useful for any reverse engineer is the SDA assumption. As discussed earlier, many prospectuses use SDA and SDA stress scenarios on assets. Enter the following text in the corresponding cells:

R6: **Defaults**
R7: **50% SDA**
S7: **100% SDA**
T7: **150% SDA**

The derivation of 100% SDA was described previously and can be implemented here. However, to save time it is acceptable to copy the values in the range of cells R9:T508 of the example model. At this point the Vectors sheet is complete. I recommend for readability that you format the sheet like the example model.

3. Back on the Inputs sheet there are a few final items to complete before we can move on to the amortization code. One item that will save time in the code later is if we know if our asset pool contains all fixed rate loans. If this is the case we do not have to load up many floating rate assumptions. In cell B11, enter the text **Assets Fixed/Floating**. We want the user to select Fixed, Variable, or Custom. The best way to do this is by implementing a data validation list. Go to the Hidden sheet and enter the following text in the corresponding cells:

A15: **IntStruc**
A16: **Fixed**
A17: **Variable**
A18: **Custom**

Name the range of cells A16:A18 **lst_FxdFlt**. Go back to the Inputs sheet and in cell C11, create a data validation list using the range **lst_FxdFlt**. Name this cell **assets_FxdFlt**.

4. Another valuable item for use in the code is how many assets we have to amortize. Because we have two loan groups we should parse each value out. Enter **Total Number of Group 1 Loans** in cell B13 and **Total Number of Group 2 Loans** in cell B14. Rather than entering a value each time we enter new assets on the Group Assets sheets we should use a formula. Enter the following formulas in cells C13 and C14, respectively:

C13: **=COUNT('Group 1 - Assets'!A2:A65536)**
C14: **=COUNT('Group 2 - Assets'!A2:A65536)**

Name cell C13 **gbl_LoanID1** and cell C14 **gbl_LoanID2**.

5. Finally, there is one other assumption to include, which may or may not be used in the modeling: Servicer Advances. For most transactions the servicers must advance delinquent interest and principal payments. Page S-9 introduces this concept under the section titled "P&I Advances" and is excerpted here:

P&I Advances

The servicer is required to advance delinquent payments of principal and interest on the mortgage loans, subject to the limitations described under "Description of the Certificates—P&I Advances" in this prospectus supplement. The servicer is entitled to be reimbursed for these advances, and therefore these advances are not a form of credit enhancement.

However, as can be read, servicer advances are not forms of credit enhancement because they should be fully reimbursable when cash is available. The other problem with servicer advances is found when we explore the section "Description of the Certificates—P&I Advances" in detail. This section, on page S-104 of the prospectus supplement, states that the servicer may not have to advance monies if they believe the advance may be nonrecoverable. The relevant wording is excerpted here:

. . . except to the extent the servicer determines any such advance to be nonrecoverable from future payments on the mortgage loan for which such advance was made.

If this is the case then there is no guarantee that the servicer must make an advance on any specific shortfall. Combined with this problem is the idea that if the servicer defaults there would be no advance. For all these reasons the benefit of including servicer advances is questionable.

Regardless, we will build in the option for servicer advances. Enter the text **Servicer Advances** in cell B15 of the Inputs sheet. A data validation list should also be used here to select Yes or No. Go to the Hidden sheet and enter the following text in the corresponding cells:

C15: **YesNo**
C16: **Yes**
C17: **No**

Name the range of cells C16:C17 **lst_YesNo**. Go back to the Inputs sheet and create a data validation list in cell C15 using the range **lst_YesNo**. Name cell **C15 gbl_ServicerAdv**. The Securitization Inputs section should look like Figure 3.11.

SECURITIZATION INPUTS			
Assets Fixed/Floating	Fixed	Default Multiple	1.0x
Maximum Periods	500	Prepayment Multiple	1.0x
Total Number of Group 1 Loans	55		
Total Number of Group 2 Loans	115		
Servicer Advances	No		

FIGURE 3.11 Controls relating the assets are stored on the Inputs sheet.

MODEL BUILDER 3.4: INTRODUCING VBA AND MOVING DATA IN AND OUT OF THE MODEL

1. With all the necessary inputs created, we are ready to utilize the power and flexibility of VBA code to create cash flow. Most of the work in this section will be created in the VBE, where code is written to perform calculations and interact with the worksheets. Activate the VBE by pressing **Alt-F11**. There are four primary windows that we should have an understanding about before giving specific code instructions: the Project Window, the Properties Window, the Code Window, and the Watch Window. Figure 3.12 shows the VBE with all four windows open. If one of the windows is not open on your system you can open it by selecting the **View** menu and left-clicking on the window name you want shown.

   Project Window: This is where a user selects the object they want to work with in the VBE. The most top-level item is the project that we are working in, which is denoted by statement VBAProject ([FILENAME]). The filename is whatever name the workbook has been saved under. There will be two files of objects within the VBA project that will be part of the example model: Microsoft Excel Objects and Modules. The Microsoft Excel Objects should already be created and lists the sheets and the workbook itself. We can write code that is related to specific sheets or the workbook itself, but all the code written for this project is in modules. The default setting for Excel workbooks is to have no modules, so we must insert at least one to view the Modules file. Do this by going to the **Insert menu** and left-clicking on **Module**. A module is where code is stored.

   Properties Window: This window changes properties of objects in the VBE. We will only use it to change the names of the modules to make them more relevant and easy to identify. Make sure Module1 is selected by left-clicking on it in the Project Window and then left-click on the **Name:** section in the Properties Window. Delete the name Module1 and replace it with Loader_Data1.

   Code Window: The large window that takes up most of the screen is where VBA code is written. A different code window will appear for every module

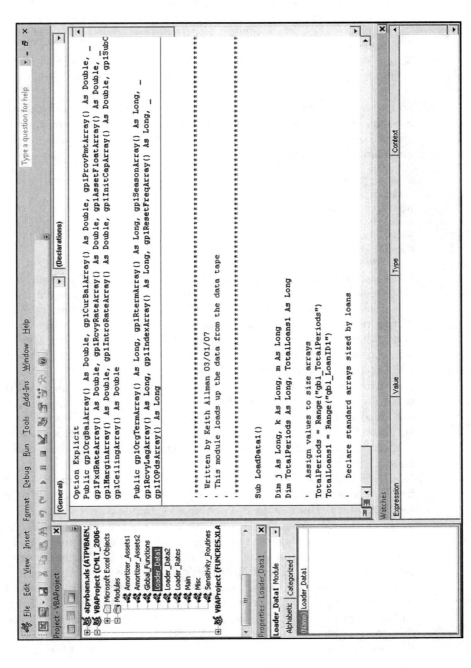

FIGURE 3.12 The Visual Basic Editor with the Project, Properties, Code, and Watch windows open.

51

in the Project Window, so be cognizant of which module is selected. Also, to select a module you must double left-click on the module to activate it. Double left-click on the module `LoaderData1`. You can see the name of the module that is selected on the top of the VBE window.

Watch Window: The watch window is used to see the values that code is returning. It is a good auditing tool that we will use later in the chapter.

2. So far we have explained the layout of the VBE and created and named a single module. We will be working in multiple modules to stay organized, so we should create them and name them now. Repeat the process described in Step 1 to insert and name the following modules:

```
Loader_Data2
Loader_Rates
Amortizer_Assets1
Amortizer_Assets2
Main
Global_Functions
```

We should now take a moment to think about our overall goal and the process that we need to implement. My philosophy in using VBA is to only use it when it is necessary. For this reason, we will only use it to create the asset cash flow as this requires multiple calculations for each loan, each period. The liability waterfall will be done on the Excel sheet. To create the asset cash flow efficiently we need to take the data that we know about the loans, which is contained on the Excel worksheets, load that data into a useable VBA form, perform loan amortization calculations, and export the completed schedules back to Excel worksheets. Although it is possible to create code that performs calculations on the Excel worksheets, this is an inefficient method that causes the code to run very slowly. As we work through each module the overall process will become clearer. For now, the next step is to jump right in and create code for the `Loader_Data1` module.

3. Double left click on the `Loader_Data1` module to make sure it is selected. The first step we need to do is create space in VBA's memory to store the data from the Excel sheet. This is done by creating code that loads the data from the Excel ranges to VBA arrays. Arrays are created by making up a name for the array followed by a `()` and then an optional declaration of a variable type. Declaring variable types are important because different types of variables take up different amounts of memory. If a variable is not declared then it will become a variant type, which takes up the most amount of memory. We will also use the `Public` statement in the beginning, as we will want to access the arrays in other modules. Although the code can be copied directly from the example model, I recommend that you type all the code out. Enter the code provided here in the Code Window for the `Loader_Data1` module. Note that all code has been formatted for easy

text viewing, which may make the spacing look different then what is in the VBE. Try to space the code in the VBE so it is easily readable, but be careful how you use underscores to break lines up.

```
Option Explicit
Public gp1OrgBalArray() As Double, gp1CurBalArray() As
Double, gp1ProvPmtArray() As Double, gp1FxdRateArray()
As Double, gp1RcvyRateArray() As Double, gp1AssetFloatArray()
As Double, gp1MarginArray() As Double, gp1IntroRateArray()
As Double, gp1InitCapArray() As Double, gp1SubCapArray()
As Double, gp1CeilingArray() As Double

Public gp1OrgTermArray() As Long, gp1RtermArray() As Long,
gp1SeasonArray() As Long, gp1RcvyLagArray() As Long,
gp1IndexArray() As Long, gp1ResetFreqArray() As Long,
gp1IOPdsArray() As Long
```

4. The next step is to create the first subroutine for the model. There are two main types of code that are written in VBA: subroutines and functions. A subroutine is similar to writing out a list of commands that the computer executes. A function returns a value when certain parameters are entered. The first subroutine sizes the arrays correctly and then fills them with the data from the Excel sheets. The first step to accomplish this is to initialize the subroutine, declare variables, and then assign values to the variables. This process is shown in the next section of code here.

```
'*****************************************************************
' Written by Keith Allman 03/01/07
' This module loads up the data from the data tape
'
'*****************************************************************

Sub LoadData1()

Dim j As Long, k As Long, m As Long
Dim TotalPeriods As Long, TotalLoans1 As Long

'    Assign values to size arrays
TotalPeriods = Range("gbl_TotalPeriods")
TotalLoans1 = Range("gbl_LoanID1")
```

The code does a number of things. The subroutine was initialized by using the Sub command with the name LoadData1, followed by open and close parentheses. Two variables were assigned values by writing the variable name, an equal sign, and then a reference to a value on the sheet. The references here use named ranges from the Excel sheet. Also notice that there is green text in the example model that begins with an apostrophe. These are comments to help code readers understand what each section does. They do not have an impact on the actual code in anyway. The other nuance to notice is the use of the underscore, which is used after a space in the code so a continuous code statement can be continued to the next line down.

5. In Step 4, we declared and assigned values to the variables `TotalPeriods` and `TotalLoans1`. The purpose of this next step is to size arrays. Whereas we declared the arrays earlier in Step 3, we did not create the size for them. Most of the arrays for Loan Group 1 come from the Group 1 – Assets sheet, where the size depends on the number of loans. In VBA, we size arrays with variables using the `ReDim` statement. Notice in the code here we use the `ReDim` statement, the name of the array, and then insert sizing parameters between the parentheses.

```
'    Declare standard arrays sized by loans
ReDim gp1OrgBalArray(1 To TotalLoans1, 0)
ReDim gp1CurBalArray(1 To TotalLoans1, 0)
ReDim gp1OrgTermArray(1 To TotalLoans1, 0)
ReDim gp1RtermArray(1 To TotalLoans1, 0)
ReDim gp1SeasonArray(1 To TotalLoans1, 0)
ReDim gp1ProvPmtArray(1 To TotalLoans1, 0)
ReDim gp1FxdRateArray(1 To TotalLoans1, 0)
ReDim gp1RcvyRateArray(1 To TotalLoans1, 0)
ReDim gp1RcvyLagArray(1 To TotalLoans1, 0)

'    Declare optional arrays
ReDim gp1IndexArray(1 To TotalLoans1, 0)
ReDim gp1AssetFloatArray(0 To TotalPeriods, 2)
ReDim gp1MarginArray(1 To TotalLoans1, 0)
ReDim gp1IntroRateArray(1 To TotalLoans1, 0)
ReDim gp1ResetFreqArray(1 To TotalLoans1, 0)
ReDim gp1InitCapArray(1 To TotalLoans1, 0)
ReDim gp1SubCapArray(1 To TotalLoans1, 0)
ReDim gp1CeilingArray(1 To TotalLoans1, 0)
ReDim gp1IOPdsArray(1 To TotalLoans1, 0)
```

We could have used numbers to size the arrays and the `Dim` statement, but because the number of periods and total number of loans could change from deal to deal, we should base the size on the variables we created. Every time the number of periods and total number of loans are changed on the Excel sheet and the subroutine run, the change will populate through the code.

6. Just because we declared and sized the arrays, does not mean that the data exists in the VBA's memory. The next step introduces two powerful and straightforward techniques that allow users to read in data: FOR-NEXT loops and OFFSET.

The first technique, FOR-NEXT loops perform a section of code repetitively, until the loop's limit is reached. The beginning of the first FOR-NEXT loop can be seen in the code here.

```
'*************************************************************
*******************************************
'    GLOBAL ARRAY READER
'*************************************************************
*******************************************

'    Read arrays based on TotalLoans1

For j = 1 To TotalLoans1
  gp1OrgBalArray(j, 0) = Range("strt_gp1_OrgBal").Offset(j, 0)
  gp1CurBalArray(j, 0) = Range("strt_gp1_CurBal").Offset(j, 0)
  gp1OrgTermArray(j, 0) = Range("strt_gp1_OrgTerm").Offset(j, 0)
  gp1RtermArray(j, 0) = Range("strt_gp1_Rterm").Offset(j, 0)
  gp1SeasonArray(j, 0) = Range("strt_gp1_Season").Offset(j, 0)
  gp1ProvPmtArray(j, 0) = Range("strt_gp1_ProvPMT").Offset(j, 0)
  gp1FxdRateArray(j, 0) = Range("strt_gp1_IR").Offset(j, 0)
  gp1RcvyRateArray(j, 0)= Range("strt_gp1_RcvyRate").Offset(j, 0)
  gp1RcvyLagArray(j, 0) = Range("strt_gp1_RcvyLag").Offset(j, 0)
  gp1IOPdsArray(j, 0) = Range("strt_gp1_IO").Offset(j, 0)
```

Notice that a counter variable j is used to start the loop. The statement starts j as 1 and increases it by 1 every time the code reaches a Next j. When the NEXT statement is reached, the order the code is run loops back to the beginning of the FOR statement. However, on the next iteration j becomes a 2. Once j reaches the value of TotalLoans1 the FOR-NEXT loop will stop and the code progresses below the NEXT statement.

What occurs in between the FOR and NEXT statement is incredibly important. Notice the first line of code below the FOR statement:

```
gp1OrgBalArray(j, 0) = Range("strt_gp1_OrgBal").Offset(j, 0)
```

In this section of code, we are loading up values into the array gp1OrgBal-Array. We are creating a two-dimensional array, which goes down by rows. VBA uses its own sense of data ordering by starting with 0 and creating one dimensional arrays on a horizontal basis. Because of this standard we will want to create the data in a way that is easy to understand and manipulate. Here we use the counter variable j, which starts at 1 and grows. For example, in the first iteration of the loop, if j was equal to 1, then we would be filling up the first row (single column as the column value is 0) of gp1OrgBalArray. The value that it would be is derived from the Offset method.

The `Offset` method in VBA works similar to the `Offset` function in Excel. `Offset` in VBA takes an object, such as a cell reference (in this case the named cell `strt_gp1_OrgBal`) as an anchor reference point and points to data depending on the value of the `Offset`. In this case we use the same counter variable `j` to determine the value of the `Offset`. As `j` increases and creates the order in the VBA array it also moves down the Excel sheet and reads in the data that is being Offset from the anchor value. This process continues for every array until the `FOR-NEXT` loop terminates.

7. There is a statement in the `FOR-NEXT` loop, the `IF-THEN` statement, which is used to build in efficiency. `IF-THEN` statements in VBA work similarly to the `IF` function in Excel. Look at the continuation of the code as depicted here.

```
'   If assets are variable rate or have a floating/
custom structure additional fields are read
 If Range("assets_FxdFlt") <> "Fixed" Then
  gp1IndexArray(j, 0) = Range("strt_gp1_Index").Offset(j, 0)
  gp1MarginArray(j, 0) = Range("strt_gp1_Margins").Offset(j, 0)
  gp1IntroRateArray(j, 0) = Range("strt_gp1_OrgRate").Offset(j, 0)
  gp1ResetFreqArray(j, 0) = Range("strt_gp1_ResetFreq").Offset(j, 0)
  gp1InitCapArray(j, 0) = Range("strt_gp1_PCap").Offset(j, 0)
  gp1SubCapArray(j, 0) = Range("strt_gp1_SubsCap").Offset(j, 0)
  gp1CeilingArray(j, 0) = Range("strt_gp1_Ceiling").Offset(j, 0)
 End If
Next j
```

The `IF-THEN` statement tests whether or not the cell named `assets_FxdFlt` has a value of `Fixed`. If the loans are not only fixed rate, then it proceeds to load up the floating rate arrays. Notice that the symbols < > were used to denote "does not equal" in the conditional statement. This allows us to only have to write one conditional statement because we have two alternatives to fixed rate assets: variable and custom. `IF-THEN` statements in VBA must always be finished off with an `End If` statement. If this is omitted then the subroutine will not compile and an error will be generated. Also notice that the `FOR-NEXT` loop is finished off at the bottom with the `Next` statement.

8. Two final lines of code complete the `LoadData1` subroutine, as seen in the code after this paragraph. The first line is used to control the Status Bar on the Excel sheet. The Status Bar is the bottom left area of the Excel workbook that typically says "Ready" or "Calculate" if the sheet has not been calculated. This can be changed by VBA to inform model users of the current progress of a macro. In this subroutine, we only inform readers that loan data is loading. Later we will see how to show looping progress in the Status Bar. Finally, every subroutine must end with an `End Sub`, which is declared at the bottom.

```
Application.StatusBar = "Loading Loan Data..."
End Sub
```

9. Steps 1 through 8 should be replicated for a new subroutine named `LoadData2` that should be saved in the `Loader_Data2` module. The difference between the two is that all the arrays and variables that contain *gp1* (a convention for Group 1), should be converted to **gp2**. Because this was done on the Excel sheets the changed code will pick up and run completely new arrays of potentially different sizes and values.

MODEL BUILDER 3.5: LOADING LOAN PERFORMANCE ASSUMPTIONS INTO VBA

1. The next step is to create a subroutine to load up the prepayment and default assumptions from the sheet. Because of the size and uniformity of the data, we will use a slightly different technique to load this data. However, many of the techniques remain the same. Begin by declaring more public arrays at the top of the `Loader_Rates` module. Here is the code that should be entered.

```
Option Explicit
Public gp1PrepayRange() As Double
Public gp1DefaultRange() As Double
Public gp2PrepayRange() As Double
Public gp2DefaultRange() As Double
```

This code creates four sets of arrays: prepayment and default arrays for both loan groups.

2. The next step is to comment the module, initialize it with the `Sub` statement, and declare standard variables. The standard variables are counter variables for loops and the ultimate loop limits for total loans in each group and the total periods. There are two additional variables in this subroutine that are specialized for performance: `PrepayMultiple` and `DefaultMultiple`. These will be values that are used to stress the performance curves. These variables can be seen in the next section of code here.

```
'*************************************************************
' Written by Keith Allman 03/01/07
' This module loads up the prepay and default curves for each
loan
'
'*************************************************************

Sub LoadPpayDefRates()

Dim aLoans As Long, bLoans As Long, bPeriods As Long
Dim TotalPeriods As Long, TotalLoans1 As Long, TotalLoans2
As Long

Dim PrepayMultiple As Double, DefaultMultiple As Double
```

3. After declaring the variables, we still need to point them to a location on the Excel sheet where values can be read. This is done in the next section of code here.

```
'    Assign values to size arrays
TotalPeriods = Range("gbl_TotalPeriods")
TotalLoans1 = Range("gbl_LoanID1")
TotalLoans2 = Range("gbl_LoanID2")

'    Assign values for stresses
PrepayMultiple = Range("ppay_Mult")
DefaultMultiple = Range("loss_Mult")
```

4. The following step, sizing arrays for performance data, causes confusion because it is slightly different then before and takes advantage of multidimensional arrays in VBA. Instead of sizing single arrays for each prepayment and default curve, we size two giant arrays that are organized by loan and period. Essentially, there will be a space for a unique loss and prepayment curve to be loaded up for each loan. The code here shows that this is done using the ReDim statement as before.

```
'    Declare arrays for prepays and defaults
ReDim gp1PrepayRange(0 To TotalLoans1, 0 To TotalPeriods)
ReDim gp1DefaultRange(0 To TotalLoans1, 0 To TotalPeriods)
ReDim gp2PrepayRange(0 To TotalLoans2, 0 To TotalPeriods)
ReDim gp2DefaultRange(0 To TotalLoans2, 0 To TotalPeriods)
```

Notice once again that we size separate arrays for prepayments and defaults for each loan group.

5. Step 4 sized arrays for each loan, but we also need a method to determine which curve to assign to each loan. Earlier, on the Excel sheet, we created flags on the Assets sheets that are numeric fields to be entered by the user to select curves stored in the model. We must size arrays for these flags to automate the selection process. The code here shows how this is done.

```
'    Declare loan arrays for prepays and defaults
ReDim PrepayFlagArray1(1 To TotalLoans1, 0) As Long
ReDim DefFlagArray1(1 To TotalLoans1, 0) As Long
ReDim PrepayFlagArray2(1 To TotalLoans2, 0) As Long
ReDim DefFlagArray2(1 To TotalLoans2, 0) As Long
```

6. Up to this point, we have sized arrays for curves to be assigned to each loan and to the flags to map the curves to loans, but we have yet to size an array for the actual performance data. We will do this in a more efficient method than before,

by sizing an array as a variant and taking in entire data tables at once. These methods are shown in the code here.

```
'    Define performance arrays for taking all loan data
Dim PrepayExcelRange As Variant
Dim DefaultExcelRange As Variant

'    Assign arrays to ranges from workbook, which essen-
tially loads up all curve data
PrepayExcelRange = Range("ppay_Table")
DefaultExcelRange = Range("rng_DefaultCurveTable")
```

7. The next step in this subroutine is to read the data into the arrays that have just been sized. We begin with the prepayment and default flags for both loan groups as seen in the code here.

```
'    Loop through each loan to determine which curve to use
For aLoans = 1 To TotalLoans1
 PrepayFlagArray1(aLoans, 0) =
 Range("strt_gp1_PPayFlag").Offset(aLoans, 0)
 DefFlagArray1(aLoans, 0) =
 Range("strt_gp1_DefFlag").Offset(aLoans, 0)
Next aLoans

For aLoans = 1 To TotalLoans2
 PrepayFlagArray2(aLoans, 0) = Sheets("Group 2 -
 Assets").Range("strt_gp2_PPayFlag").Offset(aLoans, 0)
 DefFlagArray2(aLoans, 0) = Sheets("Group 2 -
 Assets").Range("strt_gp2_DefFlag").Offset(aLoans, 0)
Next aLoans
```

8. The next major part of the code is where everything comes together. We introduce two major concepts in this section of the code: using nested loops and using arrays of VBA data that we just created. The code here starts by looping through each loan and then each period for each loan. The purpose of this is to fill the prepayment and default curve ranges for each loan for each period. We have an array that contains all the curve data and an array that contains flags for mapping loans to the curves. We then set the empty array that has been sized for loans and periods to take in values based on references using the other two arrays and a counter variable.

   The counter variable locates the correct period from the performance arrays, whereas the flag arrays locate the correct curve to use from the performance arrays. Finally, the stressors are applied to each period as the percentages are read into the organized array.

```
'    Fill prepay and default arrays prior to computation
For bLoans = 1 To TotalLoans1
 For bPeriods = 1 To TotalPeriods
```

```
    gp1PrepayRange(bLoans, bPeriods) = PrepayExcelRange
    (bPeriods, PrepayFlagArray1(bLoans, 0)) * PrepayMultiple
    gp1DefaultRange(bLoans, bPeriods) = DefaultExcelRange
    (bPeriods,DefFlagArray1(bLoans, 0)) * DefaultMultiple
  Next bPeriods
Next bLoans

For bLoans = 1 To TotalLoans2
  For bPeriods = 1 To TotalPeriods
    gp2PrepayRange(bLoans, bPeriods) = PrepayExcelRange
    (bPeriods,PrepayFlagArray2(bLoans, 0)) * PrepayMultiple
    gp2DefaultRange(bLoans, bPeriods) = DefaultExcelRange
    (bPeriods,DefFlagArray2(bLoans, 0)) * DefaultMultiple
  Next bPeriods
Next bLoans

End Sub
```

A few programming tips can be drawn from this example. The first is to be mindful of the order of nested loops. The subroutine would be difficult to conceptualize if we first looped through periods and then through loans. There is even a chance that inefficiency can be introduced depending on which loops are nested. The second programming concept to be mindful of is that we created this subroutine in a specific order. We needed to dimension, size, and fill certain arrays before we could use them in the code itself later.

9. Make sure to end the subroutine with an End Sub, which should automatically be created when we entered the Sub statement.

MODEL BUILDER 3.6: GLOBAL FUNCTIONS

1. There are two functions that should be created prior to writing the main amortization code. The reason for this is that functions run slowly when they are called from the Excel library. We can speed code up if we create our own custom functions. Of course the trade-off is the complexity of the function versus its implementation. The two easiest functions to develop on your own are MIN and MAX functions. These functions are created in the Global_Functions module. Enter the code here in the Global_Functions module to create the MAX function.

```
'****************************************************************
'General Max Function
'****************************************************************
Function max(var1 As Variant, var2 As Variant, Optional var3
  As Variant)
```

```
If var1 >= var2 Then
    max = var1
Else
    max = var2
End If

If (Not IsMissing(var3)) Then
    If max < var3 Then
        max = var3
    End If
End If

End Function
```

2. Now repeat the same for the MIN function but reverse all the less than or greater than signs as seen in code here.

```
'*************************************************************
'General Min Function
'*************************************************************
Function min(var1 As Variant, var2 As Variant,
  Optional var3 As Variant)

    If var1 <= var2 Then
        min = var1
    Else
        min = var2
    End If

    If (Not IsMissing(var3)) Then
        If min > var3 Then
            min = var3
        End If
    End If

End Function
```

We can now use MAX and MIN later in our code for asset amortization.

MODEL BUILDER 3.7: LOAN-LEVEL ASSET AMORTIZATION

1. With all auxiliary modules to the asset amortization modules complete, now we can actually create the asset amortization code. As with the loader subroutines,

we will create the code for the first loan group and then repeat the process for the second. Double left-click on the `Amortizer_Assets1` module and begin the preliminary code for the `Amort1` subroutine. The code here shows how it begins.

```
Option Explicit
Public DayFactorArray() As Double
Sub Amort1()


'*************************************************************
' Written by Keith Allman 03/01/07
' This is a custom amortization engine for fixed and
  floating rate transactions.
'
'*************************************************************
```

2. Next, just as we did earlier in the beginning of most subroutines, we declare variables and assign values to some of them. This process is shown in the code here.

```
'    Declare variables
Dim i As Long, j As Long, k As Long, m As Long, l As Long,
z As Long, d As Long, q As Long, u As Long,
TotalPeriods As Long, TotalLoans1 As Long
Dim FixedFloat As String, ServAdv As String

'    Assign values to size arrays
TotalPeriods = Range("gbl_TotalPeriods")
TotalLoans1 = Range("gbl_LoanID1")

'    Assign Values to run constants
FixedFloat = Range("assets_FxdFlt")
ServAdv = Range("gbl_ServicerAdv")
```

3. With a few key values loaded into the variables we can now start declaring arrays as seen in the code here.

```
'    Declare standard arrays sized by periods
ReDim DayFactorArray(0 To TotalPeriods, 0) As Double
ReDim PrepayArray(0 To TotalPeriods, 0) As Double
ReDim DefaultArray(0 To TotalPeriods, 0) As Double
ReDim CurRateArray(0 To TotalPeriods, 0) As Double
'    Dim arrays for notional amort
ReDim NotionalBegBal(0 To TotalPeriods, 0)
ReDim NotionalPMT(0 To TotalPeriods, 0)
ReDim NotionalInt(0 To TotalPeriods, 0)
ReDim NotionalPrin(0 To TotalPeriods, 0)
ReDim NotionalEndBal(0 To TotalPeriods, 0)
ReDim NotionalAmortFact(0 To TotalPeriods, 0)
```

We will use the ReDim statement for each array so we can make them dynamic. The key to this section is to notice the names of the arrays that we are declaring, as they give us an idea of what data we will fill them with. We will need a day count factor for all the rates related to the collateral, the performance data, and finally an array to store the current rate. We will go into more detail on the current rate as we use it later in the code, but for now we should understand that we need a space to store the current rate of each security, regardless of the rates in the market.

The next section of arrays curiously begins with the word Notional. This is because we are going to first amortize the loans assuming no prepayment and default, and then introduce the performance factors to create the actual amortization. There are six notional arrays. The first five are standard amortization arrays: beginning balance, payment, interest, principal, and ending balance. The final notional array is the payment factor, which is a fractional representation of the notional amortizing balance.

4. The next section is to declare and size the arrays for the actual amortization as shown in the code here. We will go through what each array means as we see it in the body of the code later, but for now notice that the array is being sized by the total number of periods.

```
'    Dim arrays for actual calcs
ReDim ActualBegBal(0 To TotalPeriods, 0)
ReDim ActualNewDef(0 To TotalPeriods, 0)
ReDim ActualNewDefDelay(0 To TotalPeriods, 0)
ReDim ActualADB(0 To TotalPeriods, 0)
ReDim ActualLoss(0 To TotalPeriods, 0)
ReDim ActualIntPerf(0 To TotalPeriods, 0)
ReDim ActualIntAdv(0 To TotalPeriods, 0)
ReDim ActualPrinPerf(0 To TotalPeriods, 0)
ReDim ActualPrinAdv(0 To TotalPeriods, 0)
ReDim ActualRecovery(0 To TotalPeriods, 0)
ReDim ActualAdvOwed(0 To TotalPeriods, 0)
ReDim ActualPrepay(0 To TotalPeriods, 0)
ReDim ActualPrepayPen(0 To TotalPeriods, 0)
ReDim ActualDefRoll(0 To TotalPeriods, 0)
ReDim ActualPMT(0 To TotalPeriods, 0)
ReDim ActualEndBal(0 To TotalPeriods, 0)
```

5. Once we have the arrays for actual amortization, there is another set of arrays that are required. These are the aggregation arrays. Conceptually, we must loop through each loan to get its amortization schedule. We could technically figure out a way to do this by making cumulative arrays, but to aid in auditing, it is preferred to have separate arrays for the current loan of the loop and aggregation

arrays for all the loans that have been amortized. The aggregation arrays are declared and sized in the code here.

```
'   Dim arrays for aggregation
ReDim AggBegBal(0 To TotalPeriods, 0)
ReDim AggNewDef(0 To TotalPeriods, 0)
ReDim AggNewDefDelay(0 To TotalPeriods, 0)
ReDim AggADB(0 To TotalPeriods, 0)
ReDim AggLoss(0 To TotalPeriods, 0)
ReDim AggIntPerf(0 To TotalPeriods, 0)
ReDim AggIntAdv(0 To TotalPeriods, 0)
ReDim AggPrinPerf(0 To TotalPeriods, 0)
ReDim AggPrinAdv(0 To TotalPeriods, 0)
ReDim AggRecovery(0 To TotalPeriods, 0)
ReDim AggAdvOwed(0 To TotalPeriods, 0)
ReDim AggPrepay(0 To TotalPeriods, 0)
ReDim AggPrepayPen(0 To TotalPeriods, 0)
ReDim AggDefRoll(0 To TotalPeriods, 0)
ReDim AggPMT(0 To TotalPeriods, 0)
ReDim AggEndBal(0 To TotalPeriods, 0)
```

6. The next step is to start loading up data using the subroutines that we created earlier. Creating subroutines with simple, specific purposes is a better practice than building a single large subroutine. Modular creation reduces error and is faster to edit in the future. In VBA, once we create subroutines we can run them using the `Call` statement. In the code here we call two subroutines we created earlier: `LoadData1` and `LoadPpayDefRates`.

```
Application.ScreenUpdating = False

'****************************************************************
'   DATA LOAD
'****************************************************************

'   Load up asset data
    Call LoadData1

'   Load up all prepayment and default rates
    Call LoadPpayDefRates

'   Read arrays based on TotalPeriods
    For m = 0 To TotalPeriods
      DayFactorArray(m, 0) = Range("strt_DayFactor").Offset(m, 0)
      gp1AssetFloatArray(m, 0) = Range("strt_AssetFloat1").
      Offset(m, 0)
    Next m

    Application.StatusBar = False
```

Whereas we load a majority of the necessary input data using the `LoadData1` and `LoadPpayDefRates`, there are two universal arrays related to amortization that we should load up to amortize loan group 1: the day factor and the floating interest rate assumption. This is done with a `For-Next` loop as seen in the code. Also notice the code to turn off screen updating to save time and the control of the status bar. In this instance, the status bar is reset to "Ready" using the `FALSE` statement because the `LoadData1` and `LoadPpayDefRates` subroutines change the status bar as they are run.

7. With all the necessary assumption data loaded we can begin working with the amortization arrays. Be aware that the loan loop is initiated using k as the counter variable. It is important to track the loop that the counter variables are related to because they will be used throughout the code. The k loop is going to loop through every loan first. Immediately after initiating the k loop the q loop is started to clear out any data that might exist in the notional arrays. The code here shows the k and q loops.

```
'****************************************************************
'    NOTIONAL LOAN AMORTIZATION
'****************************************************************

'    Loop through each loan
     For k = 1 To TotalLoans1

'    Clear the notional amort arrays
        For q = 0 To TotalPeriods
            NotionalBegBal(q, 0) = 0
            NotionalPMT(q, 0) = 0
            NotionalInt(q, 0) = 0
            NotionalPrin(q, 0) = 0
            NotionalEndBal(q, 0) = 0
            NotionalAmortFact(q, 0) = 0
            CurRateArray(q, 0) = 0
        Next q
```

Always keep in mind that code written with loops must anticipate future iterations of the loop. Clearing arrays is a perfect example of the attention that must be paid to the possible future effects of the loop. For example, if the first loan had a term of 360 periods, the amortization schedule would be created and stored for 360 periods. If the second loan only had 240 periods, then the first 240 periods of the array would be rewritten, but the remaining 120 periods would remain. These remaining periods would be incorrectly added to the aggregate amortization later.

8. For each loan we will loop through a period, perform calculations, and then move onto the next period. To do this we need to create another `For-Next` loop for the periods. The counter variable for this loop is z. We start the loop from 0 because period 0 is the closing date. Upon closing there are a couple

of values that should be captured. The first is the balance of the loan, which is stored as the ending balance for period 0. There is no beginning balance for period 0 because it is not a "full" period. The second is setting the amortization factor to 1, because no amortization takes place on the closing date. If we are not in the 0 period, then the next array to fill is the beginning balance. The beginning balance is always the ending balance from the previous period. This is easy to do in code because the previous period's value can be referenced directly by subtracting 1 from the current loop's value in the ending balance array. All this code is shown here.

```
'    Begin the notional amortization with the zero period
balance ' and the amort factor set to one
  For z = 0 To TotalPeriods
   If z = 0 Then
    NotionalEndBal(z, 0) = gp1CurBalArray(k, 0)
    NotionalAmortFact(z, 0) = 1
     Else
       NotionalBegBal(z, 0) = NotionalEndBal(z - 1, 0)
```

9. Before we can start doing any calculations involving payments or rates, we must know the correct interest rate. The example transaction is simplified as all the loans are fixed rate, however, we should build in floating rate capability. To do this, we need to write a series of statements to account for the reset periodicity and caps related to a floating rate loan. The first step as seen in the code here saves running time by avoiding all the forthcoming floating rate calculations if we are dealing with a fixed rate pool. This is done by using an If-Then statement connected to an option that is selected on the Inputs sheet. If all the loans are fixed rate, then the fixed rate for each loan should be loaded as the rate for each period.

```
'    Determine the current period interest rate.  If fixed rate
'use given rate, otherwise variable tests need to be run
If FixedFloat = "Fixed" Then
 CurRateArray(z, 0) = gp1FxdRateArray(k, 0)
  Else
'    Floating rate assets in the first period use the
introductory interest rate
    If z = 1 Then
     CurRateArray(z, 0) = gp1IntroRateArray(k, 0)
      Else
```

If there are floating rate loans then the first period rate should be the introductory interest rate. This could be a low teaser rate or simply the current rate of the loan. Something very important to notice, from a programming perspective, is that we are loading up data for the loans using the k loop, but using the z loop for the periods. In the case of a fixed rate the z loop will go through all its iterations for a single k (a loan) and then move on to the next loan and go through all the iterations again, most likely loading a different value.

10. If assets are floating rate they actually remain fixed until the first reset period. In this period the loan rate changes to the market rate, taking into account rate caps. An `If-Then` statement is used to check for this period against the loan's first reset period. If the current z loop is equal to the first reset period for the loan, then the loan rate is the index rate plus margin, capped by the previous period's rate plus the cap amount and the absolute ceiling. The code for this section is shown here.

```
'    Floating rate assets at their first reset are bound
by the initial cap
If z = gplResetFreqArray(k, 0) Then
 CurRateArray(z, 0)= min(gplAssetFloatArray(z, gplIndexArray(k,
 0)) + gplMarginArray(k, 0), CurRateArray(z - 1, 0) +
 gplInitCapArray(k, 0), gplCeilingArray(k, 0))
  Else

'    Otherwise the assets are bound by the subsequent
cap and the ceiling
   If z Mod gplResetFreqArray(k, 0) = 0 Then
    CurRateArray(z, 0) = min(gplAssetFloatArray(z,
    gplIndexArray(k, 0)) + gplMarginArray(k, 0),
    CurRateArray(z - 1, 0) + gplSubCapArray(k, 0),
    gplCeilingArray(k, 0))
     Else
       CurRateArray(z, 0) = CurRateArray(z - 1, 0)
   End If
End If
End If
End If
```

Notice that this is the first time we use the MIN statement created in the `Global_Functions` module. This saves calculation time by avoiding a worksheet function call.

The next major section of the floating rate determination is if the z loop is in a reset period after the initial reset period. To determine whether the z loop is in a reset period, the MOD operator can be used. MOD is short for *modulus*, which is a calculation that determines the remainder of dividing two numbers. If the z loop is perfectly divisible by the reset periodicity, then the loan should reset. For instance, if the reset periodicity is 12 and the z loop is on month 23, then the MOD returns 11 and is known to be not perfectly divisible. However, when the z loop hits 24 with a reset periodicity of 12, the MOD returns a zero. The same is true when z hits 36, 48, and so on. With a reliable pattern we can use an IF statement to initiate the resetting of the loan as seen in the lower part of the previous code.

Finally, if the loan is not in a reset period then the rate is the previous period's rate. Also, all the `If-Then` statements that were created must be ended with `End If` statements. This is also shown in the previous code.

11. Once the rate is determined we can now start doing calculations. The first one is the periodic payment. Recall that we created an array for the possibility of a payment that has already been calculated. The first section of code for the payment calculation should check if there is a value that has already been calculated in the provided payment column on the Inputs sheet. This is done using an If-Then statement checking if a value greater than zero is entered in that column. If it is left at zero then a level payment should be calculated. Here we can use the Pmt function, which can be called from the VBA library. It works exactly the same as the Pmt function on the Excel sheet:

Pmt(periodic rate, total number of periods, present value).

Because we have the current rate for the period and the day factor, we can calculate the periodic rate. The total number of periods is the loan's original term and the present value is the loan's original balance. This section of code is depicted here.

```
'    If the payment is already provided then use it, other-
wise 'calculate it based on Original Term, Rate, and Balance
If gp1ProvPmtArray(k, 0) > 0 Then
 NotionalPMT(z, 0) = min(gp1ProvPmtArray(k, 0), NotionalBeg-
Bal(z,
 0) + (CurRateArray(z, 0) * DayFactorArray(z, 0)) *
 NotionalBegBal(z, 0))
  Else
    NotionalPMT(z, 0) = min(VBA.Pmt(CurRateArray(z, 0) *
    DayFactorArray(z, 0), gp1OrgTermArray(k, 0),
gp1OrgBalArray(k,
    0) * -1), NotionalBegBal(z, 0) + (CurRateArray(z, 0) *
    DayFactorArray(z, 0)) * NotionalBegBal(z, 0))
End If
```

12. The next calculation that should be completed is the interest component of the payment. This is one of the easiest calculations in the code. It is the current rate multiplied by the day factor multiplied by the beginning balance of the period. This is shown in the top portion of the code here.

```
'    Pay notional interest
NotionalInt(z, 0) = (CurRateArray(z, 0) *
DayFactorArray(z, 0)) * NotionalBegBal(z, 0)


'    Check if loan is in an interest only period, if so do not
pay 'principal.  Otherwise principal is payment less interest
 If z <= gp1IOPdsArray(k, 0) Then
  NotionalPrin(z, 0) = 0
   Else
     NotionalPrin(z, 0) = NotionalPMT(z, 0) - NotionalInt(z, 0)
 End If
```

The bottom half of the code shows the principal calculation. As this transaction has loans that have IO periods, we must build in that functionality. We know when the IO period of each loan expires based on the data we loaded up into the `IOpdsArray`. If a loan is still in its IO period then no principal should be paid. However, once the IO period is done, the principal is the payment less the interest.

An interesting point to consider here, from a programming point of view, is that we are using arrays that we have created in the code in calculations for other arrays. Any programmer must be careful to map this process out earlier to avoid requiring an array for a calculation that has not been created yet. For example, to calculate the principal we need to calculate the payment and interest first. There are other methods, but this is the most precise and error can be introduced when using custom functions to overcome illogical calculation order.

13. The notional amortization is nearly complete, except for two arrays. The first of these is the ending balance, which is the beginning balance minus the current period's principal. The second array is calculating the amortization factor, which is the current period's ending balance divided by the closing balance. Notice that all `If-Then` statements are closed off using `End If` statements and the z loop is set to iterate using the `Next z` statement. This is shown in the code here.

```
'   Calculate ending balance and amortization factor
NotionalEndBal(z, 0) = NotionalBegBal(z, 0) -
NotionalPrin(z, 0)
NotionalAmortFact(z, 0) = NotionalEndBal(z, 0)
/NotionalEndBal(0, 0)
 End If
Next z
```

14. With notional amortization done for every period, we now have an excellent basis to begin the actual amortization. Performance factors such as default, prepayment, and recovery will require many additional calculations. Also note that we must now capture every final calculation for each period to store in separate aggregated arrays. Still we begin by doing as we did for the notional amortization arrays and clear out the arrays from the start. The code here shows this next section.

```
'*************************************************************
'   ACTUAL LOAN AMORTIZATION
'*************************************************************

'   Clear actual amortization arrays
    For m = 1 To TotalPeriods
        ActualBegBal(m, 0) = 0
        ActualNewDef(m, 0) = 0
        ActualNewDefDelay(m, 0) = 0
        ActualADB(m, 0) = 0
```

```
        ActualLoss(m, 0) = 0
        ActualIntPerf(m, 0) = 0
        ActualIntAdv(m, 0) = 0
        ActualPrinPerf(m, 0) = 0
        ActualPrinAdv(m, 0) = 0
        ActualRecovery(m, 0) = 0
        ActualAdvOwed(m, 0) = 0
        ActualPrepay(m, 0) = 0
        ActualPrepayPen(m, 0) = 0
        ActualDefRoll(m, 0) = 0
        ActualPMT(m, 0) = 0
        ActualEndBal(m, 0) = 0
    Next m
```

15. The first real step of the actual amortization is looping through the periods (i loop) and performing all the necessary calculations for each period. Recall that we never exited the first loan (k loop). In memory we have the first loan's notional amortization for every period. We begin filling the actual amortization arrays in a very similar pattern, with the balance for period 0. Once again, if we are not in period 0 then the beginning balance is the prior month's ending balance. This concept is transformed into the code here.

```
'    Loop through each period
    For i = 0 To TotalPeriods

'    If in period 0 use the current balances from the data tape
'rather than calculating the beginning balance
    If i = 0 Then
      ActualEndBal(i, 0) = gp1CurBalArray(k, 0)
      AggEndBal(i, 0) = ActualEndBal(i, 0) + AggEndBal(i, 0)
      Else
        ActualBegBal(i, 0) = ActualEndBal(i - 1, 0)
        AggBegBal(i, 0) = ActualBegBal(i, 0) + AggBegBal(i, 0)
```

Notice the arrays beginning with Agg, which equal one of the actual arrays, plus itself. This technique is how we store information across loans. The Agg arrays will never be cleared by setting every period to 0 using loops. Instead, each loans' value for each period will be aggregated, producing a single amortization schedule for the entire pool of loans.

16. A unique section to the actual amortization is that we have to do some work on the recovery array first. This is because there are situations that need to be anticipated prior to ending the period loop. Logically, we should end the loan loop when the beginning balance is paid off. However, if we do this, we would miss any recovery that would result from a late-stage default. For instance, if the default curve for the loan had a value in period 239 and the loan's balance went

to 0 in period 240 and there was a recovery assumption with a 6-month lag, we would miss 5 months of recovery. To overcome this, we initialize a loop for all recovery periods after the loan pays off, as seen in the code here.

```
'    If the remaining balance of the loan is zero, begin a
loop 'for recoveries post amortization.  Do not start any
recoveries 'until after the lag period
    If ActualBegBal(i, 0) < 0.01 Then
    For u = 1 To gp1RcvyLagArray(k, 0)
    ActualRecovery(i, 0) = 0
    AggRecovery(i, 0) = ActualRecovery(i, 0) +
AggRecovery(i, 0)
```

You may wonder why we make the recovery value 0 to start with in each period. This is to make sure that the recovery array is clear prior to any late stage calculation from a previous loan.

17. Another unique situation to consider for recoveries is if the loan pays off prior to the first recovery. Any period prior to the first recovery will attempt to reference an invalid negative period for recovery. We cut this off with the code here.

```
'    If the loan has a short tenor and it pays off before
the 'recovery lag, there should be no recovery until the
period after 'the lag
    If (i - gp1RcvyLagArray(k, 0)) <= 0 Then
    ActualRecovery(i, 0) = 0
    i = i + 1
    Else
```

18. If the other conditions have not been met, then there must be a default that should be recovered. Instead of using an Offset function like on the Excel sheet, we can just reference the new default array (NewDef) by subtracting out the recovery lag. You may be asking yourself, "We have not created the NewDef array yet, so how is this possible." Remember to think in loops and that this specialized recovery code only runs if the balance of the loan is already zero. It would be virtually impossible to not run the code that fills the NewDef array prior to this section of code, which is shown here.

```
'    Otherwise, the recovery amount is the recovery rate
times the 'defaulted amount for the current time period
less the lag period
ActualRecovery(i, 0) = gp1RcvyRateArray(k, 0) * Actual-
NewDef(i -
gp1RcvyLagArray(k, 0), 0)
AggRecovery(i, 0) = ActualRecovery(i, 0) + AggRecovery(i, 0)
i = i + 1
```

```
        End If
     Next u
     Exit For
  End If
```

Also in the code is the first use of the `Exit For` statement. This is to end the period loop for a loan if the specialized recovery loop is complete. There is no more calculation to be done. Be very careful on the use of `Exit For` statements—they end all procedures related to a loop the minute the statement is read.

19. The next section of code shown here is to calculate default. Multiple concepts are turned into code here. The first is that we are calculating defaults using an original balance methodology. This means that the periodic percentages of the loss curves are multiplied against the original balance of the loan. With regard to default, there are many methods to choose from, but this is the one most seen by sell side structurers. Because we are using an original balance methodology there is the possibility that the default curve could exceed the balance of the loan. If this situation ever occurs, the code here caps the default to the current balance of the loan.

```
'    Calculate defaults.  In high default scenarios where
defaults 'can exceed the beginning balance, force the
default to equal the 'beginning balance.
ActualNewDef(i, 0) = min(gp1DefaultRange
(k, (i + gp1SeasonArray(k, 0))) * gp1OrgBalArray(k, 0),
ActualBegBal(i, 0))
AggNewDef(i, 0) = ActualNewDef(i, 0) + AggNewDef(i, 0)
```

Also of importance in this section is the use of the seasoning array (`gp1SeasonArray`). It is added to the `i` counter variable to reference the correct point of time on the loan's default curve. Seasoned loans in pools should not take loss like a new loan. The loss percentage should be determined based on the loan's seasoning and the correct percentage referenced. Using the seasoning array as shown in the previous code achieves this.

20. Losses are realized when the recovery is expected. We should, therefore, track the default amount as it is delayed by recovery. For each default there will be a recovery lag period where the recovery rate will be realized and the loss passed through the structure. Keep in mind that the timing of realized loss can differ between deals. The method shown here is standard for U.S. mortgage transactions as this is the type of deal that we are reverse engineering. The code here shows how to delay defaults.

```
'    Calculate delayed defaults.  These are essentially
the new defaults at their delay period.
If i > gp1RcvyLagArray(k, 0) Then
ActualNewDefDelay(i, 0) = ActualNewDef(i -
```

```
gp1RcvyLagArray (k, 0), 0)
AggNewDefDelay(i, 0) = ActualNewDefDelay(i, 0) +
AggNewDefDelay(i, 0)
 Else
  ActualNewDefDelay(i, 0) = 0
  AggNewDefDelay(i, 0) = ActualNewDefDelay(i, 0) +
AggNewDefDelay(i, 0)
  End If
```

21. The next section of code is only for those who are reverse engineering a deal with the assumption that the servicer advances delinquent payments. Earlier we explained why this might not be the case, but if it is, the reverse engineer should track the amortizing default balance (ADB). This is how much of the defaulted loans should be amortizing each period. The code here should be inserted to implement servicer advances.

```
'    Calculate the amortized defaulted balance (ADB).
If ServAdv = "Yes" Then
 If i > gp1RcvyLagArray(k, 0) Then
  ActualADB(i, 0) = ActualNewDefDelay(i, 0) *
  (NotionalAmortFact(i - 1, 0) / NotionalAmortFact(i - 1 -
  gp1RcvyLagArray(k, 0), 0))
  AggADB(i, 0) = ActualADB(i, 0) + AggADB(i, 0)
   Else
    ActualADB(i, 0) = 0
    AggADB(i, 0) = ActualADB(i, 0) + AggADB(i, 0)
  End If
   Else
    ActualADB(i, 0) = ActualNewDefDelay(i, 0)
    AggADB(i, 0) = ActualADB(i, 0) + AggADB(i, 0)
End If
```

If servicer advances are not assumed, then the ADB is equal to the delayed defaults.

22. The final step for loss is calculating what the periodic loss amount should be. This is actually quite simple, as it is the lesser of the ADB and the new defaults delay multiplied by the severity of loss. This is shown in the code here.

```
'    Calculate the actual loss amount after giving effect to
recovery
ActualLoss(i, 0) = min(ActualADB(i, 0), ActualNewDefDelay(i, 0)
* (1 - gp1RcvyRateArray(k, 0)))
AggLoss(i, 0) = ActualLoss(i, 0) + AggLoss(i, 0)
```

23. After loss is calculated, we can continue on to a more familiar calculation, interest. There are two special calculations to keep in mind. The first is that new defaults do not pay interest, so we must subtract any defaults from the

beginning balance of the period. The other calculation is that if servicer advances are assumed, then the interest portion must be paid. All of these additions to the calculation are shown in the code here.

```
'   Calculate interest based on performing principal times
current rate
ActualIntPerf(i, 0) = (CurRateArray(i, 0) *
DayFactorArray(i, 0)) * (ActualBegBal(i, 0) -
ActualNewDef(i, 0))
AggIntPerf(i, 0) = ActualIntPerf(i, 0) + AggIntPerf(i, 0)

If ServAdv = "Yes" Then
 ActualIntAdv(i, 0) = (ActualDefRoll(i - 1, 0) +
ActualNewDef(i, 0)) * (CurRateArray(i, 0) * DayFactorAr-
ray(i, 0))
 AggIntAdv(i, 0) = ActualIntAdv(i, 0) + AggIntAdv(i, 0)
  Else
   ActualIntAdv(i, 0) = 0
   AggIntAdv(i, 0) = ActualIntAdv(i, 0) + AggIntAdv(i, 0)
End If
```

24. The next step is to pay principal. If we are in the closing period there should be no principal outflow. This is included in the code using an IF statement because of a nuance where the period 0 was paying principal. We should also use an IF statement to not pay principal if we are in an IO period. Another special consideration is if we are in the final period of the loan. If this is the case, we should first apply our default assumption. Once this is complete, we can apply our remaining balance for principal payment. Preventing too much principal payment is completed by using the MIN function with the remaining balance less default and the normal principal payment. Notice that the regular principal payment is calculated by taking the beginning balance less defaults (defaulted loans do not pay principal) and multiplying it by a fraction of the current period's amortization factor over the last period's amortization factor. This fraction represents the expected periodic amortization of the loan and can be used rather than recalculating the principal amount. The code here shows all of these code sections.

```
'   Calculate principal as payment less interest
If i = 0 Then
 ActualPrinPerf(i, 0) = 0
  Else
   If i < gp1IOPdsArray(k, 0) Then
    ActualPrinPerf(i, 0) = 0
     Else
      If NotionalAmortFact(i, 0) = 0 Then
       ActualPrinPerf(i, 0) = min((ActualBegBal(i, 0) -
```

```
ActualNewDef(i, 0)) * (1 - (NotionalAmortFact
  (i, 0) / 1)),
ActualBegBal(i, 0) - ActualNewDef(i, 0))
AggPrinPerf(i, 0) = ActualPrinPerf(i, 0) +
AggPrinPerf(i, 0)
 Else
  ActualPrinPerf(i, 0) = min((ActualBegBal(i, 0) -
  ActualNewDef(i, 0)) * (1 - (NotionalAmortFact(i, 0) /
  NotionalAmortFact(i - 1, 0))), ActualBegBal(i, 0) -
  ActualNewDef(i, 0))
  AggPrinPerf(i, 0) = ActualPrinPerf(i, 0) +
  AggPrinPerf(i, 0)
```

The final portion of the principal calculation is in the case of servicer advances. If the servicer is advancing principal, we need to keep track of this in a separate array. The principal the servicer advances is calculated by adding the new defaults to the rolling default balance, subtracting the ADB, and multiplying that amount by the periodic amortization factor ratio. If servicer advances are not assumed then the array value should be zero. This is seen in the code here.

```
If ServAdv = "Yes" Then
  ActualPrinAdv(i, 0) = (ActualDefRoll(i - 1, 0) +
  ActualNewDef(i, 0) - ActualADB(i, 0)) * (1 -
  (NotionalAmortFact(i, 0) /
  NotionalAmortFact(i - 1, 0)))
  AggPrinAdv(i, 0) = ActualPrinAdv(i, 0) + AggPrinAdv(i, 0)
   Else
     ActualPrinAdv(i, 0) = 0
     AggPrinAdv(i, 0) = ActualPrinAdv(i, 0) + AggPrinAdv(i, 0)
   End If
  End If
 End If
End If
```

25. We should next calculate the recovery from default during the normal loops. Earlier, we calculated the recovery under unique circumstances. This section is for the mainstream defaults. We definitely do not want to calculate recoveries prior to the lag. This would cause us to go beyond the boundaries of the array we defined and generate an error. To prevent this we include an IF statement that makes the recovery amount equal to zero if the current period is less than the recovery lag. Otherwise the recovery amount is the actual ADB minus the actual loss amount, as seen in the code here.

```
'   Recoveries on defaults are based off individual
rates and 'lags
 If i <= gp1RcvyLagArray(k, 0) Then
```

```
  ActualRecovery(i, 0) = 0
    Else
      ActualRecovery(i, 0) = ActualADB(i, 0) - ActualLoss(i, 0)
      AggRecovery(i, 0) = ActualRecovery(i, 0) +
      AggRecovery(i, 0)
  End If
```

26. Because we have been calculating advance amounts we should take time to aggregate the advances owed in a single array. This is the last period's advances owed, plus the current period's principal and interest advances, less the current period's recovery amount. We need to bound this in case of any small negative amounts by using the MAX function. The code here shows this section.

```
'    Keep track of the advances owed to the servicer.
ActualAdvOwed(i, 0) = max(0, (ActualAdvOwed(i - 1, 0) +
ActualIntAdv(i, 0) + ActualPrinAdv(i, 0) -
ActualRecovery(i, 0)))
AggAdvOwed(i, 0) = ActualAdvOwed(i, 0) + AggAdvOwed(i, 0)
```

27. Prepayments are the next major section to code. We will be running the prepayment scenarios that were suggested in the prospectus, so we must build in the functionality. Prepayment amounts definitely have a few considerations: if the default amount is greater than the current balance, then there is no amount for prepayment. Note that we recalculate the default amount so we do not create any dependency on the calculated default array. Also, if we are in the closing period, then there is no prepaid principal. Otherwise, the prepayment amount is equal to the correct prepayment rate (based on the loan's seasoning) multiplied by the current balance, further multiplied by the periodic amortization factor ratio. The multiplication by the periodic amortization factor ratio is because when we calculated SMM, we did not include scheduled amortization. Therefore, when we apply the rate, we must take out the scheduled amortization. The prepayment amount should be a pure prepayment amount and not influenced by scheduled principal. This section of code is shown here.

```
'    Calculate the prepayment for each loan.  This amount uses
the 'individual loan's SMM rate (as determined by period
and product 'type) multiplied against the current balance
adjusted by the 'amort factor
If gp1DefaultRange(k, (i + gp1SeasonArray(k, 0) - 1)) *
gp1OrgBalArray(k, 0) > _
  ActualBegBal(i, 0) Then
    ActualPrepay(i, 0) = 0
      Else
        If i = 0 Then
        ActualPrepay(i, 0) = 0
          Else
```

```
      ActualPrepay(i, 0) = max(min(gp1PrepayRange(k, (i +
      gp1SeasonArray(k, 0))) * ((ActualBegBal(i, 0) *
      (NotionalAmortFact(i, 0) / NotionalAmortFact
      (i - 1, 0))))),
      ActualBegBal(i, 0) - ActualNewDef(i, 0)), 0)
      AggPrepay(i, 0) = ActualPrepay(i, 0) + AggPrepay(i, 0)
   End If
 End If
```

28. We next need to calculate the amount in foreclosure, known as our `ActualDefRoll` array. This is the last period's amount in foreclosure, plus the new defaults, minus the servicer advances and recovery. In case of slight zero amounts, this calculation should be capped by a `MAX` function and 0 as seen in the code here.

```
 '    Calculate foreclosure balance.  This is essentially
 the rolling balance of assets in foreclosure/repo.
 ActualDefRoll(i, 0) = max(0, ActualDefRoll(i - 1, 0) +
 ActualNewDef(i, 0) - ActualPrinAdv(i, 0) - ActualLoss(i, 0) -
 ActualRecovery(i, 0))
 AggDefRoll(i, 0) = ActualDefRoll(i, 0) + AggDefRoll(i, 0)
```

29. Two more arrays need to be calculated as displayed in the code here: the payment aggregation and the ending balance. Because we calculated the actual interest and principal separately, we may, at some point, want to check on the combined payment that was submitted. This is done by adding the actual interest and principal arrays together. Note that this is not what the obligors are contracted to pay, but what they submit. The final array is the actual ending balance, which is the current period's balance, minus new defaults, minus prepayments, and minus scheduled principal.

```
 '    Calculate ending balance and aggregate payments for
 presentation.
 ActualPMT(i, 0) = ActualIntPerf(i, 0) + ActualIntAdv(i, 0)
    + ActualPrinPerf(i, 0) + ActualPrinAdv(i, 0)
 AggPMT(i, 0) = ActualPMT(i, 0) + AggPMT(i, 0)
 ActualEndBal(i, 0) = ActualBegBal(i, 0) - ActualNewDef(i, 0) -
 ActualPrinPerf(i, 0) - ActualPrepay(i, 0)

 AggEndBal(i, 0) = ActualEndBal(i, 0) + AggEndBal(i, 0)
 End If
  Next i

 Application.StatusBar = "Group 1 - Amortizing Loan"
 & Str(k) & " of " & Str(TotalLoans1)

 Next k
```

Notice that we also include a progress indicator by writing code that changes the status bar. The status bar is what a model user sees in the bottom-left corner of Excel that typically reads "Ready." Programmers can change this to update as code is run. In our case, we update it whenever the k loop increases. Also notice that we are done with the i and k loops. This means we are done with the main body of code as everything for a loan will be repeated on the next iteration of the k and i loops.

30. Although the primary section of calculation code is complete, there are still a few steps that are required to finish of the asset amortization. We have yet to write anything out to the Excel sheets. To write out all the arrays, we need to create the following named ranges on the Group 1 – Waterfall sheet. Note that we will have to do this for Group 2 as well, changing all the names appropriately.

G9:G509:	**rng_gp1_BegBal**
H9:H509:	**rng_gp1_NewDef**
I9:I509:	**rng_gp1_NewDefDelay**
J9:J509:	**rng_gp1_ADB**
K9:K509:	**rng_gp1_Loss**
L9:L509:	**rng_gp1_IntPerf**
M9:M509:	**rng_gp1_IntAdv**
N9:N509:	**rng_gp1_PrinPerf**
O9:O509:	**rng_gp1_PrinAdv**
P9:P509:	**rng_gp1_Recovery**
Q9:Q509:	**rng_gp1_AdvOwed**
R9:R509:	**rng_gp1_Prepay**
S9:S509:	**rng_gp1_DefRoll**
T9:T509:	**rng_gp1_EndBal**
G9:T509:	**rng_gp1_OutputTable**

Once we have the ranges named we can write them out using the code here.

```
'   Write the outputs
Range("rng_gp1_BegBal") = AggBegBal
Range("rng_gp1_NewDef") = AggNewDef
Range("rng_gp1_NewDefDelay") = AggNewDefDelay
Range("rng_gp1_ADB") = AggADB
Range("rng_gp1_Loss") = AggLoss
Range("rng_gp1_IntPerf") = AggIntPerf
Range("rng_gp1_IntAdv") = AggIntAdv
Range("rng_gp1_PrinPerf") = AggPrinPerf
Range("rng_gp1_PrinAdv") = AggPrinAdv
Range("rng_gp1_Recovery") = AggRecovery
Range("rng_gp1_AdvOwed") = AggAdvOwed
Range("rng_gp1_Prepay") = AggPrepay
Range("rng_gp1_DefRoll") = AggDefRoll
Range("rng_gp1_EndBal") = AggEndBal
```

	Beginning Balance	New Defaults	New Defaults Delay	ADB	Loss	Performing Interest	Advanced Interest	Performing Principal	Advanced Principal	Rec
5										
6	*Group I - Actual Asset Amortization*									
7										
8		-	-	-	-	107,143,617	-	16,673,492	-	
9										
10	532,064,773	-	-	-	-	3,422,503	-	425,250	-	
11	525,899,842	-	-	-	-	3,382,886	-	423,354	-	
12	518,507,958	-	-	-	-	3,335,376	-	420,417	-	
13	509,903,750	-	-	-	-	3,280,067	-	416,428	-	
14	500,110,292	-	-	-	-	3,217,107	-	411,384	-	
15	489,159,237	-	-	-	-	3,146,699	-	405,289	-	

FIGURE 3.13 Once the subroutines amortize the assets in VBA, they are exported at one time to the Waterfall sheets.

31. The final code that needs to be inserted is largely clean-up. We need to take all the outputs that we just wrote and format them correctly; otherwise they may be difficult to interpret. We should make sure the sheet is calculated by forcing it with a `Calculate` statement, and then complete the code with an `End Sub`. This code should be repeated for loan group 2, but it should be created in the `Amortizer_Assets2` module as the `Amort2` subroutine, with all the *gp1* references changed to **gp2**, and the arrays written out to the Group 2 – Waterfall sheet. The final pieces of the `Amortizer_Assets` code is seen here.

```
Range("rng_gp1_OutputTable").NumberFormat = "_(* #,##0_);_
(* (#,##0);_(* ""-""??_);_(@_)"
Worksheets("Inputs").Select

Calculate

Application.StatusBar = False

End Sub
```

32. Finally, we should run both the `Amort1` and `Amort2` subroutines in a simple `Main` subroutine, stored in the `Main` module. The main subroutine should be assigned to a button on the Inputs sheet. In the example model this is done in the range of cells G4:I8. The code for this simple module and subroutine is shown here.

```
Sub Main()
    Call Amort1
    Call Amort2
End Sub
```

33. We can now see the results of the asset amortization macros by going to the Group 1 – Waterfall and the Group 2 – Waterfall sheets. The subroutines should have output the asset amortization arrays to columns G through T. An example of this is shown in Figure 3.13.

CHAPTER 4

Setting Up Liability Assumptions, Paying Fees, and Distributing Interest

Reverse engineering the liability structure is just as challenging as the asset section, but in a different way. To recreate the asset cash flow we have to apply intermediate programming techniques and know concepts that are not readily defined in the prospectus. The liability structure is technically less demanding, as it can be completed entirely on the Excel sheet; however, the documentation wording is far more challenging to interpret and implement.

Our approach will be to first identify the liabilities in the prospectus, set up the liability parameters in Excel, and then go back and forth between the prospectus's description of how the liabilities get paid and how the payment structure is implemented in Excel. The liability structure is particularly well suited to reverse engineering as most prospectuses, terms sheets, or indentures have a section called the priority of payments or *waterfall*. It is a step-by-step allocation of cash flow generated by the assets. Following the priority of payments is a virtual road map to reverse engineering the liabilities.

IDENTIFYING THE OFFERED SECURITIES

Liability information is littered all over the prospectus supplement for our example transaction, which is dangerous for our purposes because some sections only provide partial liability information. Partial liability information is caused by the fact that a prospectus supplement is as its name implies, a supplement. This means that it is supplementing another document. Without delving into the legal reasoning behind this, you should understand that the prospectus supplement is often offering select securities for a transaction; not the entire securities backed by the assets.

In our example case, nearly all of the securities being offered are included in the prospectus supplement. Figure 4.1 is an excerpt from page S-5 of the prospectus supplement detailing the offered certificates.

In Figure 4.1 we see eleven tranches of debt, each with an initial principal balance and pass-through rate. We should read more to check for other tranches. As we see on page S-7, there is a description of the certificates, which include more than eleven

Class	Initial Certificate Principal Balance	Pass-Through Rate	Class	Initial Certificate Principal Balance	Pass-Through Rate
A-1	$484,445,000	6.750% per annum	A-2F	$54,559,000	5.985% per annum
A-2A	$203,118,000	5.906% per annum	M-1	$49,211,000	6.297% per annum
A-2B	$65,317,000	5.735% per annum	M-2	$22,626,000	6.446% per annum
A-2C	$83,228,000	5.852% per annum	M-3	$8,484,000	6.750% per annum
A-2D	$86,053,000	6.164% per annum	M-4	$10,747,000	6.750% per annum
A-2E	$53,316,000	6.351% per annum	M-5		

FIGURE 4.1   The securities being offered by the supplement are detailed in this table. Notice though the M-5 tranche has no information.

different sets of securities. There are six more tranches of debt that exist in the structure: an M-5 class, a CE class, a P class, an X class, and two sets of residual certificates. This is explicitly stated on page S-7 and shown in the excerpt here.

> *The Class M-5 Certificates, the Class CE Certificates, the Class P Certificates, the Class X Certificates and the Residual Certificates are not offered by this prospectus supplement.*
>
> *Information about these classes of certificates is included in this prospectus supplement solely to facilitate an understanding of the Offered Certificates.*

Interestingly, the final sentence of the excerpt states, "Information about these classes of certificates is included in this prospectus supplement solely to facilitate an understanding of the Offered Certificates." Our goal is a thorough understanding. If we were an investor in any of the offered securities, we would not be too concerned by the other six tranches of debt, as, by name, they initially appear to be subordinate in payment priority to the offered securities. However, if we were part of the subordinate class or if the nonoffered securities had any possible prioritization over the offered securities, we should be extremely concerned about the description and payment structure of the nonoffered securities.

Because we have determined that we want to reverse the entire liability structure, we should next think about what information we will need to accomplish this task. The two most important pieces of data have already been seen for the offered securities: the initial principal balance and the pass-through rate. A comprehensive list of all securities' rates are seen on page S-7 and displayed in Figure 4.2.

Notice that Figure 4.2 includes the M-5 class, however, two items are missing: the rates for the other four classes and their initial principal balances. The missing rates are not a problem as those certificates do not pay a coupon, but are unique tranches in a structure that we will discuss later. The missing initial principal balances can be determined on page S-8 of the prospectus supplement, under each security's description.

	Pass-Through Rate	
Class	1	2
A-1	6.750% per annum	7.250% per annum
A-2A	5.906% per annum	6.406% per annum
A-2B	5.735% per annum	6.235% per annum
A-2C	5.852% per annum	6.352% per annum
A-2D	6.164% per annum	6.664% per annum
A-2E	6.351% per annum	6.851% per annum
A-2F	5.985% per annum	6.485% per annum
M-1	6.297% per annum	6.797% per annum
M-2	6.446% per annum	6.946% per annum
M-3	6.750% per annum	7.250% per annum
M-4	6.750% per annum	7.250% per annum
M-5	6.750% per annum	7.250% per annum

FIGURE 4.2 The complete liability information, including pass-through rates (column 1) and post-clean-up call pass-through rates (column 2).

Also of interest in the securities' descriptions in Figure 4.2, are a second set of pass-through rates. We will discuss the implementation later, but we should understand what they are and why they exist. The pass-through rates in the second column are applicable to the securities when the assets have amortized to less than 10% of their original principal balance. Such a point in time is when the optional clean-up call is active. This is officially described on page S-10, which has been excerpted here.

Optional Termination

At its option, the majority holder of the Class X Certificates may purchase all of the mortgage loans in the trust, together with any properties in respect of the mortgage loans acquired on behalf of the trust, and thereby effect termination and early retirement of the certificates, after the aggregate principal balance of the mortgage loans and properties acquired in respect of the mortgage loans has been reduced to less than 10% of the aggregate principal balance of the mortgage loans as of the cut-off date.

The optional clean-up call allows the residual Certificate X holders to purchase all of the mortgage loans in the trust and terminate the transaction. The reasoning behind an optional clean-up call is because at a certain point a transaction becomes inefficient. With fixed fees and cash being generated on a percentage basis, it is often better to curtail a transaction earlier than maturity. There are other reasons behind a clean-up, some of which we will discuss in Chapter 6.

To incentivize the residual holder to exercise the call, the transaction increases the rates for the securities. This also compensates the certificate holders for extended maturities of their certificates, which could have gone beyond the certificate holders' expectations. To properly reverse engineer the deal we should build in the possibility of passing a clean-up call and not having the deal called.

Thus far we see that we need the following information to model the liability section: the initial principal balances, the pass-through rates under normal conditions, and the pass-through rates post clean-up call. The day-count system is the final piece of information necessary to set up the liabilities. To find this information we turn to page S-86 for a description of the pass-through rates. The key sentence of this section states:

> *Interest will accrue on each class of Fixed Rate Certificates on the basis of a 360 day year consisting of twelve 30-day Interest Accrual Periods.*

We should be very careful whenever we see capitalized words or phrases, as this often indicates a defined term. In this sentence the terms Fixed Rate Certificates and Interest Accrual Periods are capitalized. The Fixed Rate Certificates are easy to identify on page S-7, where it states in italic that the fixed rate certificates are the Class A and Mezzanine Certificates. To find the Interest Accrual Periods definition we have to turn to page S-91. The excerpt here shows this definition as seen in the prospectus supplement.

> *"Interest Accrual Period": The Interest Accrual Period for any distribution date and each class of Fixed Rate Certificates will be the calendar month preceding the month in which the distribution date occurs, and each such Interest Accrual Period will be deemed to be 30 days regardless of its actual length.*

Two interesting points come out of the definition: the first being that the accrual month is the month preceding the distribution and the second is reconfirmation that each month is assumed to have 30 days regardless of the actual number of days. Both are important to make sure we are calculating the correct amount and periods of interest.

MODEL BUILDER 4.1: TRANSFERRING THE LIABILITY INFORMATION TO A CONSOLIDATED SHEET

1. Given the large number of liabilities in the example transaction, we should create an entirely separate sheet to store the basic descriptive information. Insert a new worksheet and name it **Liabilities**.
2. To make the sheet easy to comprehend enter the text, **Liabilities** in cell A1. Also, enter the text **Tranches** in cell C3.

3. Label the following cells with the corresponding text:

C4: **ID**
C5: **Name**
C6: **Advance Rate**
C7: **Initial Certificate Principal Balance**
C8: **Price**
C9: **Interest Type**
C10: **Day Count System**
C11: **Fixed Rate**
C12: **Fixed Rate Post Clean-Up Pct**
C13: **Index**
C14: **Margin**

4. We want to be able to identify all of the liabilities by both name and number. The number will be useful when we set up a subroutine later, which automatically creates names for each liability item. In cell D4 enter a **1** and increase it by 1 in each of the cells through the range of cells D4:T4. Next enter the liability names in the range of cells D5:T5. This should include:

D5: **A-1**	M5: **M-3**
E5: **A-2A**	N5: **M-4**
F5: **A-2B**	O5: **M-5**
G5: **A-2C**	P5: **CE**
H5: **A-2D**	Q5: **P**
I5: **A-2E**	R5: **X**
J5: **A-2F**	S5: **R**
K5: **M-1**	T5: **R-X**
L5: **M-2**	

5. Next we should enter the amounts of each tranche. It is useful to have both the dollar amount of each certificate and a percentage representation, otherwise known as the advance rate. Figure 4.1 had the starting certificate principal balances for each tranche up to and including the M-4 tranche. Enter these balances in the corresponding cell in the range of cells D7:T7. We can complete the balances of the remaining certificates by going to page S-8, where the descriptions of those certificates include the certificate balances.

   Converting the dollar amounts to advance rates is simple. Divide the dollar balance of the tranche by the aggregate asset balance. Do this for each cell in the range of cells D6:T6. This has been represented as a hard-coded value in the example model.

6. Each liability may sell for less than or more than 100% of its par. We should represent this as a percentage. For now let's assume that each liability is priced at 100% of par. Enter **100%** for each cell in the range of cells D8:T8.

7. The next section to create for each liability is a cell noting whether the liability's interest payment is fixed, variable, or custom. We completed a similar task for the assets and now we should implement the same for each liability. Create a data validation list using the named range **lst_FxdFlt** for each cell in the range of cells D9:T9.

8. Also similar to the assets, we need to assume a day count system for each liability. Create a data validation list using the named range **lst_DayCountSys** for each cell in the range of cells D10:T10.

9. Two very important fields of data need to be entered for the interest rate: the fixed rate under normal circumstance and the fixed rate after the clean-up call. These rates are detailed in Figure 4.2. Enter the correct rate for each tranche (for both circumstances) in the range of cells D11:T12.

10. Cell range D13:T13 is where we would enter the floating rate index and cell range D14:T14 is for the margin that is in addition to the index. Because we have no floating rate certificates in the example model, we can enter 0% for the margin and create drop-down lists for the index, although they will not be used for this example.

11. Notice that we did not name any of the liability cells or ranges in the instructions. This is because there are so many different liability cells that it would take a long time and be very tedious to enter each one individually. Although entering each one is an option, the Appendix details how to write a VBA subroutine to automatically name all of these cells. If you do not want to implement the additional code in the Appendix, you should name each cell as in the example model. It is critical to name these cells either by hand or using the method described in the Appendix as many parts of the upcoming chapters are referenced with these names in formulas. Thus far the Liabilities sheet should look like Figure 4.3.

	A	C	D	E	F	G
1	**Liabilities**					
2						
3		Tranches				
4		ID	1	2	3	4
5		Name	A-1	A-2A	A-2B	A-2C
6		Advance Rate	42.82%	17.95%	5.77%	7.36%
7		Initial Certificate Principal Balance	484,445,000	203,118,000	65,317,000	83,228,000
8		Price	100.00%	100.00%	100.00%	100.00%
9		Interest Type	Fixed	Fixed	Fixed	Fixed
10		Day Count System	30 / 360	30 / 360	30 / 360	30 / 360
11		Fixed Rate	6.75%	5.91%	5.74%	5.85%
12		Fixed Rate Post-Clean Up Pct	7.25%	6.41%	6.24%	6.35%
13		Index				
14		Margin	0.00%	0.00%	0.00%	0.00%
15						
16		Create Cell Names for Liabilities				
17						
18						

FIGURE 4.3 The Liabilities sheet stores all of the descriptive information of the liabilities. Note that the button will be created later in the Appendix.

THE LIABILITY WATERFALL: A SYSTEM OF PRIORITY

Listing out each liability is of little use unless we build in functionality to see how the deal performs under different assumptions. The only way of seeing how the deal performs is by modeling out the monthly cash flows of each liability. Risk is often parsed in Wall Street transactions by a system of priority. Cash that is paid to one entity prior to another is considered to be more secure. In a structured transaction, such as we are looking at in the example model, the standard priority is payment of fees first and then interest and principal. The priority of payments is well defined, but in various places throughout the prospectus supplement.

Fees: No Transaction is Free

It would be a bizarre world if transactions were free. In most transactions the parties who keep the deal working expect to get paid first. This is no different in the example transaction. The excerpt here is from page S-82, which clearly states that the fees are paid prior to any distributions to the certificate holders.

Fees and Expenses of the Trust

The following fees and expenses will be paid from amounts received on the Mortgage Loans prior to distributions to certificateholders ...

In the example transaction, there are three key entities that we should assume receive fees: the servicer, the primary mortgage insurer, and the credit risk manager. Without any of these parties the transaction would fall apart. We are introduced to the fees on page S-82 of the prospectus supplement, where the servicing fee, the credit risk manager fee, and the Primary Mortgage Insurance (PMI) fee are outlined.

The servicer is responsible for the monthly collection of payments from obligors and the continued collection of payments in arrears. The first instance of how the servicing fee is structured has been excerpted here.

For each mortgage loan, a monthly fee paid to the servicer out of interest collections received from the related mortgage loan. The monthly fee is calculated as one-twelfth of the Servicing Fee Rate on the unpaid principal balance of the mortgage loan at the end of the applicable Due Period.

A number of important facts about the servicing fee structure can be garnered from this excerpt. We see basic elements such as the periodicity of the payment and that the fee is applied on the balance of mortgage loans. However, there are more subtle details such as the source of funds for the servicing fee coming only from the interest collected on the mortgages. There is also reconfirmation that the fee is paid prior to distributions to the certificate holders.

We still have yet to see the actual servicing fee rate. This is in the excerpt here from page S-94.

> *"Servicing Fee Rate": The Servicing Fee Rate on each mortgage loan is 0.375% per annum.*

The next fee seen in the transaction is paid to the credit risk manager, who monitors the transaction's other fiduciary entities. The credit risk manager is paid similarly to the servicer, as shown in the excerpt here from page S-82. The fee rate of 0.01125% per annum is defined on page S-89.

> *For each mortgage loan, a monthly fee payable to the credit risk manager. The monthly fee is calculated as one-twelfth of the Credit Risk Manager Fee Rate on the unpaid principal balance of the mortgage loan at the end of the applicable Due Period.*

The final fee that we should incorporate into our analysis is the PMI fee. PMI is typical for mortgage obligors whose properties have LTVs greater than 80%. PMI does not eliminate all default risk of the obligor. The excerpt from page S-16 gives us the first indication of how the PMI policy works.

> *Unlike a financial guaranty policy, coverage under a mortgage insurance policy is subject to certain limitations and exclusions including, for example, losses resulting from fraud and physical damage to the mortgaged property and to certain conditions precedent to payment, such as notices and reports. As a result, coverage may be denied or limited on covered mortgage loans. In addition, since the amount of coverage depends on the loan-to-value ratio at the time of origination of the covered mortgage loan, a decline in the value of a mortgaged property will not result in increased coverage, and the trust may still suffer a loss on a covered mortgage loan.*

The example model will account for the fee for the policy, but the actual loss mitigation is not included. For now we have to understand how the fee for the PMI policy works. There are a number of indications in the prospectus supplement that suggest that the precise fee amount will be difficult to pinpoint. Take a look at the defined PMI Insurer Fee Rate on page S-93, detailed in the excerpt here.

> *"PMI Insurer Fee Rate": With respect to any distribution date and any mortgage loan covered by the PMI Policy, the PMI Insurer Fee Rate will range from approximately 0.176% per annum to approximately 2.467% per annum. The weighted average PMI Insurer Fee Rate as of the Closing Date is approximately 0.9023%.*

In this excerpt, we see that the rate can vary and it is only applied to the loans that are covered by PMI. Earlier in the prospectus supplement, on page S-9, we see that 47.43% of the Group I loans and 48.02% of the Group II loans have PMI. There are further stratifications of the loans and their PMI policies on page S-34 and S-44. The payment of the PMI fee is also detailed in the same familiar format as the servicing and credit risk manager fees, as seen in the excerpt here from page S-82.

> *For each mortgage loan covered by the PMI Policy, a monthly fee payable to the PMI Insurer. The monthly fee is calculated as one-twelfth of the applicable PMI Insurer Fee Rate on the unpaid principal balance of the related mortgage loan at the end of the applicable Due Period.*

A reverse engineer at this point could try to determine the PMI-covered loans and calculate the balance as they amortize, or they can estimate the fees. The original structurer of the deal estimated the fees. This is known from page S-73 where the prospectus supplement lays out the transaction's modeling assumptions. In this section, we see that regardless of the actual fee calculations the fee rates assumed for modeling purposes are collapsed into a single weighted rate described in the excerpt here. This blended rate should be first converted to a periodic rate using the 30 / 360 day count factor and then further multiplied by the current balance of the mortgages each month. We will see this later in Model Builder 4.2.

> *the sum of the Servicing Fee Rate, the PMI insurer fee rate and the Credit Risk Manager Fee Rate is 0.81705% per annum . . .*

MODEL BUILDER 4.2: STARTING THE WATERFALL WITH FEES

1. We have just described the fees section, so it makes sense to go ahead and implement it as the start of the waterfall. The first step is to go to the Inputs sheet to enter in the fee assumptions. In the following cells, enter the corresponding text:

   B19: **Fixed Mthly Fees**
   B20: **Servicing Fees**
   B21: **PMI Fee**
   B22: **WA Combined Fees**

   In cell B19, we are creating an area for the possibility of fixed monthly fees if we want to add additional fees to the model. The two primary fees are listed: the servicing fee and the PMI fee. The credit risk manager fee is not singled out because it is usually such a small component. However, all of the individual fees are trumped by the WA Combined Fees assumption in cell B22, which we will take directly from the modeling assumptions section of the prospectus supplement.

Fxd Mtlhly Fees	-
Servicing Fees	0.375%
PMI Fee	0.90273%
WA Combined Fees	0.81705%

FIGURE 4.4 The fees section on the Inputs sheet.

2. In the following cells enter the corresponding values:

C19: **0**
C20: **0.375%**
C21: **0.90273%**
C22: **0.81705%**

Name cell C19 **fees_FixedMthly**, cell C20 **fees_ServicingFee**, cell C21 **struc_WAPMIFee**, and cell C22 **struc_WACombFees**. The fees section of the Inputs sheet should look like Figure 4.4.

3. Next go to the Group 1 – Waterfall sheet. In cell V10, enter the following formula:

=MIN((struc_WACombFees*C10)*G10,(L10+M10))

This formula multiplies the combined weighted average fee assumption by the 30/360 day count factor. This converts the annual fee rate to a monthly rate. The formula then multiplies the monthly fee rate by the beginning of period balance for the Group 1 assets. A MIN statement is used because we are determining how much can be paid. We can only pay the lesser of what we have and what we owe. Because the first part of the formula calculates what we owe, all we need to reference is what we have, which are the interest distributions from the assets. Recall that the fees were only paid for by the interest amounts collected from the loans. Copy this formula over the range of cells V10:V509. Also, enter the text **Fees Paid** in cell V7 for labeling purposes. Repeat Step 3 for the Group 2 assets on the Group 2 – Waterfall sheet. Figure 4.5 is an example of what the fees section should look like.

   What we have started here is the movement of cash through the liability waterfall. We will approach each liability in the waterfall in a similar manner, but broken down in a bit more detail than the way we implemented the fee calculations. The normal method will be to calculate what is due in one column, what can be paid in the next, what is unpaid, and then how much cash is remaining. The reason we did not bother with such detail for fees is that we should never run a scenario where the fees are unpaid. It would be a ridiculously stressed scenario that would essentially shut down the transaction as none of the key parties get paid.

	V
6	*Fees*
	Fees Paid
7	
8	11,337,896
9	
10	362,270
11	358,072
12	353,039
13	347,181
14	340,513
15	333,056

FIGURE 4.5
The top of the
fees section on the
Waterfall sheets.

INTEREST: NO FINANCING IS FREE

Much like the fact that a party would rarely work on a transaction for free, few people would provide money for free. Astute investors also want to get paid for the risk that they take. Interest paid to investors for their risk in the transaction typically comes right after fees. This is where we start seeing a more developed interplay between the terms in the prospectus. Often there is a section that describes specific instructions on how cash should flow, but embedded in those instructions are defined terms that require a reader to jump to the definitions. Within the definitions are also references to more defined terms. This process can get very confusing, but it is something that we will work through in a detailed and diligent manner.

The first indication of how interest is paid to investors comes from page S-95, which is excerpted here.

Interest Distributions

On each distribution date, the trust administrator will withdraw from the Distribution Account that portion of Available Distribution Amount for such distribution date consisting of the Interest Remittance Amount for such distribution date and make the following disbursements and transfers in the order of priority described below, in each case to the extent of the Interest Remittance Amount remaining for such distribution date.

As mentioned earlier, the capitalized phrases are defined terms. To truly understand what is meant by each of these defined terms we must locate the definition (usually spread out all over the prospectus supplement). In the case of this excerpt, we see that we must take funds from the Distribution Account. We encountered this term earlier when we discussed fees, but did not actually find the definition for it. If we go to page S-108 we see the following sentence:

> *The trust administrator will establish an account (the "Distribution Account") into which will be deposited amounts withdrawn from the Collection Account for distribution to certificate holders on a distribution date and payment of certain fees and expenses of the trust.*

We read earlier in the same paragraph that the Collection Account contains funds from the mortgages. However, the amount each period is constrained by the term Available Distribution Amount, which is defined on page S-86. The key idea behind this definition is that the Available Distribution Amount includes:

1. The scheduled monthly payments from the mortgages for the related due date, *after* deducting the servicing fee, credit risk manager fee, and PMI insurer fee.
2. Unscheduled amounts from prepayment, liquidation, or repurchase.
3. All advanced amounts.

The model is currently set up with this information because we have calculated the periodic amount for each of these three components, including the fees to be deducted. To fully determine the amount we start with we have to look up one more definition: the Interest Remittance Amount. The prospectus supplement defines this for each loan group (for example, "Group 1 Interest Remittance Amount"), rather than as "Interest Remittance Amount." We can find the definition for Group 1 Interest Remittance Amount on page S-90, which is captured in the excerpt here.

> *"Group I Interest Remittance Amount": The Group I Interest Remittance Amount for any distribution date will be (i) interest received or advanced on the Group I Mortgage Loans and (ii) amounts paid by the servicer in respect of Prepayment Interest Shortfalls on the Group I Mortgage Loans (in each case, to the extent remaining after payment of an allocable portion of (A) the servicing fees for such distribution date and any unpaid servicing fees in respect of prior periods collected by the servicer, (B) the Credit Risk Manager Fee for such distribution date and (C) the PMI insurer fee, if applicable, for such distribution date).*

This statement isolates the Interest Remittance Amount to just the interest paid and advanced from the mortgage loans. It also reinforces that the three fees we calculated earlier should be deducted first. In sum, all we know thus far is that the interest from the mortgage loans should first be applied to fees, which we have done, and next is paid to certificate holders in some type of priority. Now we must identify that priority, what amount should be paid, and how that amount should be paid.

The priority is immediately started after the Interest Distributions on page S-95 is initiated. Here there are specific instructions for dispersing funds from the Distribution Account based on the Group 1 Interest Remittance Amount. We see that the Group I certificate holders (the A-1 certificates only) are due the Senior Interest Distribution Amount. When we read the definition of Senior Interest Distribution Amount on page S-94, it leads us to another defined term, the Interest Distribution Amount. The excerpt shows the definition for the Interest Distribution Amount on page S-92.

"Interest Distribution Amount": The Interest Distribution Amount for each class of certificates on any distribution date will be equal to interest accrued during the related Interest Accrual Period on the Certificate Principal Balance of such class of certificates immediately prior to the distribution date at the then applicable pass-through rate for such class, reduced, to not less than zero, in the case of each class, by the allocable share for such class of Prepayment Interest Shortfalls to the extent not covered by Compensating Interest paid by the servicer and shortfalls resulting from the application of the Relief Act or any state law providing for similar relief.

This definition states that each security gets paid periodically based on its monthly pass-through rate. At this point, we will just use one of the two rates for each security, determined by being in an optional call state or not. The last piece of information we need, which we have briefly discussed and partially implemented, is the day count system. The definition of the Interest Distribution Amount indicated that the amount is paid based on the Interest Accrual Period. When we look this definition up on page S-91, we see that the 30 / 360 day count system is used for the Fixed Rate certificates.

Given that we know which rates to use, the balances of the certificate balances, the day count system, and the source to pay the interest, we can now implement the interest calculations in the example model.

MODEL BUILDER 4.3: CONTINUING THE WATERFALL WITH INTEREST PAID TO THE CERTIFICATE HOLDERS

1. We will start the Interest section with the Group 1 certificates on the Group 1 – Waterfall sheet. Skip a few columns from where we left off on Fees to column Y. In cell Y7, enter the text **Group 1 Interest Remittance Amount**.

2. In cell Y9 enter the following formula:

=(L10+M10)-V10

This formula takes the interest from the mortgage loans, plus the interest advanced and subtracts out the servicing, credit risk manager, and PMI insurer fees. This is the Interest Remittance Amount each period. Copy and paste this formula over the range of cells Y9:Y510.

3. Next we need to figure out the appropriate interest rate. In cell Z7, enter the text **A-1 Interest Rate**. The next formula will return the correct interest rate for the tranche. This formula needs to assess whether or not the transaction is in an optional call state. We have yet to track the optional call state and should do so on a separate sheet. Insert a worksheet and name it **Balances**.

4. On the Balances sheet, enter the following text in the corresponding cells to create labels:

A11: **Timing**
A12: **Period**
B12: **Date**

5. The period and date columns (A and B) can be set to reference other sheets where this is calculated. Enter the following formula into cell A14:

=‘Group 1 - Waterfall’!A9

Copy and paste the formula over the range of cells A14:A514. Also create following formula in cell B14:

=‘Group 1 - Waterfall’!B9

Copy and paste the formula over the range of cells B14:B514.

6. Next, in cell D11, enter the text **Collateral**. In cell D12, enter **EOP Balance**. This column is going to be the summary of both asset loan groups. Enter the following formula in cell D14:

=‘Group 1 - Waterfall’!T9+’Group 2 - Waterfall’!T9

Copy and paste the formula over the range of cells D14:D514.

7. In cell E12, enter the text **% of Original Balance**. In cell E14, enter the following formula:

=D14/$D$14

This formula tracks the current aggregate asset balances as a percentage of the original balance. Copy and paste this formula over the range of cells E14:E514.

8. Once we know the percentage of current assets to original, we are almost set up to create the optional clean-up call test. First we should jump to the Inputs sheet and enter the following text in the corresponding cells:

G19: **% of Collateral for Call**
G20: **Call On/Off**

9. Enter the value **10%** in cell H19 and name this cell **struc_CallPct**. In cell H20 we want to have an On/Off option, so go to the Hidden sheet and enter the text **OnOff** in cell A21, **On** in cell A22, and **Off** in cell A23. Name the range of cells A22:A23 **lst_OnOff**. Now go back to the Inputs page and create a data validation list in cell H20 using the range **lst_OnOff**.

10. Now we can go back to the Balances sheet and continue with the call trigger. Enter the following formula in cell F15:

=IF(AND(E14<struc_CallPct,struc_CallOnOff="On"),TRUE,FALSE)

Copy and paste this formula over the range of cells F15:F514. This formula checks to see if the beginning of period asset balance is 10% of the original balance. If so, and if the optional clean-up call is turned on, then a TRUE value is returned. Also, enter the text **Clean-up Call Possible** in cell F12.

11. We should also track the aggregate interest and amortization on the mortgage loans. Notice the word amortization is used because it includes all items that reduce the principal balance of the loan pool. Enter the following formulas in the corresponding cells:

G15: =('Group 1 - Waterfall'!L10+'Group 1 - Waterfall'!M10)+
    ('Group 2 - Waterfall'!L10+'Group 2 - Waterfall'!M10)
H15: =('Group 1 - Waterfall'!H10+'Group 1 - Waterfall'!N10+
    'Group 1 - Waterfall'!O10+'Group 1 - Waterfall'!P10+
    'Group 1 - Waterfall'!R10)+('Group 2 - Waterfall'!H10+
    'Group 2 - Waterfall'!N10+'Group 2 - Waterfall'!O10+
    'Group 2 - Waterfall'!P10+'Group 2 - Waterfall'!R10)

Copy the formula in cell G15 over the range of cells G15:G514 and the formula in cell H15 over the range of cells H15:H514. Enter the text **Interest** in cell G12 and **Amortization** in cell H12. So far the Balances sheet should look like Figure 4.6.

	A	B	C	D	E	F	G	H
11	*Timing*			*Collateral*				
12	Period	Date		EOP Balance	% of Original Balance	Clean Up Call Possible	Interest	Amortization
13							229,457,429	1,131,286,782
14	0	05/25/06		1,131,286,782	100.00%			
15	1	06/25/06		1,117,841,233	98.81%	FALSE	7,331,655	13,445,549
16	2	07/25/06		1,101,784,557	97.39%	FALSE	7,244,616	16,056,676
17	3	08/25/06		1,083,150,024	95.74%	FALSE	7,140,654	18,634,533
18	4	09/25/06		1,061,988,952	93.87%	FALSE	7,019,982	21,161,073
19	5	10/25/06		1,038,370,966	91.79%	FALSE	6,882,934	23,617,986

FIGURE 4.6 The Balances sheet is started to track balances and deal states.

12. While we are on this page, we should take a moment to step back and look at the big picture of the modeling. We are working on the Balances sheet, which is where we will store the aggregate balances of the assets throughout time, all of the balances of the liabilities throughout time, and information that is tied to those balances that affects the payment structure. This last set of information is usually calculations for triggers or tests that the deal sets up. We have already seen this with the optional clean-up and will see it more.

Because we will soon return to the waterfall sheets to complete the interest calculations, we should think whether we have enough information to actually calculate periodic interest. Although we have the rate, whether the deal is in an optional call state or not, and the day count system, we do not have a balance to multiply against. We should now create the balances for all of the liabilities on the Balances sheet.

On the Balances sheet, skip over to column P. There is a lot of repetitive information that will need to be entered here, so there will be multiple cell references for the same text (instructed in a reverse manner than usual). Make sure to enter the following text in the corresponding cell references:

P10: **Group I**, T10: **Group II**
P11: **A-1**, T11: **A-2A**, Y11: **A-2B**, AD11: **A-2C**, AI11: **A-2D**, AN11: **A-2E**, AS11: **A-2F**, AY11: **M-1**, BC11: **M-2**, BG11: **M-3**, BK11: **M-4**, BO11: **M-5**, BS11: **CE**, BV11: **P**, BY11: **X**, CB11: **R**, CE11: **R-X**
EOP Balance: D12, P12, T12, Z12, AF12, AL12, AR12, AX12, BE12, BI12, BM12, BQ12, BU12, BY12, CB12, CE12, CH12, CK12
% of Original Tranche Balance: E12, Q12, U12, AA12, AG12, AM12, AS12, AY12, BF12, BJ12, BN12, BR12, BV12
Group II Interest Pro Rata Share: V12, AB12, AH12, AN12, AT12, AZ12
Group II Principal Pro Rata Share: W12, AC12, AI12, AO12, AU12, BA12
Interest: G12, R12, X12, AD12, AJ12, AP12, AV12, BC12, BG12, BK12, BO12, BS12, BW12, BZ12, CC12, CF12, CI12, CL12
Principal: S12, Y12, AE12, AK12, AQ12, AW12, BD12, BH12, BL12, BP12, BT12, BX12, CA12, CD12, CG12, CJ12, CM12
BB12: **Lockout Distribution Percentage**

13. In cell P14, we will start entering the balance data for the first liability. Enter the following formula into cell P14:

=IF($A14=0,liab1_Balance,P13-S14)

Notice that this checks to see if the current period is the closing period and enters that starting balance of the first liability if true. Otherwise it is the previous period's balance less the current period's principal. Copy this formula over the range of cells P14:P514. This step should be repeated for each column where we

	P	Q
11	*A-1*	
12	EOP Balance	% of Original Tranche Balance
13		
14	484,445,000	
15	478,003,776	99%
16	470,336,422	97%
17	461,458,540	95%
18	451,394,063	93%
19	440,175,436	91%
20	427,844,082	88%

FIGURE 4.7 The liabilities should be entered on the Balances sheet.

entered the title "EOP Balance" in row 12. For instance, cell T14 should have the following variation of the same formula:

=IF($A14=0,liab2_Balance,T13-X14)

Repeat Step 13 for all of the EOP Balance columns.

14. Next we want a fractional representation of each tranches' current balance versus original balance. This is easily done by entering the following formula into cell Q15:

=P15/$P$14

Copy this formula over the range of cells Q15:Q514. This step should be repeated for each column with the title "% of Original Tranche Balance" in row 12. Make sure that the denominator changes when creating this formula multiple times for different columns. This section of the Balances sheet should look like Figure 4.7.

15. We see that for the A-1 tranche, the only two missing items are interest and principal. Because we have yet to calculate either we will have to move away from the Balances sheet temporarily and back to the Group 1 - Waterfall sheet. Determining the correct interest rate is the next step toward calculating the correct interest amounts. However, this is not as clear as you might expect. The interest rates for the tranches are generally determined by three possible factors: if the deal is in a normal state, if it is in an optional clean-up call state, or if the mortgages are generating less interest than the fixed liabilities demand.

The last part of the statement, where the mortgages generate less interest than the fixed liabilities require, is a problem solved by a concept called the Net

WAC Pass-Through Rate. This term is defined on page S-92 and captured in the excerpt here.

> *"Net WAC Pass-Through Rate": The Net WAC Pass-Through Rate for any distribution date and (a) the Group I Certificates is a per annum rate equal to the weighted average of the Expense Adjusted Mortgage Rates on the then outstanding Group I Mortgage Loans, weighted based on their principal balances as of the first day of the related Due Period;*
>
> *(b) the Group II Certificates is a per annum rate equal to the weighted average of the Expense Adjusted Mortgage Rates on the then outstanding Group II Mortgage Loans, weighted based on their principal balances as of the first day of the related Due Period; and*
>
> *(c) the Mezzanine Certificates is a per annum rate equal to the weighted average (weighted in proportion to the results of subtracting from the aggregate principal balance of each loan group the current aggregate Certificate Principal Balance of the related Class A Certificates) of (i) the Net WAC Pass-Through Rate for the Group I Certificates and (ii) the Net WAC Pass-Through Rate for the Group II Certificates.*

Reading this excerpt for the Group I certificates suggests that the Net WAC Pass-Through Rate is based on the rates from the Group I mortgages rates. There is another defined term within this term called "Expense Adjusted Mortgage Rates", which we should look into further. We find this term on page S-89 and understand that an expense adjusted mortgage rate is a mortgage rate less servicing, credit risk manager, and PMI Insurer fees.

So, does this mean that we have to create more code to pull out each mortgagor's rate, weight it by the periodic balance, and then aggregate and export it? Although that is a solution, we could just take the interest that has been paid and advanced each period and divide it by the beginning balance of that period and the day factor (in order to get an annual rate). Enter this formula in cell X10 of the Group 1 - Waterfall sheet:

=IF(G10<0.001,0,MAX((SUM(L10:M10)-V10)/G10/Vectors!E9,0))

Copy and paste this formula over the range of cells X10:X509. Note that this formula starts with an IF function that returns a zero in case of the amortization being off by fractions of a penny and the balance not quite becoming 0. Label this formula by entering the text **Group I Net WAC Pass-Through Rate** in cell X7.

16. With the Net WAC Pass-Through Rate known, there are still the other two possible rates that we must calculate in case they are used. Enter the following formula in cell Z10:

=IF(G10<0.001,0,MIN(X10,IF(Balances!F14,liab1_FxdRateClnUp, liab1_FxdRate)))

Copy and paste this formula over the range of cells Z10:Z509. Also enter the text in **A-1 Interest Rate** in cell Z7. The first part of the formula, the MIN function, is very important. Earlier we just assumed that there are only two possible rates, a pass-through rate for normal circumstances and one if the optional clean-up call period is activated. If we read the Pass-Through Rate section of page S-86 we see that the actual pass through rate for each period is the lesser of the Formula Rate and the Net WAC Pass-Through rate. The Formula Rate is defined on page S-90 and is the same as what we have entered on the Liabilities sheet. The Net WAC Pass-Through rate we calculated in Step 15. We must construct the actual rate formula to take the lesser of the Net WAC Pass-Through rate and the Formula rate. This is written out as the prospectus states on page S-86, also excerpted here.

Pass-Through Rates

The pass-through rate for any class of Fixed Rate Certificates and any distribution date will be the lesser of (i) the related Formula Rate for such distribution date and (ii) the related Net WAC Pass-Through Rate for such distribution date.

The formula in cell Z10 ends with an IF function checking to see whether the optional clean-up call is activated on the Balances sheet. If the clean-up call is activated, then it populates the post clean-up call rate, otherwise it is the pre clean-up call rate.

17. Once the rate is determined, we have all the information necessary to calculate the interest dollar amount. The only challenge we have is that each tranche of debt may have a different day count system (this is unlikely, but we should build in the option to alter each one). To do this we use a combination of the OFFSET-MATCH functions. To understand the complete formula enter the following in cell AA10:

=(Z10*OFFSET(\$B10,0,MATCH(liab1_DayCtSys,grp1_DayCountSys, 0))*Balances!P14)+AC9

This formula takes the periodic rate we created in Step 15 and multiplies it by the day count system. The day count system is selected by using OFFSET on the possible day count systems starting in the B column of the same sheet and matching the OFFSET column reference with the type of day count system selected on the Liabilities sheet. That product is then multiplied by the balance we created for the A-1 tranche on the balances sheet for the end of the previous period. A final step that you will notice is the addition of AC9.

Remember that the prospectus supplement stated that the certificate holders are due the Senior Interest Distribution Amount. To fully understand the nuances of this defined term we should turn to page S-94. On this page, we can read that the Senior Interest Distribution Amount includes an item called the Interest Carry Forward Amount. In the excerpt here, from page S-92, we can see that the

Interest Carry Forward Amount is the unpaid portion of interest from the prior period. Thus we must add this amount to what interest is currently due. Copy and paste the complete formula over the range of cells AA10:AA509. Enter the text **A-1 Interest Due** in cell AA7.

> *"Interest Carry Forward Amount": The Interest Carry Forward Amount with respect to any class of Fixed Rate Certificates and any distribution date will be equal to the amount, if any, by which the Interest Distribution Amount for that class of certificates for the immediately preceding distribution date exceeded the actual amount distributed on the certificates in respect of interest on the immediately preceding distribution date, together with any Interest Carry Forward Amount with respect to that class of certificates remaining undistributed from the previous distribution date, plus interest accrued thereon at the related pass-through rate on such class of certificates for the most recently ended Interest Accrual Period.*

18. In Step 16, we calculated what interest is due, but we are mostly concerned with the amount paid. This formula is much simpler because we will only take the lesser of what we have and what we owe. We have calculated the interest due and we know how much we have available from the assets and can therefore create the following formula in cell AB10:

=MIN(Y10,AA10)

Copy and paste this formula over the range of cells AB10:AB509. Make sure to enter the text **A-1 Interest Paid** in cell AB7.

19. In Step 17, we looked at the concept of the Interest Carry Forward Amount and how it was unpaid interest that was added to the interest due for the next period. We need to calculate the unpaid interest in a separate column. This is relatively easy to implement, but a bit convoluted when you read the previous excerpt. The definition states that the amount is "... equal to the amount, if any, by which the Interest Distribution Amount for that class of certificates for the immediately preceding distribution date exceeded the actual amount distributed on the certificates in respect of interest on the immediately preceding distribution date." The use of the word *exceeded* is confusing but it simply means that if the amount that is due is greater than what was paid, the difference should be carried forward. The formula to capture this concept is in cell AC10:

=AA10-AB10+AC9+(AC9*X10*OFFSET($B10,0,
MATCH(liab1_DayCtSys,grp1_DayCountSys,0)))

Notice that this formula also adds the interest due on the unpaid from the previous period. The latter part of the definition states that interest should be

	Group I Net WAC Pass Through Rate	Group I Interest Remittance Amount	A-1 Interest Rate	A-1 Interest Due	A-1 Interest Paid	A-1 Interest Carry Forward Amount
	W	X	Y	Z	AA	AB	AC
6	*Interest - Green Indicates Pre-Principal Waterfall Events*					
7						
8		95,805,721		77,673,276	77,673,276	-
9						
10	6.90%	3,060,233	6.75%	2,725,003	2,725,003	-
11	6.90%	3,024,814	6.75%	2,688,771	2,688,771	-
12	6.90%	2,982,337	6.75%	2,645,642	2,645,642	-
13	6.90%	2,932,886	6.75%	2,595,704	2,595,704	-
14	6.90%	2,876,594	6.75%	2,539,092	2,539,092	-
15	6.90%	2,813,643	6.75%	2,475,987	2,475,987	-

FIGURE 4.8 The A-1 tranche's interest distribution is reverse engineered in the Group 1 - Waterfall sheet.

charged on unpaid interest. Copy and paste this formula over the range of cells AC10:AC509. Enter the text **A-1 Interest Carry Forward Amount** in cell AC7. Figure 4.8 shows how the Group 1 – Waterfall sheet should be developing.

20. Column AD we will skip over until later in this chapter, and columns AE through AG we will come back to in Chapter 6. Let us look back at the Interest Distribution steps on page S-95. We have essentially finished step I (i) of the interest section of the prospectus. The next substep (ii) directs the cash to the Group II certificates after substep (i) has been completed. This is an important feature of a multiple loan group transaction. Certificates are directly supported by the mortgages in their respective loan group, but there is the possibility of cross support if excess cash exists in one loan group and the other needs it.

For this reason, we must build in a system to track the available cash for the other loan group. In our example, we have been working on the interest distributions for the Group I liabilities, which consist of a single A-1 tranche. We have calculated how much is due, paid, and unpaid, and therefore know how much is available for loan group II. Label this section by entering the text **Undistributed Interest Sent to Group II** in cell AH7 and then enter the following formula in cell AH10:

=Y10-AB10

Copy this formula over the range of cells AH10:AH509.

21. We should now move immediately to the Group II interest calculations as we are at a point on the Group I interest waterfall that interacts with the Group II waterfall. These next few steps can be confusing as there will now be interaction between two sheets with similar names, so pay careful attention to which sheet and loan group is being referenced in the instructions. We are going to switch over to the Group 2 – Waterfall sheet now. So far this sheet has been developed as

far as Fees in column V. Repeat Steps 15 and 16 for the A-2A class making sure to replace any reference to an assumption for the A-1 certificate to assumptions for the A-2A certificate.

The first difference we will encounter for the Group II liabilities is that they are paid on a pro rata basis. To help understand this concept, look at the etymology of the phrase pro rata, which is derived from two Latin words: pro meaning "by" and rata meaning "of calculation" (in reference to a rate or change). The next logical question is "What rate or change?" The answer to this question resides in the wording of the pro rata payment instructions. Notice the excerpt here from page S-95 states that the Group II interest should be paid in section II (i) "... on a *pro rata* basis based on the entitlement of each such class."

> *II. On each distribution date, the Group II Interest Remittance Amount will be distributed in the following order of priority: (i) concurrently, to the holders of each class of Group II Certificates, on a pro rata basis based on the entitlement of each such class, the Senior Interest Distribution Amounts allocable to the Group II Certificates; and (ii) to the holders of the Group I Certificates, the Senior Interest Distribution Amount related to such certificates, to the extent remaining undistributed after the distribution of the Group I Interest Remittance Amount, as set forth in clause I above.*

The entitlement in this case is the interest amount that is due to each class of certificates. You might think that this whole section is absurd because how can we have an interest amount that is based off a percentage of entitlement, when we haven't calculated the entitlement? Although it seems circular, the answer is relatively easy. Each class of notes is due their interest entitlement, which is essentially their periodic certificate rate multiplied by the beginning of period balance. If there is enough cash to pay everyone, then everyone gets their entitlement. However, if there is a shortfall of cash, we must restrict the payment in such a way that everyone gets paid a share based on what they would have been entitled.

This is effected in the model by making the Interest Due calculation the same as always, but restricting the Interest Paid calculation. Go to the Group 2 – Waterfall sheet and enter the following formula in cell AA10:

=(Z10*OFFSET(\$B10,0,MATCH(liab2_DayCtSys,grp2_DayCountSys, 0))*Balances!T14)+AC9

This formula should look similar to the one we did for Group 1. In fact it's virtually identical aside from references being changed for the A2-A class. Copy and paste this formula over the range of cells AA10:AA509. Also enter the text **A-2A Interest Due** in cell AA7.

We know the initial balances and rates, so now we can perform this calculation for all of the Group II certificates. To calculate the next step, we will need to perform Step 16 and this last step in order to get interest rates and interest due amounts for each of the Group 2 certificates. We already have the balance information on the Balances sheet, so this can be mostly completed. The word *mostly* is used because we have not calculated any principal at this point and the balances will look odd since they will be capitalizing interest and not amortizing down. Do not worry about this as it is normal during model construction; it will all make sense by the end!

22. With initial interest calculations for each Group 2 tranche, we can now calculate the interest entitlement of each class. Go to the Balances sheet and enter the following formula in cell V15:

=IF(SUM(T14,Z14,AF14,AL14,AR14,AX14)<0.001,0,'Group 2 - Waterfall'!AA10/(SUM('Group 2 - Waterfall'!AA10,'Group 2 - Waterfall'!AI10,'Group 2 - Waterfall'!AQ10,'Group 2 - Waterfall'!AY10,'Group 2 - Waterfall'!BG10,'Group 2 - Waterfall'!BO10)))

This formula looks far worse than it really is. The initial IF function checks to see if the certificates are paid off. If they are it forces a 0 rather than allowing division by zero, which causes a #DIV/0! error. The main part of the formula takes a tranche's interest entitlement for a period and reflects it as a fraction of the aggregate interest entitlement for the same period for all of the Group 2 tranches. Copy and paste this formula over the range of cells V15:V514. Enter the text **Group II Interest Pro Rata Share** in cell V12. This section should look like Figure 4.9.

23. We can now jump back to the Group 2 – Waterfall sheet to finish off the A-2A interest calculation. On the Group 2 – Waterfall sheet go to cell AB10 and enter the following formula:

=MIN(Y10*Balances!V15,AA10)

Notice that this formula takes the lesser of the remittance amount multiplied by the A-2A's interest pro rata share and the amount of interest that is due. This is the same concept as taking the lesser of what we have and need. Only this time, what we have is constrained by the interest pro rata share percentage, which will allow the other tranches to receive interest based on their interest entitlement percent if there is a shortfall of cash.

Another clue that this is how the cash should flow is from the use of the word *concurrently* in the Interest Distribution steps on page S-95. Concurrently is synonymous to "at the same time," meaning that the cash is not paid in any order, but distributed at the same time on a pro rata basis. Finalize this column by copying and pasting the formula in cell AB10 over the range of cells AB10:AB509 and entering the text **A-2A Interest Paid** in cell AB7.

	V
11	
12	**Group II Interest Pro Rata Share**
13	
14	
15	36.83%
16	35.95%
17	34.87%
18	33.59%
19	32.08%
20	30.31%

FIGURE 4.9 The pro rata percentages are required to calculate the correct distribution amounts to the Group II liabilities.

24. The next section, the Interest Carry Forward calculation, is the same as the A-1 class as long as each reference is changed to reflect the A-2A tranche. Enter the variation of the formula over the range of cells AC10:AC509 and enter the text **A-2A Interest Carry Forward Amount** in cell AC7.

25. Column AD is where we will see the first interaction between the two loan groups. The idea is that if there is a shortfall of one loan group, then the other loan group can support it in so far as there is cash available. Once again, we can rely on the concept of taking the lesser of what you have and need. In this case, you need to cover any unpaid amounts for the A-2A tranche and you have the excess cash from the Group 1 tranche. However, keep in mind that the Interest Distributions section I (ii) states that the amount must be paid to the Group 2 tranches in a pro-rata fashion based on entitlement. We have gone through the creation of the pro rata percentage and can create the following formula in cell AD10 on the Group 2 – Waterfall sheet:

=MIN(AC10,'Group 1 - Waterfall'!AH10*Balances!V14)

Copy and paste this formula over the range of cells AD10:AD509. Also, enter the text **A-2A Interest Covered by Excess Group I** in cell AD7. This section of the Group 2 – Waterfall sheet should look like Figure 4.10.

26. At this point, we have the concept of cross support down and implemented for the A-2A certificate, but we should clean up some open-ended areas and replicate the formulas for other tranches. Go back to the Balances sheet and

	X	Y	Z	AA	AB	AC	AD
6	*Interest - Green Indicates Pre-Principal Waterfall Events*						
7	Group 2 Net WAC Pass Through Rate	Group 2 Interest Remittance Amount	A-2A Interest Rate	A-2A Interest Due	A-2A Interest Paid	A-2A Interest Carry Forward Amount	A-2A Interest Covered by Excess Group I
8		109,553,291		8,464,170	8,464,170	-	-
9							
10	7.01%	3,501,157	5.91%	999,679	999,679	-	-
11	7.01%	3,458,692	5.91%	962,240	962,240	-	-
12	7.01%	3,408,139	5.91%	918,006	918,006	-	-
13	7.01%	3,349,606	5.91%	867,070	867,070	-	-
14	7.01%	3,283,258	5.91%	809,574	809,574	-	-
15	7.01%	3,209,315	5.91%	745,708	745,708	-	-

FIGURE 4.10 The Group 2 interest and cross support from Group I comes together in the example model.

repeat Step 22 for each Group 2 tranche where we created a column header titled "Group 2 Interest Pro Rata Share."

27. Next go to the Group 2-Waterfall sheet and repeat Steps 23 through 25 for each of the Group 2 certificates. Be very careful when doing this to make sure each formula is adjusted for the correct tranche.

28. To finish off the senior certificate interest section, we need to create an area to track how much interest is left after cross supporting; this will be done at the beginning of Model Builder 4.4. For both loan groups there can be instances where money has been made available to the other loan group, but goes unused. In fact, under a normal performing transaction, there should be no need for money to switch between loan groups. However, we always direct the cash there in case it is needed and if it is not needed it will get directed elsewhere. The next area it can get directed to is in accordance with part III of the interest distributions section on page S-95 of the prospectus supplement.

29. One final step prior to moving on is to reference the aggregate interest paid to the Senior certificates on the Balances sheet. Go to the Balances sheet and enter the following formula in cell R15:

='Group 1 - Waterfall'!AB10+'Group 1 - Waterfall'!AD10

Copy and paste this formula over the range of cells R15:R514. Enter the text **Interest** in cell R7. Notice that this is how much interest was paid to the A-1 tranche, plus an additional column. The additional column will be created in Chapter 6. Repeat this step for all of the Class A tranches making sure to reference the correct columns, copy and paste across the appropriate range, and to add text for labeling purposes in row 7.

MORE ON WATERFALLS AND WALL STREET'S RISK PARSING

We should take a brief moment to pull ourselves from the minutiae of the model and talk about what we are doing and where we stand in the reverse engineering process. Thus far, we have created a system for generating cash flow from assets and have been applying that cash flow to fees and senior liabilities as dictated by the transaction documents. We began to see at the end of the last Model Builder section that the way the prospectus supplement is worded instructs us to pay cash to liabilities in different orderings of priority. This system is exactly how Wall Street has made innovations in parsing risk.

It becomes clear from the Model Builder exercises that this system is incredibly complex and that making assumptions about how a specific liability will perform without modeling the transaction at this level of detail is risky. Combined with intricate mechanics is how each tranche may perform when various stress assumptions on default and prepayment are introduced. Making buy or sell decisions on these securities without understanding how the assumptions and structure work in tandem is risky and has been shown to create market problems as evinced by the subprime mortgage securities fallout in 2007.

Although we are looking at an Alt-A transaction as an example, which tend to be less problematic than subprime deals, the mezzanine tranches that we will explore next are where the real risk is dispersed. These tranches are considered credit support for the senior tranches and can take principal write-downs when loss resulting from defaulted mortgages exceeds credit enhancement in the deal. Even the interest on these mezzanine tranches is subordinate to the senior tranches as we will see in the Model Builder exercise.

MODEL BUILDER 4.4: MEZZANINE INTEREST

1. We begin the mezzanine interest waterfall where we left off on the senior interest waterfall for both loan groups. Using the Group 1 – Waterfall sheet as an example, go to cell AH10. Here, we sent money to the Group II – Waterfall sheet in case the Group 2 certificates needed support. If they do not need the support the money should be sent down the waterfall to the Mezzanine Certificates. This means that we should collect the unused money for each loan group so it can be used as the primary resource to pay the Mezzanine Certificates' interest. In cell AI10 on the Group 1 – Waterfall sheet enter the following formula:

=AH10-'Group 2 - Waterfall'!AD10-'Group 2 - Waterfall'!AL10-'Group 2 - Waterfall'!AT10-'Group 2 - Waterfall'!BB10-'Group 2 - Waterfall'!BJ10-'Group 2 - Waterfall'!BR10

This formula starts with the interest funds that are sent to offer support to the Group 2 certificates and deducts all possible uses of the funds that could take

	Period	Date	30 / 360	Actual / 360	Actual / 365
Mezzanine - Waterfall					
Dates & Timing		**Day Count Systems**			
	0	5/25/2006			
	1	6/25/2006	0.083	0.086	0.085
	2	7/25/2006	0.083	0.083	0.082
	3	8/25/2006	0.083	0.086	0.085
	4	9/25/2006	0.083	0.086	0.085
	5	10/25/2006	0.083	0.083	0.082

FIGURE 4.11   The newly inserted Mezzanine – Waterfall sheet should take form after Step 3.

place in the Group 2 waterfall. This will return the remainder of the interest funds that can be passed to the Mezzanine Certificates. Copy and paste this formula over the range of cells AI10:AI509. Label cell AI7 **Undistributed Sent to Mezz.**

2. Repeat Step 1 for the Group 2 – Waterfall sheet. This should be done in column BW.

3. Insert a new sheet and name it **Mezzanine – Waterfall**. Columns A through E of this new sheet should be identical to the Group 2 – Waterfall sheet. Repeat the steps necessary to complete this task. The one difference is cell A1 should read **Mezzanine – Waterfall**. Take a look at Figure 4.11, as the model should progress to this state.

4. Because we left off aggregating the cash available for the Mezzanine Certificates, we should begin the Mezzanine waterfall with the cash that we amassed. The following formula should be entered in cell G10 of the Mezzanine – Waterfall sheet:

=‘Group 1 - Waterfall’!AI10+‘Group 2 - Waterfall’!BW10

Copy and paste this formula over the range of cells G10:G509. Notice that this concept is reinforced by the wording in section III of the Interest Distributions section, where it states, ". . . the sum of the Group I Interest Remittance Amount and the Group II Interest Remittance Amount remaining." Label cell G7, **Aggregate Interest Remittance Amount.** The full excerpt of Section III follows here:

III. On each distribution date, following the distributions made pursuant to clauses I and II above, the sum of the Group I Interest Remittance Amount and the Group II Interest Remittance Amount remaining will be distributed sequentially, to the Class M-1, Class M-2, Class M-3, Class M-4 and Class M-5 Certificates, in that order, in an amount equal to the Interest Distribution Amount for each such class.

Also from the excerpt, we see that the amount remaining should be distributed sequentially to the Mezzanine Certificates. So far we have seen the word *concurrently*, which directs cash at the same time, typically in a pro rata style. *Sequentially* is the opposite and pays out cash in a specific order. Here the order is listed, "Class M-1, Class M-2, Class M-3, Class M-4, and Class M-5 Certificates, in that order."

5. We know that we must begin to calculate interest for the Class M-1 tranche. The amount of interest that each mezzanine tranche should be paid is referenced on S-95. In Section III of the Interest Distributions section it states "...an amount equal to the Interest Distribution Amount for each such class." This wording is familiar—it was used for the senior class. We must repeat similar steps for the Mezzanine Certificates as with the senior classes: determine the Mezzanine Net WAC Pass-Through Rate, determine the tranche rate, calculate the interest due, calculate the interest paid, determine the interest carry forward, and then move on to the next tranche to repeat the steps.

   The first step that will be applicable to all five mezzanine tranches is calculating the Mezzanine Net WAC Pass-Through rate. The purpose of a Net WAC Pass-Through rate is to try to make sure the certificates are earning a minimum yield based on the yield of the mortgages. The calculation is a direct relation to the mortgage yield for the seniors, but because the interest must pay out the senior class prior to the mezzanine, the Net WAC Pass-Through must be based on the senior tranche yields. The wording used by the prospectus supplement to capture this idea is on the bottom of page S-92:

   (c) the Mezzanine Certificates is a per annum rate equal to the weighted average (weighted in proportion to the results of subtracting from the aggregate principal balance of each loan group the current aggregate Certificate Principal Balance of the related Class A Certificates) of (i) the Net WAC Pass-Through Rate for the Group I Certificates and (ii) the Net WAC Pass-Through Rate for the Group II Certificates.

This is where wording can make you think for a while. Breaking apart this excerpt we understand that we are seeking an annual rate that is the weighted average of (i) and (ii). This means that we must take the sum of multiplying the Net WAC Pass-Through Rate for each loan group by weights and then divide by the sum of the weights. The Net WAC Pass-Through rate of the Group I and II certificates has already been calculated, so all that we must interpret is what constitutes the weights.

   The weights are determined individually for each loan group by taking the current total principal of the mortgages that support the loan group and subtracting the related certificates current principal balance. When we put all of this together for the first period we get the following formula in cell H10 of the Mezzanine – Waterfall sheet:

=IF((‘Group 1 - Waterfall’!G10+‘Group 2 - Waterfall’!G10)<0.001,0,
　(‘Group 1 - Waterfall’!X10*(‘Group 1 - Waterfall’!G10-Balances!P14)+
　‘Group 2 - Waterfall’!X10*(‘Group 2 - Waterfall’!G10-
　SUM(Balances!T14,Balances!Z14,Balances!AF14,Balances!AL14,
　Balances!AR14,Balances!AX14)))/(‘Group 1 - Waterfall’!G10-
　Balances!P14+‘Group 2 - Waterfall’!G10-SUM(Balances!T14,
　Balances!Z14,Balances!AF14,Balances!AL14,Balances!AR14,
　Balances!AX14)))

This formula looks a bit horrendous, but this is primarily because it is referencing cells that are on sheets with long names. Note that the beginning IF function is in place to force the rate to zero when the mortgage loans are paid off. Copy and paste this formula over the range of cells H10:H509. Label cell H7, **Mezzanine Net WAC Pass-Through Rate.**

6. The next rate we need to implement is the stated rate of the security. Recall that this can vary depending on an optional clean-up call. The calculation is virtually identical to the senior certificates, except in this case we force the rate to 0 only when the collateral for both Group I and II is fully paid off. Enter the following formula in cell I10:

=IF((‘Group 1 - Waterfall’!G10+‘Group 2 - Waterfall’!G10)<0.001,0,
　MIN(H10,IF(Balances!F14,liab8_FxdRateClnUp,liab8_FxdRate)))

Copy and paste this formula over the range of cells I10:I509. Label cell I7, **M-1 Interest Rate.**

7. With the proper rate determined and the balances established on the Balances sheet earlier, we can now calculate the periodic interest due on the first mezzanine tranche. The formula for this looks familiar and should be entered in cell J10:

=I10*OFFSET($B10,0,MATCH(liab8_DayCtSys,mezz_DayCountSys,0))
　*Balances!BE14

Copy and paste this formula over the range of cells J10:J509 and label cell J7, **M-1 Interest Due.** Prior to moving on, there is a slight difference in this formula. Notice that there is no addition of unpaid interest as we have done in the senior certificates. Remember that the senior certificates were paid under the definition for the Senior Interest Distribution Amount. This is defined on S-94 and includes the key wording, "...and the Interest Carry Forward Amount, if any, for that class for that distribution date." This wording is definitely missing for the Interest Distribution Amount definition on page S-92.

So the question arises, "If a mezzanine tranche does not receive an interest payment, is it gone forever and not capitalized?" The answer to this is unfortunately a maybe. What we will see later is that the transaction structurers have subordinated mezzanine unpaid interest. It will appear later in the waterfall structure and may or may not get paid depending on the cash flow scenario run. Mezzanine investors should realize that this functionality adds additional risk to their tranche.

8. Moving on to paying interest, we invoke the "lesser of what you have and need" principle. Enter the following formula in cell K10:

=MIN(G10, J10)

Copy and paste this formula over the range of cells K10:K509. Label cell K7, **M-1 Interest Paid**. Figure 4.12 shows how the mezzanine section should be developing.

9. Although we have not read about the "Interest Carry Forward Amount" for the mezzanine tranches, we will assume readers have skimmed over the entire prospectus supplement as suggested in Chapter 1 and noted that the concept comes up later in the waterfall. We will not fully implement the concept now since it will rely on some future calculations, but we will put the system in place. Label cell L7 **Interest Carry Forward Amount Due** and enter the following formula in cell L10:

=J10-K10+L9+(L9*H10*OFFSET($B10,0,MATCH(liab8_DayCtSys, grp2_DayCountSys,0)))-M9

This formula is very similar to the senior interest carry forward formula where we add the current period's unpaid amount to the previous unpaid balance and

	F	G	H	I	J	K
5						
6		*Interest - Green Indicates Pre-Principal Waterfall Events*				
7		Aggregate Interest Remittance Amount	Mezzanine Net WAC Pass Through Rate	M-1 Interest Rate	M-1 Interest Due	M-1 Interest Paid
8		48,919,664			13,731,798	13,731,798
9						
10		1,122,358	6.96%	6.30%	258,235	258,235
11		1,118,145	6.96%	6.30%	258,235	258,235
12		1,112,478	6.96%	6.30%	258,235	258,235
13		1,105,369	6.96%	6.30%	258,235	258,235
14		1,096,837	6.96%	6.30%	258,235	258,235
15		1,086,914	6.96%	6.30%	258,235	258,235

FIGURE 4.12   The Mezzanine – Waterfall sheet starts with the M-1 tranche interest.

then add the capitalized interest. However, there is an amount subtracted at the end of the formula that differs from what was implemented for the seniors. This cell references the prior period's interest carry forward amount that was paid. Why is this implemented differently? In the senior tranches, the interest carry forward amount is integrated directly in the interest payment. For the mezzanines there will be a different source of payment later in the waterfall. For this reason it is easiest to implement and avoid circular references in Excel by creating a due and paid accounting system. Copy and paste the formula over the range of cells L10:L509.

10. Paying the interest carry forward is the same as paying any other liability. Take the lesser of what you have and need. Enter the following formula in cell M10:

=MIN(L10,AL10)

Copy and paste this formula over the range of cells M10:M509 and label cell M7, **M-1 Interest Carry Forward Amount Paid**. Notice that the source of the funds to pay this is column BA, which we have not calculated or entered information yet. This is fine as we will do so later in Chapter 6. The M-1 tranche should look like Figure 4.13.

11. We have finished the interest calculation for the first mezzanine tranche and need to replicate this for the remaining tranches. Create the following labels by entering the text provided here that corresponds with the cell references:

Q7:	**M-2 Interest Rate**	AG7:	**M-4 Interest Rate**
R7:	**M-2 Interest Due**	AH7:	**M-4 Interest Due**
S7:	**M-2 Interest Paid**	AI7:	**M-4 Interest Paid**
T7:	**M-2 Interest Carry Forward Amount Due**	AJ7:	**M-4 Interest Carry Forward Amount Due**
U7:	**M-2 Interest Carry Forward Amount Paid**	AK7:	**M-4 Interest Carry Forward Amount Paid**
Y7:	**M-3 Interest Rate**	AO7:	**M-5 Interest Rate**
Z7:	**M-3 Interest Due**	AP7:	**M-5 Interest Due**
AA7:	**M-3 Interest Paid**	AQ7:	**M-5 Interest Paid**
AB7:	**M-3 Interest Carry Forward Amount Due**	AR7:	**M-5 Interest Carry Forward Amount Due**
AC7:	**M-3 Interest Carry Forward Amount Paid**	AS7:	**M-5 Interest Carry Forward Amount Paid**

12. For all Interest Rate, Interest Due, and Interest Carry Forward Amount Due columns, the formulas will be variations of the M-1 tranche. Create these formulas, being very careful to replace all references that pertain to the M-1 tranche with the current tranche under consideration.

13. The Interest Paid columns are going to be different from what we have seen. For the Group II tranche, when we had multiple tranches of debt, we paid them on

	L	M
6	**Dark Blue Indicates Post Pri**	
7	**M-1 Interest Carry Forward Amount Due**	**M-1 Interest Carry Forward Amount Paid**
8	-	-
9		
10	-	-
11	-	-
12	-	-
13	-	-
14	-	-
15	-	-

FIGURE 4.13 The first mezzanine tranche's interest distributions.

a pro rata basis using share rates calculated on the Balances sheet. In the case of the Mezzanine Certificates, we should pay them sequentially. This means that the M-2 tranche should not receive any interest unless the M-1 tranche has been paid. To implement this in the model enter the following formula in cell S10:

=MIN(G10-K10,R10)

Copy and paste this formula over the range of cells S10:S509. Notice that this formula subtracts what was paid to the M-1 tranche from the amount available. This upholds the lesser of what you have and what you need principle, because you do not have cash that is first distributed to a mezzanine tranche with priority. Replicate this formula for all of the Interest Paid columns and make sure that each time the aggregate of what is paid to priority tranches is subtracted. For instance, the M-3 tranche should subtract the amount paid to the M-1 and M-2 tranches.

14. The Interest Carry Forward Amount Paid is the other column that must be adjusted because of the sequential nature of the Mezzanine Certificates. In Chapter 6, we will see the wording, but assume for now that the Interest Carry Forward Amount should also be paid sequentially. If this is the case, then we must subtract out amounts paid to priority mezzanine tranches. As an example, enter the following formula into cell U10:

=MIN(T10,BA10-M10)

Copy and paste this formula over the range of cells U10:U509. Notice that regardless of the source of the funds to pay the Interest Carry Forward Amount, we subtract the M-1 tranche's Interest Carry Forward Amount Paid prior to paying the M-2's Interest Carry Forward Amount. Think about the implications of this as a junior mezzanine investor. Not only is unpaid interest pushed back and subordinated to other items, but if there is cash to pay the unpaid interest later in the waterfall any mezzanine tranche higher in the waterfall must be fully reimbursed its unpaid interest.

At this point we have completed a majority of the interest calculations. Careful readers will notice that we left out explaining a few items including advanced concepts such as Net WAC Carryover, Prepayment, and Relief Act shortfalls. Net WAC Carryover will be explained in Chapter 6. Prepayment shortfalls have actually been included in the asset amortization calculations by using the current asset principal balance less prepaid amounts to determine the interest available. We calculate our Senior Net WAC Pass-Through Rates using the asset amortization numbers, so they are already reduced by amounts not covered by the servicer. Notice that we also put the option of servicer advances in the asset amortization and included this in the Senior Net WAC Pass-Through Rate formulas. Finally, the Relief Act is not being modeled in this transaction because it has no quantitative trigger.

15. As with the Class A tranches, we should summarize the interest paid on the Balances sheet. Go to the Balances sheet and enter the following formula in cell BG15:

='Mezzanine - Waterfall'!K10

Copy and paste this formula over the range of cells BG15:BG514. Repeat this step for all of the Mezzanine Certificates, making sure to change the reference for the appropriate tranche. Note that this amount is strictly the regular interest paid. We will see later in Chapter 7 that we will include more amounts when summarizing the interest paid to the Mezzanine Certificates. Figure 4.14 shows the progress on the Balances sheet.

	BE	BF	BG	BH
10				
11	*M-1*			
12	EOP Balance	% of Original Tranche Balance	Interest	Principal
13			13,731,798	49,211,000
14	49,211,000			
15	49,211,000	100%	258,235	-
16	49,211,000	100%	258,235	-
17	49,211,000	100%	258,235	(0)
18	49,211,000	100%	258,235	-
19	49,211,000	100%	258,235	-
20	49,211,000	100%	258,235	-

FIGURE 4.14 The M-1 tranche is tracked on the Balances sheet.

CONTINUING THE WATERFALL: IT ONLY GETS MORE COMPLICATED

By now you may be wondering why Wall Street has instituted such a complex system. Each step is designed to instill a specific measure of risk for each security being offered. Changes in priority of payment are especially pertinent to the interest waterfall because the first major source of credit enhancement is called *excess spread*. The simple definition for excess spread is any amount that exists in a transaction from interest generated by the assets after netting out fees and certificate interest. Transactions are designed with higher yielding assets than liabilities, so this excess flow of cash exists at each stage in the waterfall. We will see that this excess amount can sometimes compensate tranches for interest shortfalls because of defaults, but more importantly it also helps pay principal.

Principal is the next topic and has been organized into a separate chapter because more complex structures and features will be introduced. As we go through the prospectus and reverse out the principal repayment, try to keep the interest waterfall and flow of funds in the back of your mind. When the waterfall is complete by the end of Chapter 6, it is worth going back over each section of the waterfall starting with the one we just implemented in this chapter.

CHAPTER 5

Principal Repayment and the Shifting Nature of a Wall Street Deal

Principal in many structured transactions is directly passed through from the assets, meaning that whatever dollar amount comes in from a mortgage because of scheduled principal or voluntary prepayment is used to pay liability principal. This is the reason the prospectus supplement defines different distribution accounts for interest and principal. Reverse engineering a transaction like this can be done by creating a single waterfall structure, but it is always much easier to reverse a deal by following exactly what was done in the documentation.

The principal waterfall often changes based on certain conditions, which is perhaps the most elusive part of understanding a capital markets transaction on Wall Street. This is typically the case for principal repayment as senior investors are expected to have more security than subordinate investors. When a deal is performing poorly, the transaction designers try to build in mechanisms to mitigate loss according to senior prioritization. However, the converse can be true for subordinate investors when a transaction is performing well.

Reverse engineering this part of the transaction means keeping track of something I have termed the deal "state." A deal state is a categorization of a deal depending on specific conditional tests. For the most part, there are common conditional tests, but what defines the deal state can vary between banks and within the same bank's transactions. For instance, many transactions change the deal state depending on whether there is a certain amount of senior credit enhancement in the deal. This means there is a predefined calculation for the balance of the subordinate bonds versus the collateral and when that ratio dips below a certain level, the transaction switches deal states. The repercussion of a change in deal state is typically a reordering of the waterfall in some way, usually in respect to the principal payments. The concept of a deal state is captured in Figure 5.1.

Another challenge of reverse engineering principal distributions is that principal repayment is directly where collateral loss affects investors, making calculations difficult. Reductions in liability yield from defaulted assets only affect a bondholder in respect to opportunity cost, but a reduction in principal can mean an actual loss of investor principal. As we will see in this chapter, Mezzanine Certificates are particularly affected by loss because their principal balance can often be written

Deal States		
State:	Normal Pay	Accelerated Pay
Trigger:	After Stepdown Date Trigger Event Not in Effect	Prior to Stepdown Date Trigger Event in Effect
Effect:	Pays Seniors slower since no overcollateralization is required. Mezzanines receive distributions.	Pays Seniors faster to build overcollateralization or avoid loss. Mezzanines most likely locked out.

FIGURE 5.1 The deal state is typically determined by triggers and dates, which cause effects on cash flow.

down based on allocated losses from the assets. A write-down means that the value of the investors note is physically changed in the time period that the write-down takes place. Even senior liabilities are exposed to losses. Although they may not take a periodic write-down based on the deal documentation, the transaction may not have enough cash to return all the principal the senior liabilities are owed. At maturity, if the senior liability has not been paid off, the remaining balance is lost.

Complicating this section further is that mortgages default at different times and with different severity. This can cause variations in loss amounts over time and in the possibility of recovery. Excess funds can become available to try to ensure senior investors are paid by transaction maturity or that subordinate investors get reimbursed for written-down principal. All these intricacies are detailed in the prospectus supplement allowing us to reverse engineer the flow of principal.

It is extremely important that you review the full Principal Distributions section of the prospectus supplement, starting on page S-96, prior to beginning the following Model Builder sections. Much of the Principal Distributions section has been excerpted, but the complete wording has not been replicated. Reading through the Principal Distribution section once or even a few times will provide an excellent contextual foundation for implementing it using the Model Builder instructions.

MODEL BUILDER 5.1: THE DEAL STATE AND SENIOR PRINCIPAL

1. The first indication that there is a deal state concept comes on page S-96. If we read the first section of the Principal Distributions, we come across this wording:

   I. On each distribution date (a) prior to the Stepdown Date or (b) on which a Trigger Event is in effect, distributions in respect of principal to the extent of the Group I Principal Distribution Amount will be made in the following amounts and order of priority . . .

The excerpt has two conditions (a and b) to determine the deal state. The first condition (a) checks to see whether the current date is prior to the Stepdown Date. The Stepdown Date is defined on page S-94 and has been excerpted here:

"Stepdown Date": The Stepdown Date will be the earlier to occur of (i) the distribution date on which the aggregate Certificate Principal Balance of the Class A Certificates has been reduced to zero and (ii) the later to occur of (x) the distribution date occurring in June 2009 and (y) the first distribution date on which the Senior Enhancement Percentage (calculated for this purpose only prior to any distribution of the Group I Principal Distribution Amount and the Group II Principal Distribution Amount to the holders of the certificates then entitled to distributions of principal on the related distribution date) is greater than or equal to approximately 19.30%.

Let's pick the Stepdown Date definition apart step-by-step. First we see that the Stepdown Date is the earlier of (i) and (ii). Section i is easy to understand—it is simply the date on which the Class A Certificates are fully paid off. This could be a long time, so we should see what could possibly occur earlier in (ii). Section ii provides two possible dates (x) and (y) and confuses the reader by taking the later of those two dates. The first date (x) is a fixed date, the distribution date occurring in June 2009. In most transactions this date is 36 months after deal closing. The second date (y) is a conditional test on whether the Senior Enhancement Percentage is greater than or equal to a fixed percentage in the deal documentation.

In the previous assessment of the Stepdown Date, we determined there are three possible dates that need to be understood. The first two are straightforward, but the last one that tests whether the Senior Enhancement Percentage exceeds a specific value requires more investigation. We should go back to page S-94 in the prospectus supplement and look at the Senior Enhancement Percentage definition, which is excerpted here.

"Senior Enhancement Percentage": The Senior Enhancement Percentage for any distribution date is the percentage obtained by dividing (x) the aggregate Certificate Principal Balance of the Mezzanine Certificates and the Class CE Certificates, calculated after taking into account distribution of the Group I Principal Distribution Amount and the Group II Principal Distribution Amount to the holders of the certificates then entitled to distributions thereof on the related distribution date by (y) the aggregate principal balance of the mortgage loans as of the last day of the related Due Period (after giving effect to scheduled payments of principal due during the related Due Period, to the extent received or advanced, and unscheduled collections of principal received during the related Prepayment Period).

When we read this definition we see that the Senior Enhancement Percentage is calculated by adding up all the Mezzanine Certificate balances for a given time period and dividing by the corresponding period's total mortgage collateral balance. What is very tricky about this is that the Senior Enhancement Percentage clarifies that the Mezzanine Certificate balances should be reduced by the possible payment of principal for that period, whereas the Stepdown Date definition tells us otherwise. If we go back to the Stepdown Date definition. we see in parentheses that, for the purpose of the Stepdown Date definition, all principal distributions should not be taken into account. This is a very important distinction, because if it is missed, the Stepdown Date could be modeled earlier than it would occur, thereby making any scenario more aggressive.

To begin the implementation of the Stepdown Date, go to the Inputs sheet and enter the following text into the corresponding cells:

D23: **Stepdown Hard Date**
D24: **Stepdown Sr Enh Pct**
D25: **Stepdown Pct Date**

The Stepdown Hard Date is the date directly from the prospectus supplement. It is section (ii) (x) of the Stepdown Date definition, where it states the distribution date in June 2009. Recall from page S-72 that the modeling assumptions assume that all distribution dates are on the 25th of the month, so we should enter the date **6/25/2009** in cell E23. Name cell E23 **struc_StepDnDate**.

The other important figure provided in the Stepdown Date definition is the test for the Senior Enhancement Percentage. Section (ii) (y) tests if the Senior Enhancement Percentage exceeds 19.30%. Enter **19.30%** in E24 and name the cell **struc_StepDnSrPct**.

We will come back to entering a formula for cell E25 after creating the Senior Enhancement Percentage calculations.

2. Go to the Balances sheet and enter the following formula in cell I15:

=IF(D15<0.001,0,(SUM(BE14,BI14,BM14,BQ14,BU14,BY14))/D15)

Copy and paste this formula over the range of cells I15:I514. This formula calculates the Senior Enhancement Percentage by first checking to see if there is any collateral left. If not then the value is 0 to prevent #DIV/0! errors. Otherwise the formula sums up all the subordinate certificate balances for a period and divides that amount by the end of period aggregate collateral balance. Notice that the formula takes the beginning of period balances for the subordinate debt. This is to ensure that the calculation adheres to the Stepdown Date definition exception. Enter the text **Senior Enhancement %** in cell I12 for labeling purposes.

3. Go back to the Inputs sheet to finish off cell E25. After running a scenario, we may want a quick indication of when the Senior Enhancement Percentage

	D	E
23	Stepdown Hard Date	**6/25/2009**
24	Stepdown Sr Enh Pct	**19.30%**
25	Stepdown Pct Date	4/25/2008

FIGURE 5.2 The Stepdown Date section of the Inputs sheet, where a user controls Stepdown functionality, is largely complete.

exceeds the percentage provided in the prospectus supplement. Enter the following array formula in cell E25:

{=MIN(IF(struc_StepDnSrPct<Balances!I15:I514,Balances!B15:B514, 1000000))}

Note that this is an array formula and CTRL-SHFT-ENTER should be pressed to enter it in correctly. The formula should be written without the braces. Once CTRL-SHFT-ENTER is pressed, the braces should appear in the formula bar. Keep in mind that this formula returns the date when the Senior Enhancement Percentage exceeds the value listed in the prospectus. It is not the actual Stepdown Date as there are more tests required. Thus far we have created a section on the Inputs sheet that should look like Figure 5.2.

4. All the tests come together on the Balances sheet. Go to the Balances sheet and enter the following formula in cell K15:

=IF(SUM(P14,T14,Z14,AF14,AL14,AR14,AX14)<0.001,TRUE,IF (AND(B15>=struc_StepDnDate,I15>=struc_StepDnSrPct), TRUE, FALSE))

This formula transforms the Stepdown Date definition into a logical statement in Excel. First it checks to see if the sum of the Senior certificates have paid off. If this is the case, then the Stepdown Date has definitely occurred regardless of any other test. If it is not the case, then we must check if the current period being tested is beyond the Stepdown Date provided in the prospectus supplement. At the same time, we should check if the current period's Senior Enhancement Percentage is greater than the value defined in the prospectus supplement. When both of these previous two conditions are true then the Stepdown Date is active and a TRUE value populates. Copy and paste this formula over the range of cells K15:K514. Also, label cell K12 by entering the text **Stepdown Date Active**.

5. We now know if the Stepdown Date is active, but looking at the Principal Distributions section I (b), we see we have to also determine if a Trigger Event is in effect. Turning to page S-94 of the prospectus supplement we see the definition

for Trigger Event. It is a complex definition divided into the two sections. The first section is excerpted here:

> *"Trigger Event": With respect to any distribution date, a Trigger Event is in effect if: (i) (A) the percentage obtained by dividing the aggregate principal balance of mortgage loans delinquent 60 days or more (including mortgage loans delinquent 60 days or more and in foreclosure, in bankruptcy or REO properties) by the aggregate principal balance of all of the mortgage loans, in each case, as of the last day of the previous calendar month, exceeds (B) 36.00% of the Senior Enhancement Percentage for the prior distribution date; or . . .*

We interpret this definition as another conditional test during a distribution date. There are two parts to the test, the first one checking on delinquent, foreclosed, bankrupt, and real estate-owned loans. Because of the strong possibility that loans in this category will default the original structurer of the deal wanted to make sure that at any point of time there was enough enhancement for the Senior certificates.

To properly reverse a deal one would need to have performed a thorough collateral analysis including an analysis of delinquency and default. Earlier we built the possibility of calculating loss for the assets through the use of loss curves. When calibrating these curves we can also measure the delinquency. Alternative methods also include stationary or better yet, nonstationary transition matrices to create delinquency and default assumptions. Instead of deviating to calibrate these curves, which could be a book in itself, we will enter in a delinquency assumption. Also, if the deal that you are reverse engineering is well seasoned then there can be plenty of actual delinquency information that can be entered instead of an assumption. Any transpired data should be used in a deal that is seasoned.

Go to the Vectors sheet and enter the text **Delinquencies** in cell AE6 and **60+ Day Delinquencies** in cell AE7. For purposes of the model we do not want to trip the trigger yet, so we will enter a very low delinquency assumption. In cell AE9 enter the value **0.05%**. Grow this value in subsequent rows below by 0.0125%; cell AE508 should have 6.288% as a value. The beginning of the delinquency curve is shown in Figure 5.3.

6. Go back to the Inputs sheet and in cell G25, enter the text **Delinquency Trigger Pct**. In cell H25, enter the value **36%** and name the cell **struc_DelTrigPct**.

7. We are now prepped to enter the first part of the Trigger Event formula to implement the definition in the example model. Go to the Balances sheet and enter the text **Trigger Active** in cell M12. The first part of the formula that we will enter in cell M16 follows, but do not enter this yet as there will be a second step for the test. Just keep this part of the formula in mind:

=IF(SUM(P15,T15,Z15,AF15,AL15,AR15,AX15)<0.001,FALSE,IF (Vectors!AE9>(struc_DelTrigPct*Balances!I15),

	AE
1	
2	
3	
4	
5	
6	**Delinquencies**
7	**60+ Day Delinquencies**
8	
9	0.050%
10	0.063%
11	0.075%
12	0.088%
13	0.100%
14	0.113%
15	0.125%

FIGURE 5.3 The delinquency curve is an estimate that we have created for the example model. In actuality one would perform a historical study to calibrate this curve.

Notice that we first want to test if there are any Senior certificates left. If there are not, then the trigger is useless and should be deactivated. If there are Senior certificates, we then want to first test if the transpired or assumed delinquency curve that we entered on the Vectors sheet is greater than 36% of the Senior Enhancement Percentage of the prior period.

8. Although delinquency is a good metric as a precursor to default and loss, loss itself should be carefully monitored. This is built into the Trigger Event definition as well. Section (ii) of the definition is excerpted here:

> *(ii) the aggregate amount of Realized Losses incurred since the cut-off date through the last day of the related Prepayment Period (after giving effect to scheduled payments of principal due during the related Due Period, to the extent received or advanced, and unscheduled collections of principal received during the related Prepayment Period), reduced by the aggregate amount of Subsequent Recoveries received since the*

Realized Loss Percentages			
6/25/2008 through	5/25/2009	0.25%
6/25/2009 through	5/25/2010	0.60%
6/25/2010 through	5/25/2011	1.05%
6/25/2011 through	5/25/2012	1.50%
6/25/2012 and	thereafter	1.80%

FIGURE 5.4 The realized loss
percentages with corresponding dates.

*cut-off date through the last day of the related Prepayment Period,
divided by the aggregate principal balance of the mortgage loans as of the
cut-off date exceeds the applicable percentages set forth below with
respect to such distribution date . . .*

In the prospectus supplement, this excerpt is followed by the table on page S-95
depicted in Figure 5.4.

To integrate section (ii) into the Trigger Event formula, we need to replicate
the table on the Inputs sheet. Go to the Inputs sheet and enter the following date
values in the corresponding cells:

E29: **6/25/2008**	G29: **5/25/2009**
E30: **6/25/2009**	G30: **5/25/2010**
E31: **6/25/2010**	G31: **5/25/2011**
E32: **6/25/2011**	G32: **5/25/2012**
E33: **6/25/2012**	

Also enter the text **thereafter** in cell G33 and **Realized Loss Percentages** in cell
E28. Then enter the following values into the corresponding cells:

H29: **0.25%**
H30: **0.60%**
H31: **1.05%**
H32: **1.50%**
H33: **1.80%**

9. Next go to the Balances sheet and enter the text **Loss Trigger Pct** in cell L12.
Some of you may have picked up that we are going to compare the current loss
rate to the values provided in the prospectus. We already entered the values from
the prospectus, now we need to calculate each period's loss rate as defined in the
Trigger Events definition. Enter the following formula in cell L16:

=(SUM('Group 1 - Waterfall'!$K$10:K10)+SUM('Group 2 - Waterfall'!
$K$10:K10)-SUM('Group 1 - Waterfall'!$P$10:P10)-SUM('Group 2 -
Waterfall'!$P$10:P10))/SUM(grp1_TotalBal, grp2_TotalBal)

This formula aggregates the loss each period for both loan groups and takes out recoveries. It then divides this amount by the total mortgage balances as of the cut-off date. Copy and paste this formula over the range of cells L16:L514.

10. The strategy for triggers and varying waterfalls is to break up the conditional testing so it is easier to visualize. We have calculated both the delinquency and loss component to the trigger test and can now implement the actual trigger. Enter the text, **Trigger Active** in cell M12 and then enter the following formula in cell M16:

=IF(SUM(P15,T15,Z15,AF15,AL15,AR15,AX15)<0.001,FALSE,
 IF(Vectors!AE9>(struc_DelTrigPct*Balances!I15),TRUE,
 IF(B16<Inputs!$E$29,FALSE,IF(L16>OFFSET(Inputs!$H$28,MATCH
 (Balances!$B16,Inputs!$E$29:$E$33,1),0),TRUE,FALSE))))

The first part of this formula checks to see if the Senior certificates are all paid off. If they have, then the trigger is turned off. Next the delinquency is checked against the limits set forth in the prospectus supplement. If the limit is breached, then the trigger is activated with a TRUE. The date is then checked to see if it is prior to the start of the table on the Inputs sheet. If it is then the formula returns a FALSE. It would be unlikely to realize so much loss in the first two years without the delinquency rate breaching the trigger. Finally, the loss rate in the L column is compared against the table we entered on the Inputs sheet using an OFFSET-MATCH combination. Copy and paste this formula over the range of cells M16:M514. The trigger section should look like the area shown in Figure 5.5.

11. Now that we know the Stepdown Date and have built in a mechanism to test if a Trigger Event has occurred, we should look at how the two concepts are used for

	K	L	M
11	**Waterfall Adjustments**		
12	Stepdown Date Active	Loss Trigger Pct	Trigger Active
13			
14			
15	FALSE		
16	FALSE	0.00%	FALSE
17	FALSE	0.00%	FALSE
18	FALSE	0.00%	FALSE
19	FALSE	0.00%	FALSE
20	FALSE	0.00%	FALSE

FIGURE 5.5 The complete area of the trigger section.

principal payment. If we look at the excerpt from Step 1 of this Model Builder we see that the Principal Distribution's first section only applies if the current period is prior to the calculated Stepdown Date or if the Trigger Event is in effect. Be extraordinarily careful with the wording in this section. The conditional test here involves the word *or* meaning that if either of these conditions is true then the payment instructions that follow should be used for calculations.

The conditional test in Section 1 of the Principal Distributions on page S-96 of the prospectus supplement only applies to the Group I certificates. If we look at Section II and III we see that the same conditional test is applicable for the Group II and Mezzanine Certificates. When we look at Sections IV, V, and VI we notice that the conditional test changes. Those sections' payment structures are activated on or after the Stepdown Date and if the Trigger Event is not in effect. Once again, be careful of the wording as the conditional statement changes from an *or* to an *and*.

Principal will be paid depending on one of these two states. Each period one of the two conditional statements will be met. For this reason we should track the current state of the transaction. Enter the text **Waterfall 1 Active** in cell N12 and **Waterfall 2 Active** in cell O12. In cell N15 enter the following formula:

=IF(OR(K15=FALSE,M15),TRUE,FALSE)

Copy and paste this formula over the range of cells N15:N514. This formula uses the OR function to activate the first waterfall if the Stepdown Date has not occurred or if a Trigger Event is in effect. Complete the second waterfall status check by entering the following formula in cell O15:

=IF(AND(K15,IF(M15=FALSE,TRUE,FALSE)),TRUE,FALSE)

Copy and paste this formula over the range of cells O15:O514. A bit more complicated than the previous waterfall status check, this formula activates the second waterfall if the current period is the Stepdown Date or beyond and if a Trigger Event is not in effect. By knowing which waterfall is in effect we are ready to begin the actual principal calculations. However, the Stepdown Date and Trigger Events are very important parts to a structured transaction and we should provide more detail on them.

The Stepdown Date and Trigger Events are features that are closely watched in structured mortgage transactions, particularly by mezzanine investors. The reason is that passing the Stepdown Date without a Trigger Event is a key hurdle in achieving additional returns. As we will see later in this chapter, once the Stepdown Date is passed in conjunction with no Trigger Events, additional cash will flow to the Mezzanine Certificates. The likelihood of a Stepdown Date being realized is a key decision for mezzanine investors, especially in distressed environments. Often deals get marked down in depressed times with the expectation of no cash being released to the mezzanine debt holders. However, if a Stepdown Date is passed with no trigger breaches, even for a few periods, then cash can flow to the mezzanine tranches. If this cash creates a yield that is more than the price paid, a savvy investor can earn a decent return.

12. We can now finally proceed through the Principal Distributions section to the first subsection (i), which states:

> *(i) to the holders of the Group I Certificates until the Certificate Principal Balance thereof has been reduced to zero; and . . .*

Recall from the first excerpt from Step 1 of this Model Builder that the amount that is available to the Group I certificates is the Group I Principal Distribution Amount. Turning to the definition on page S-90 we are met with a hefty definition:

> *"Group I Principal Distribution Amount": The Group I Principal Distribution Amount for any distribution date will be the sum of (i) the principal portion of all scheduled monthly payments due on the Group I Mortgage Loans during the related Due Period, to the extent received on or prior to the related Determination Date or advanced prior to such distribution date; (ii) the principal portion of all proceeds received in respect of the repurchase of a Group I Mortgage Loan (or, in the case of a substitution, certain amounts representing a principal adjustment) during the related Prepayment Period; (iii) the principal portion of all other unscheduled collections, including insurance proceeds, liquidation proceeds, Subsequent Recoveries and all full and partial principal prepayments, received on the Group I Mortgage Loans during the related Prepayment Period, to the extent applied as recoveries of principal on the mortgage loans and (iv) the Group I Allocation Percentage of the amount of any Overcollateralization Increase Amount for such distribution date minus (v) the Group I Allocation Percentage of the amount of any Overcollateralization Reduction Amount for such distribution date. In no event will the Group I Principal Distribution Amount with respect to any distribution date be (x) less than zero or (y) greater than the then outstanding aggregate Certificate Principal Balance of the Fixed Rate Certificates.*

Like any complex statement we will break this down in parts. The first key phrase to notice is that the Group I Principal Distribution Amount will be a sum of subsections (i, ii, iii, iv, v). The first subsection (i) is the scheduled monthly principal from the Group I mortgage loans for the period. These are principal amounts that are received from mortgagors or advanced from the servicer. Subsection (ii) is reserved for special circumstances involving loan repurchases or substitution. These would typically take place if fraud or an ineligible loan ended up in the pool of loans. We are not modeling these loans, but should note that they do frequently occur in structured mortgage transactions. Subsection (iii) is very important as it includes all unscheduled collections, which we have calculated as voluntary prepayments and recoveries. Subsections (iv) and (v) will be discussed in Chapter 6 as they are part of the credit enhancement calculations.

Go to the Group 1 - Waterfall sheet and enter the text **Group I Principal Remittance Amount** in cell AL7. Enter the following formula in cell AL10:

=N10+O10+P10+R10

Copy and paste this formula over the range of cells AL10:AL509. Notice that this sums up the Group I asset's scheduled and advanced principal, voluntary prepayments, and recovery proceeds. This covers subsections (i, ii, and iii) of the Group I Principal Distribution Amount, but is not the Group I Principal Distribution Amount. The first thought is, "So why bother calculating it?" The reason is that the formula in column AL is the Group I Principal Remittance Amount as defined a bit lower on page S-90, which will be integral to the calculations.

> *"Group I Principal Remittance Amount": The Group I Principal Remittance Amount for any distribution date will be equal to the sum of the amounts described in clauses (i) through (iii) of the definition of Group I Principal Distribution Amount.*

13. We will continue with the Principal Distribution section, but will have to skip over many columns for now because much of the principal section relies on advanced features described in Chapter 6. For now, enter the following formula in AN10:

=N10+O10+P10+R10

Copy and paste this formula over the range AN10:AN509. Note that this formula is the same as the last step. This is primarily because in Chapter 6, we will modify the formula to take into account advanced features, but need to populate the data for now. Also, label cell AN7, **Group I Principal Distribution Amount**.

14. Before we can pay any amount of principal we should jump slightly ahead in the Principal Distributions section to cases when the second waterfall state is active. This is because there is a key difference in wording that we should define now for use later. If we go to page S-96 to subsection (iv) we see the following instructions for situations when the second waterfall state is activated:

> *(i) to the holders of the Group I Certificates, the Group I Senior Principal Distribution Amount until the Certificate Principal Balance thereof has been reduced to zero; and ...*

The important difference between this excerpt and the first one described in Step 12 is that the excerpt here defines the Group I Senior Principal Distribution Amount as the amount paid to the certificates. We should check this definition to understand what we need to implement to be able to pay this amount. On page S-90 we find the definition, which reads:

> *"Group I Senior Principal Distribution Amount": The Group I Senior Principal Distribution Amount is an amount equal to the excess of (i) the aggregate Certificate Principal Balance of the Group I Certificates immediately prior to the related distribution date over (ii) the lesser of (A) the product of (i) approximately 80.70% and (ii) the aggregate principal balance of the Group I Mortgage Loans as of the last day of the related Due Period (after giving effect to scheduled payments of principal due during the related Due Period, to the extent received or advanced, and unscheduled collections of principal received during the related Prepayment Period) and (B) the aggregate principal balance of the Group I Mortgage Loans as of the last day of the related Due Period (after giving effect to scheduled payments of principal due during the related Due Period, to the extent received or advanced, and unscheduled collections of principal received during the related Prepayment Period) minus 0.50% of the aggregate principal balance of the Group I Mortgage Loans as of the cut-off date.*

No doubt this definition is a mouthful, but like all legal definitions it is worded for precision and can be followed precisely. The first key word is *excess*, which means that we will be subtracting an amount from another amount. This is tricky because *excess* is usually followed by an *over*, which is suggestive of a fraction or division. However, when *over* is paired with *excess* the intention is to subtract an amount. Here we see that (ii) should be subtracted from (i). This is made even more confusing because there are two (i)s and two (ii)s.

Clarity can be achieved by starting with (i) the aggregate Group I Certificate Principal Balance (predistribution) minus (ii) the minimum of (A), which is 80.70% multiplied by the Group I mortgage loan principal balance and (B), which is the aggregate principal balance of the Group I mortgage loans less 0.50% multiplied by the original balance of the Group I mortgage loans. To properly implement this formula we need to insert a few assumptions on the Inputs sheet. Go to the Inputs sheet and enter the following text and values in the corresponding cells:

D19: **Senior Prin Dist %**
D20: **Senior Org Prin Dist %**
E19: **80.7%**
E20: **0.5%**

Figure 5.6 shows the progress on the Inputs sheet thus far. Also, name cell E19 **struc_SrPrinPct** and cell E20 **struc_SrOrgPrinPct**.

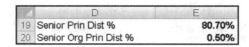

	D	E
19	Senior Prin Dist %	80.70%
20	Senior Org Prin Dist %	0.50%

FIGURE 5.6   The Inputs sheet should incorporate the principal percentages.

15. Next go to the Group 1 – Waterfall and enter the following formula in cell AO10:

    =MAX(MIN(Balances!P14-MIN(struc_SrPrinPct*T10, T10-struc_SrOrgPrinPct*grp1_TotalBal),AN10),0)

    Copy and paste this formula over the range of cells AO10:AO509. Notice that this formula captures the wording in Step 14, but also adds a MAX function in case of a rare condition where there could be a slight negative value. Also, enter the text **Group I Senior Principal Distribution Amount** in cell AO7.

16. Most likely in no loss or low loss situations, there will be little to no difference between the Principal Distribution Amount and Senior Principal Distribution Amount. We will see in the next chapter, after we modify the Senior Principal Distribution Amount formula to include credit enhancement, how the two values deviate. For now we can move on to what should actually be paid to the Group I Senior certificate holder. This is in column AP. In cell AP7, enter the text **A-1 Distribution Paid** and then enter the following formula in cell AP10:

    =MIN(Balances!P14,MIN(AL10+AK10,IF(Balances!N15,AN10,AO10)))

    Copy and paste this formula over the range of cells AP10:AP509. This formula checks to see which waterfall is activated and then pays either the Principal Distribution Amount or the Senior Principal Distribution Amount. It is constrained by the Principal Remittance Amount plus the excess spread, which we have not yet included. Finally, the formula is constrained further by only paying the balance of the tranche. This protects from overpaying when the tranche balance becomes very low. Notice that cell AK10 is referenced, but not yet complete. We will come back to this reference in the next chapter when we calculate overcollateralization increases.

17. The next step in reversing out the principal waterfall is to include the second subsection of Step I:

    (ii) to the holders of the Group II Certificates (allocated among the classes of Group II Certificates in the priority described below), after taking into account the distribution of the Group II Principal Distribution Amount already distributed, as described herein, until the Certificate Principal Balances thereof have been reduced to zero.

This wording is similar as in the interest section. It is a bit trickier given the two possible distribution amounts. Therefore the following formula must be entered in cell AR10:

=IF(Balances!N15,AN10-AP10,AO10-AP10)

Copy and paste this formula over the range of cells AR10:AR509. Also, enter the text, **Undistributed Principal Sent to Group II** in cell AR7. Thus far this section of the example model should look like Figure 5.7.

18. Notice from the excerpt in Step 17 that the money which we calculated in the formula is directed to the Group II certificates and is allocated according to a specific priority. This priority is detailed on page S-97 and excerpted here:

> *With respect to the Group II Certificates, all principal distributions will be distributed sequentially, first, to the holders of the Class A-2F Certificates, the Lockout Distribution Percentage of such principal distributions, until the Certificate Principal Balance of the Class A-2F Certificates has been reduced to zero; second, to the Class A-2A Certificates, until the Certificate Principal Balance of the Class A-2A Certificates has been reduced to zero; third, to the Class A-2B Certificates, until the Certificate Principal Balance of the Class A-2B Certificates has been reduced to zero; fourth, to the Class A-2C Certificates, until the Certificate Principal Balance of the Class A-2C Certificates has been reduced to zero; fifth, to the Class A-2D Certificates, until the Certificate Principal Balance of the Class A-2D Certificates has been reduced to zero; sixth, to the Class A-2E Certificates, until the aggregate Certificate Principal Balance of the Class A-2E Certificates has been reduced to zero and seventh, to the Class A-2F Certificates, until the Certificate Principal Balance of the Class A-2F Certificates has been reduced to zero, provided, however, on any distribution date on which the aggregate Certificate Principal Balance of the Subordinate Certificates has been reduced to zero, principal distributions will be distributed concurrently, to the Group II Certificates, on a pro rata basis, based on the Certificate Principal Balance of each such class.*

From this excerpt we can read that the normal distribution of principal to the Group II certificates is sequential, but not to the Class A-2A first as one would expect. Instead, the A-2F is allocated a special amount based on a concept called the Lockout Distribution. To completely understand the Lockout Distribution we should turn to the definition on page S-92, which states:

> *"Lockout Distribution Percentage": The Lockout Distribution Percentage for the Class A-2F Certificates and any distribution date means the indicated percentage of the Lockout Certificate Percentage for such distribution date . . .*

	AK	AL	AM	AN	AO	AP	AQ	AR
6	*Principal*							*Principal Redistributions*
7	Group I Excess	Group I Principal Remittance Amount	Group I Allocation Percentage	Group I Principal Distribution Amount	Group I Senior Principal Distribution Amount	A-1 Distribution Paid	A-1 Principal Distributed by Group II	Undistributed Principal Sent to Group II
8	3,695,280	532,064,773		529,937,557	400,304,627	484,445,000	-	40,803
9								
10	276,294	6,164,931	46%	6,441,224	6,441,224	6,441,224	-	0
11	275,469	7,391,884	46%	7,667,354	7,667,354	7,667,354	-	-
12	273,674	8,604,208	46%	8,877,882	8,877,882	8,877,882	-	0
13	271,019	9,793,458	46%	10,064,477	10,064,477	10,064,477	-	-
14	267,572	10,951,055	46%	11,218,627	11,218,627	11,218,627	-	-
15	263,402	12,067,953	46%	12,331,355	12,331,355	12,331,355	-	-

FIGURE 5.7 The Group 1 – Waterfall principal distribution section.

130

Distribution Date Occurring		Percentage
From	**To**	
6/25/2006	5/25/2009	0%
6/25/2009	5/25/2011	45%
6/25/2011	5/25/2012	80%
6/25/2012	5/25/2013	100%
6/25/2013	thereafter	300%

FIGURE 5.8 The Lockout Distribution
Percentages in table format.

The percentages the prospectus show are captured in Figure 5.8.

To fully interpret the last figure and excerpt, we now understand that the first principal distribution goes to the A-2F tranche based on the percentages shown in Figure 5.2. Prior to starting the Group II principal waterfall, we need to update the Inputs sheet to account for the special payments to the A-2F tranche.

Go to the Inputs sheet and enter the following text and dates in the corresponding cells:

B28: **Lockout Distribution Percentages**
B29: **6/25/2006**
C29: **5/25/2009**
B30: **6/25/2009**
C30: **5/25/2011**
B31: **6/25/2011**
C31: **5/25/2012**
B32: **6/25/2012**
C32: **5/25/2013**
B33: **6/25/2013**
C33: **thereafter**

Also enter the following values in the corresponding cells:

D29: **0%**
D30: **45%**
D31: **80%**
D32: **100%**
D33: **300%**

This sets up the necessary assumptions on the Inputs sheet to continue with principal amortization for Group II.

19. Go to the Group II – Waterfall sheet. The Group II Principal Remittance Amount is defined identically to the Group I Principal Remittance in the prospectus supplement. This definition is captured by entering the following formula in cell BZ10:

=N10+O10+P10+R10

Copy and paste this formula over the range of cells BZ10:BZ509. Notice that this formula on the Group II – Waterfall sheet is identical to the one on the Group I – Waterfall sheet. Also enter the text **Group II Principal Remittance Amount** in cell BZ7.

20. Just as we did for the Group I – Waterfall sheet we will enter a partial formula in the next column, which will be finished off in Chapter 6. In cell CB10 enter the following formula:

=N10+O10+P10+R10

Copy and paste this formula over the range of cells CB10:CB509. This is the same as the previous formula, as the definition for the Group II Principal Distribution Amount is virtually identical. Keep in mind that this is incomplete and we will revisit this column in Chapter 6 to add additional functionality. Enter the text **Group II Principal Distribution Amount** in cell CB7.

21. Moving on, we need to jump ahead to the second waterfall state, just as we did with the Group I loans. This is seen on page S-96, where it states:

> *V. On each distribution date (a) on or after the Stepdown Date and (b) on which a Trigger Event is not in effect, distributions in respect of principal to the extent of the Group II Principal Distribution Amount will be made in the following amounts and order of priority:*
>
> *(i) to the holders of the Group II Certificates (allocated among the classes of Group II Certificates in the priority described below), the Group II Senior Principal Distribution Amount, until the Certificate Principal Balances thereof have been reduced to zero; and . . .*

The wording is similar to what was implemented for the Group I loans in Step 14. Even the definition of the Group II Senior Distribution Amount on page S-91 is very much alike; however there are many more tranches in Group II. This translates into a formula that should be entered in CC10 on the Group II – Waterfall sheet:

=MAX(MIN(SUM(Balances!T14,Balances!Z14,Balances!AF14,Balances!
    AL14,Balances!AR14,Balances!AX14),SUM(Balances!T14,Balances!Z14,
    Balances!AF14,Balances!AL14,Balances!AR14,Balances!AX14)-MIN
    (struc_SrPrinPct*T10,T10-struc_SrOrgPrinPct*grp2_TotalBal),CB10),0)

Copy and paste this formula over the range of cells CC10:CC509. This formula is actually much simpler than it seems because it is highly repetitive. When reading the Group II Senior Distribution Amount definition, we see the word *excess* again. Recall that this means we are going to subtract two amounts. The first amount is the sum of the aggregate Group II certificates, which we are drawing from the Balances sheet. We also need to cap the formula by the current period's beginning balances of those certificates. Remember that you should never pay more principal than is due to the certificate holders. Later in the formula we reference set percentages from the Inputs sheet and apply them to the Group II collateral's current and original balances. Also enter the text **Group II Senior Principal Distribution Amount** in cell CC7 to create a label.

22. We can now proceed forward on the Group II principal distribution definition as shown in the excerpt in Step 18. We see that we have to pay the Group A-2F first based on the Lockout Certificate Percentage. We have set up the initial inputs for this, but we need to set up the actual amount each period. This is best done on the Balances sheet. Go to the Balances sheet and enter the following formula in cell BB15:

=IF(SUM(T14,Z14,AF14,AL14,AR14,AX14)<0.001,0,AX14/SUM(T14, Z14,AF14,AL14,AR14,AX14)*OFFSET(Inputs!$D$28,MATCH(B15, Inputs!$B$29:$B$33,1),0))

Copy and paste this formula over the range of cells BB15:BB514. Also enter the text, **Lockout Distribution Percentage** in cell BB12. Notice that in Step 18, we looked at the definition of the Lockout Distribution Percentage, not the Lockout Certificate Percentage. Wall Street loves details. The Lockout Certificate Percentage modifies the Lockout Distribution Percentage. Read the Lockout Certificate Percentage from page S-92, excerpted here:

> *"Lockout Certificate Percentage": The Lockout Certificate Percentage for the Class A-2F Certificates will be calculated for each distribution date to be the percentage equal to the Certificate Principal Balance of the Class A-2F Certificates immediately prior to such distribution date divided by the aggregate Certificate Principal Balance of the Group II Certificates immediately prior to such distribution date.*

Essentially this is a pro rata weighting for the Class A-2F class. It seems as if the Lockout Distribution Percentage was created for any tranche of debt and that if a tranche is allowed it, then it only receives its pro rata share. This explains why the latter part of the formula divides the prior period's balance by all the tranches' balances and then multiplies that ratio by the relevant percentage from the Inputs sheet (as determined by period). There is some clean up functionality to prevent errors. The formula first checks to see if there are any Group II certificates outstanding; if not then the percentage is zero.

23. While we are on the Balances sheet, we are going to complete some columns that will help us with the Group II principal distributions. Earlier, in the excerpt from Step 18, we read that the Group II principal distributions are sequential. However, we should read the entire payment priority instructions. Right after explaining that each tranche should be paid sequentially, the definition has a subtle ending that informs the reader that the Group II certificates will be paid concurrently on a pro rata basis, if the Mezzanine Certificates are all reduced to zero. This is a complete change in payment methodology.

In Chapter 4, we created pro rata share percentages for the Group II certificates. These percentages are created based on interest due. The last line of the excerpt from Step 18 informs the reader that if the certificates are being paid on a pro rata basis, the pro rata weighting is based on certificate balances.

We have already labeled the pertinent columns for the periodic principal pro rata percentages as "Group II Principal Pro Rata Share." Now we should enter formulas for them, beginning with W14 on the Balances sheet:

=IF(SUM(T14,Z14,AF14,AL14,AR14,AX14)<0.001,0,T14/SUM(T14,Z14, AF14,AL14,AR14,AX14))

Copy and paste this formula over the range of cells W14:W509. This formula should be repeated for each Group II certificate. The only difference between the formulas is the numerator of the weighted average calculation should change. Notice this difference for the A-2B tranche in cell AC14:

=IF(SUM(T14,Z14,AF14,AL14,AR14,AX14)<0.001,0,Z14/SUM(T14,Z14, AF14,AL14,AR14,AX14))

Make sure to copy and paste all formulas over the rows 14 to 509 for the relevant columns.

24. We can finally start paying the Group II liabilities. Go to the Group II – Waterfall sheet and enter the following formula in cell CD10:

=IF(SUM(Balances!BE14,Balances!BI14,Balances!BM14,Balances!BQ14, Balances!BU14)>0,MIN(IF(Balances!N15,CB10*Balances!BB15,CC10* Balances!BB15),Balances!AX14,BZ10),MIN(IF(Balances!N15,CB10* Balances!BA14,CC10*Balances!BA14),Balances!AX14,BZ10))

We first pay the A-2F certificate with this formula, as the prospectus supplement directs us to pay the Lockout Distribution Percentage. However, there are a number of nuances within this formula. First, we need to check if the subordinate certificates have balances. Recall that if they are paid off, then the payment priority switches to pro rata. We set up a conditional test on the subordinate certificate balances to implement this feature. If the aggregate subordinate balance is greater than zero, we pay the Lockout Distribution Percentage.

However, we have to test if we are paying the Group II Principal Distribution Amount or the Group II Senior Principal Distribution Amount. Remember that the Principal Distribution section on page S-96 shows that either can be paid depending on the Stepdown Date and Trigger Event. Because we have set both principal distribution amounts up in cells CB10 and CC10, and have logical statements for the active waterfall, we can set up a conditional test and pay the correct distribution amount multiplied by the Lockout Distribution Percentage from the Balances sheet. Keep in mind that we must always cap principal payments by the current period's beginning certificate balance using a MIN function. Finally, if the subordinate tranches are paid off, then we implement a pro rata pay system based on the Group II Pro Rata Share percentage for the A-2F certificate from the Balances sheet. Although we will come back to the A-2F tranche later in the waterfall in a sequential situation, this is the only time we will pay the pro rata share; otherwise we would overpay the A-2F tranche in a given period. Make sure to copy and paste this formula over the range of cells CD10:CD509. Also, enter the text **A-2F Distribution Paid** in cell CD7 for labeling purposes.

25. Next we should follow the sequential ordering and pay the A-2A tranche. To make this easier in sequential situations we should move the cash by adding another column to calculate what is available after paying the A-2F distribution. First enter the text **Group II Principal Distribution Remaining** in cell CF7 and then enter the following formula in cell CF10:

=CB10-CD10

Copy and paste this over the range of cells CF10:CF509. This simple formula takes the Group II Principal Distribution we started with and subtracts out the distribution to the A-2F tranche.

26. A similar formula should be entered into cell CG10:

=MAX(CC10-CD10,0)

This formula is to carry over the Group II Senior Distribution Amount. The difference is that this formula has a MAX function in case of very rare nuances where there could be a slight negative value. Copy and paste this formula over the range of cells CG10:CG509. Also, enter the text **Group II Senior Distribution Remaining** in cell CG7. The Group II principal section should be developing as seen in Figure 5.9.

27. The first tranche paid, the A-2F, tranche was a special case. The remaining Group II certificates have similar payment formulas. First we should label each column appropriately by entering the following text in the corresponding cell:

CH7: **A-2A Distribution Paid**
CJ7: **A-2B Distribution Paid**
CL7: **A-2C Distribution Paid**

	CB	CC	CD	CE	CF	CG
7	Group II Principal Distribution Amount	Group II Senior Principal Distribution Amount	A-2F Distribution Paid	A-2F Principal Distributed by Group I	Group II Principal Distribution Remaining	Group II Senior Principal Distribution Amount Remaining
8	596,862,162	445,321,676	54,559,000	-	542,303,162	395,846,455
9						
10	7,606,914	7,606,914	-	-	7,606,914	7,606,914
11	8,987,698	8,987,698	-	-	8,987,698	8,987,698
12	10,349,359	10,349,359	-	-	10,349,359	10,349,359
13	11,682,196	11,682,196	-	-	11,682,196	11,682,196
14	12,976,427	12,976,427	-	-	12,976,427	12,976,427
15	14,219,970	14,219,970	-	-	14,219,970	14,219,970

FIGURE 5.9 The Group II principal calculations that have been created thus far.

> CN7: **A-2D Distribution Paid**
> CP7: **A-2E Distribution Paid**
> CR7: **A-2F Distribution Paid**

28. In cell CH10, enter the following formula to pay the A-2A principal:

> =IF(SUM(Balances!BE14,Balances!BI14,Balances!BM14,Balances!BQ14,
> Balances!BU14)>0,MIN(IF(Balances!N15,CF10,CG10),Balances!T14),
> MIN(IF(Balances!N15,CB10*Balances!W14,CC10*Balances!W14),
> Balances!T14))

This formula has similar elements to the A-2F payment formula earlier, but the most important difference is that when there are subordinate certificates, the tranche is due the entire amount from the distribution amount, rather than a percentage. The distribution amount can vary depending on the state of the deal. What can be confusing about this formula is if there are no subordinate certificates and the Group II certificates are paying pro rata. Some will think there is an error in the formula because it is referencing the earlier distribution amount. This is actually correct because in a pro rata distribution, the tranches are taking the full distribution amount and splitting it up based on balance percentages. In the sequential system, we must deduct payments made to tranches prior to the tranche under examination. Copy and paste this formula over the range of cells CH10:CH509.

29. Let's move on to the A-2B certificate, the next sequential tranche according to the principal distribution priority. For this tranche enter the following formula in cell CJ10:

> =IF(SUM(Balances!BE14,Balances!BI14,Balances!BM14,Balances!BQ14,
> Balances!BU14)>0,IF((Balances!T14-CH10)<0.001,MIN(IF(Balances!
> N15,CF10-CH10,CG10-CH10),Balances!Z14),0),MIN(IF(Balances!N15,
> CB10*Balances!AC14,CC10*Balances!AC14),Balances!Z14))

Copy and paste this formula over the range of cells CJ10:CJ509. For the most part this formula is almost the same as the A-2A tranche aside from logical shifts in references to reflect the A-2B certificate exposures. The major difference is that there is an additional IF function right after the initial IF function to check if the subordinate tranches are paid off. An additional IF function is included to check if the tranche prior to the A-2B (the A-2A) is paid off before releasing funds for payment. Notice that the IF function looks at the A-2A balance less the amount paid in the current period. If this is less than a certain level of precision (in this case .0001), then the A-2B can start receiving money. If not, then the tranche gets nothing. Such a system only pertains to a sequential payout. If the subordinate certificates are paid off, then the payment system reverts to a pro rata payout as seen in the last part of the formula.

30. Replicate the formula in Step 29 for the A-2C, A-2D, and A-2E tranches in their respective columns. Make sure to change all references and to subtract out prior payments in the sequential section of the formula. If any of this is unclear, refer to the example model on the CD-ROM for the complete formulas.

31. Finally, there is the matter of the A-2F tranche. We see it appear twice in the prospectus supplement's priority of Group II principal payments. This is only the case for a sequential pay system. In such a system, the A-2F receives it's Lockout Distribution first and if there is money left after paying all the other Group II tranches, then it receives another distribution. In a pro rata situation, we already allocated funds to the A-2F tranche. The ordering does not matter in the pro rata case because if there are shortfalls, each tranche will only be assigned its pro rata share of the available funds. To implement these concepts enter the following formula in cell CR10:

=IF((Balances!AR14-CP10)<0.001,MIN(IF(Balances!N15,CF10-CH10-CJ10-CL10-CN10-CP10,CG10-CH10-CJ10-CL10-CN10-CP10),Balances!AX14-CE10),0)

Notice that this is the same as the part of the other Group II formulas, but only covers sequential pay. The pro rata pay was implemented earlier in column CD. Copy and paste this formula over the range of cells CR10:CR509. So far the Group II principal section should look like Figure 5.10.

32. Next we should follow the principal distribution instructions to see where the remaining cash should go. The following excerpt is from page S-96:

> *(ii) to the holders of the Group I Certificates, after taking into account the distribution of the Group I Principal Distribution Amount already distributed, as described herein, until the Certificate Principal Balance thereof has been reduced to zero.*

We have seen this language before with the Group I certificates directing remaining funds to Group II. Here the funds are directed to Group I. We incorporate

	CH	CI	CJ	CK	CL	CM	CN	CO	CP	CQ	CR	CS
	A-2A Distribution Paid	A-2A Principal Distributed by Group I	A-2B Distribution Paid	A-2B Principal Distributed by Group I	A-2C Distribution Paid	A-2C Principal Distributed by Group I	A-2D Distribution Paid	A-2D Principal Distributed by Group I	A-2E Distribution Paid	A-2E Principal Distributed by Group I	A-2F Distribution Paid	A-2F Principal Distributed by Group I
7												
8	203,118,000	0	65,317,000	-	83,228,000	-	86,053,000	-	53,313,916	2,084	-	-
9		0	-	-	-	-	-	-	-	-	-	-
10	7,606,914	-	-	-	-	-	-	-	-	-	-	-
11	8,987,698	0	-	-	-	-	-	-	-	-	-	-
12	10,349,359	-	-	-	-	-	-	-	-	-	-	-
13	11,682,196	-	-	-	-	-	-	-	-	-	-	-
14	12,976,427	-	-	-	-	-	-	-	-	-	-	-
15	14,219,970	-	-	-	-	-	-	-	-	-	-	-

FIGURE 5.10 The Group II principal section continues to develop by paying principal to each tranche.

this by entering the following formula in cell CT10 of the Group II – Waterfall sheet:

=IF(Balances!N15,CF10,CG10)-CH10-CJ10-CL10-CN10-CP10-CR10

Copy and paste this formula over the range of cells CT10:CT509. Also enter the text **Undistributed Principal Sent to Group I** in cell CT7.

33. We should now go back to the Group I – Waterfall sheet and complete the section that relies on the undistributed Group II funds. Enter the following formula in cell AQ10 of the Group I – Waterfall sheet:

=MIN('Group 2 - Waterfall'!CT10,Balances!P14-AP10)

This formula uses the "lesser of what you have and need" adage, by taking the minimum of what is available from Group II and what is needed for the A-1 tranche after the Group I distribution. Copy and paste this formula over the range of cells AQ10:AQ509. Enter the text **A-1 Principal Distributed By Group II** in cell AQ7.

34. We should now do the same for the Group II certificates. Because there are more tranches, we need to have a more systematic approach. Enter the following text in the corresponding cells:

CE7: **A-2F Principal Distributed by Group I**
CI7: **A-2A Principal Distributed by Group I**
CK7: **A-2B Principal Distributed by Group I**
CM7: **A-2C Principal Distributed by Group I**
CO7: **A-2D Principal Distributed by Group I**
CQ7: **A-2E Principal Distributed by Group I**
CS7: **A-2F Principal Distributed by Group I**

For the initial A-2F payment, we should use a custom formula to take into account that only the Lockout Distribution should be attempted to be paid. Enter the following formula in cell CE10:

**=IF(SUM(Balances!BE14,Balances!BI14,Balances!BM14,Balances!BQ14,
Balances!BU14)>0,MIN('Group 1 - Waterfall'!AR10*Balances!BB15,
Balances!AX14-CD10,'Group 1 - Waterfall'!AR10),MIN('Group 1 -
Waterfall'!AR10*Balances!BA14,Balances!AX14-CD10))**

Copy and paste this formula over the range of cells CE10:CE509. Notice that this formula applies the Lockout Distribution Percentage to the available funds from the Group I waterfall. When the subordinate certificates are paid off then the A-2F tranche only receives its pro rata share of the Group I available funds. We also cap the payment by the certificate balance less the current period's principal payment.

35. The A-2A tranche is the first tranche to get paid its full amount in sequential order so its formula will be slightly different from the others. Enter the following formula in cell CI10:

=IF(SUM(Balances!BE14,Balances!BI14,Balances!BM14,Balances!
    BQ14,Balances!BU14)>0,MIN('Group 1 - Waterfall'!
    AR10-CE10,Balances!T14-CH10),MIN('Group 1 - Waterfall'!
    AR10*Balances!W14,Balances!T14-CH10))

Copy and paste this formula over the range of cells CI10:CI509. Here the same rules apply: if the subordinates exist then the Group I remaining is provided to the A-2A first, if there are no subordinate certificates left then the Group I remaining is split pro rata.

36. The A-2B, A-2C, A-2D, and A-2E tranches will have similar formulas. For example, look at the A-2B formula that should be entered in cell CK10:

=IF(SUM(Balances!BE14,Balances!BI14,Balances!BM14,Balances!BQ14,
    Balances!BU14)>0,IF((Balances!T14-CH10-CI10)<0.001,MIN('Group 1 -
    Waterfall'!AR10-CE10-CI10,Balances!Z14-CJ10),0),MIN('Group 1 -
    Waterfall'!AR10*Balances!AC14,Balances!Z14-CJ10))

Like the normal principal payment, in a sequential pay structure, the A-2B tranche is paid only after the A-2A is completely paid off using funds from both the Group I and II sources. Otherwise it is paid in a pro rata form using the percentages from the Balances sheet. Enter variations of this formula for the other three tranches, making sure to change all references that pertain to a tranche. Also make sure to copy and paste each formula in its correct column over the rows 10 through 509. If you are lost you should definitely follow the example model formulas on the CD-ROM.

37. Once again, the final exception is the A-2F's final sequential payment. The following formula captures the concept and should be entered in cell CS10:

=IF((Balances!AR14-CP10-CQ10)<0.001,MIN('Group 1 - Waterfall'!AR10-
    CE10-CI10-CK10-CM10-CO10-CQ10,Balances!AX14-CD10-CE10-
    CR10),0)

Copy and paste this formula over the range of cells CS10:CS509. We already paid out the pro rata distribution of the Group I funds in column CE, so we should only pay the remaining sequential funds that could be distributed from Group I sources here. Always make sure to cap the payment amount by the balance of the certificate less what has been paid out already.

38. We are almost nearing the end of the Group I and II principal distribution sections, so do not think the waterfall is endless. We have amounts that can be

paid, but we have not actually applied any cash to the certificate balances. Go to the Balances sheet and enter the following formula in cell S15:

='Group 1 - Waterfall'!AP10+'Group 1 - Waterfall'!AQ10

Copy and paste this formula over the range of cells S15:S514. This formula adds up the amounts paid to the A-1 certificate from Group I and Group II sources. This should be repeated for each Group II tranche, paying special attention to the four references for the A-2F certificate (two possible payment sources from Group II funds and two possible payment sources from Group II funds).

39. Finally, we need to determine how much money to pass on to the Mezzanine Certificates, which is the next major stage of the principal distribution section. We will split this out by what remains directly from the Principal Remittance accounts and what remains after each loan group supports the other. Do this by starting on the Group I – Waterfall sheet and entering the following formula in cell AS10:

=AR10-'Group 2 - Waterfall'!CE10-'Group 2 - Waterfall'!CI10-'Group 2 - Waterfall'!CK10-'Group 2 - Waterfall'!CM10-'Group 2 - Waterfall'! CO10-'Group 2 - Waterfall'!CQ10-'Group 2 - Waterfall'!CS10

Copy and paste this formula over the range of cells AS10:AS509. This formula takes the amount that was sent to Group II and returns the remainder of all the uses in the Group II waterfall for each period. Enter the text **Undistributed Unused Sent to Mezz** in cell AS7. Do the same for the Group II certificates by entering the following formula in cell CU10 of the Group II – Waterfall sheet:

=CT10-'Group 1 - Waterfall'!AQ10

Make sure to copy and paste this formula over the range of cells CU10:CU509. Enter the text **Undistributed Unused Sent to Mezz** in cell CU7.

Now enter the following formula in cell CV10 of the Group II – Waterfall worksheet:

=BY10+BZ10-CD10-CH10-CJ10-CL10-CN10-CP10-CR10-CU10

This formula captures the amount left over after paying the Group II liabilities. Copy and paste this formula over the range of cells CV10:CV509. Also, enter the text **Unused Sent to Mezz** in cell CV7.

Go to the Group I – Waterfall worksheet and enter the following formula in cell AT10:

=AK10+AL10-AP10-AS10

	AR	AS	AT
6	*Principal Redistributions*		
7	Undistributed Principal Sent to Group II	Undistributed Unused Sent to Mezz	Unused Sent to Mezz
8	40,803	38,719	51,276,335
9			
10	0	-	-
11	-	-	-
12	0	-	-
13	-	-	-
14	-	-	-
15	-	-	-

FIGURE 5.11   The mezzanine funds come from the end of the senior waterfalls.

Copy and paste this formula over the range of cells AT10:AT509. Label AT7 by entering the text **Unused Sent to Mezz**. This section, where funds are sent to the mezzanine tranches, is shown in Figure 5.11.

MEZZANINE PRINCIPAL RETURNS

We can see from Model Builder 5.1 that the senior principal waterfall is complex and attempts to make the most funds available for the Senior certificates. This protection for the Senior certificates should be understood by mezzanine investors, because the principal that is returned to the Mezzanine Certificates must pass through the Senior certificates' waterfall first.

Mezzanine investors need to be even more careful and understand the other Mezzanine Certificates because as we will see from the prospectus supplement, the Mezzanine Certificates are always paid sequentially. The amounts that are paid each period may also change depending on the deal state, which also complicates the analysis. To really understand this section, we will jump right in with Model Builder 5.2.

MODEL BUILDER 5.2: THE MEZZANINE CERTIFICATES' PRIORITY OF PAYMENTS

1. We will begin with the funds that were left over after paying the Senior certificates. Prior to actually moving that cash over, we should set up a few labels. Go to the Mezzanine – Waterfall sheet and enter the text **Principal** in cell BK6. Also, enter the text **Aggregate Principal Distribution Amount** in cell BK7. Enter the following formula in cell BK10 to capture the cash that was left over from the Senior certificates' waterfall:

   ='Group 1 - Waterfall'!AS10+'Group 1 - Waterfall'!AT10+'Group 2 - Waterfall'!CU10+'Group 2 - Waterfall'!CV10

Copy and paste this formula over the range of cells BK10:BK509.

2. Next we should look back to the prospectus supplement to the Mezzanine certificate principal instructions detailed in Sections III and VI, on pages S-96 and S-97, respectively. To show the two possible payment structures Sections III and VI have been excerpted here:

> *III. On each distribution date (a) prior to the Stepdown Date or (b) on which a Trigger Event is in effect, distributions in respect of principal to the extent of the sum of the Group I Principal Distribution Amount and the Group II Principal Distribution Amount remaining undistributed for such distribution date will be made sequentially to the Class M-1, Class M-2, Class M-3, Class M-4 and Class M-5 Certificates, in that order, in each case, until the Certificate Principal Balance of each such class has been reduced to zero.*

> *VI. On each distribution date (a) on or after the Stepdown Date and (b) on which a Trigger Event is not in effect, distributions in respect of principal to the extent of the sum of the Group I Principal Distribution Amount and the Group II Principal Distribution Amount remaining undistributed for such distribution date will be made in the following amounts and order of priority:*

> *(i) to the holders of the Class M-1 Certificates, the Class M-1 Principal Distribution Amount, until the Certificate Principal Balance thereof has been reduced to zero;*

> *(ii) to the holders of the Class M-2 Certificates, the Class M-2 Principal Distribution Amount, until the Certificate Principal Balance thereof has been reduced to zero;*

> *(iii) to the holders of the Class M-3 Certificates, the Class M-3 Principal Distribution Amount, until the Certificate Principal Balance thereof has been reduced to zero;*

> *(iv) to the holders of the Class M-4 Certificates, the Class M-4 Principal Distribution Amount, until the Certificate Principal Balance thereof has been reduced to zero; and*

> *(v) to the holders of the Class M-5 Certificates, the Class M-5 Principal Distribution Amount, until the Certificate Principal Balance thereof has been reduced to zero.*

Read carefully to see that the mezzanine payment structure changes depending on the deal states. In Section III, when the current period is prior to the Stepdown Date or if there is a Trigger Event active, then *all* the undistributed funds will be used to pay principal to the Mezzanine Certificates in a sequential order. In Section VI, when the current period is on or after the Stepdown Date and when the Trigger is not active, then each Mezzanine Certificate should receive its defined Principal Distribution Amount.

To implement this is simple for Section III as we have already populated the remaining amounts from the Senior certificates. However, for Section VI, we need to understand how each Mezzanine Certificates' Principal Distribution Amount is defined. Take the Class M-1 Principal Distribution Amount for example, its definition from page S-87 is excerpted here:

> *"Class M-1 Principal Distribution Amount": The Class M-1 Principal Distribution Amount is an amount equal to the excess of:*
>
> *– the sum of (i) the aggregate Certificate Principal Balance of the Class A Certificates (after taking into account the distribution of the Senior Principal Distribution Amount on the related distribution date) and (ii) the Certificate Principal Balance of the Class M-1 Certificates immediately prior to the related distribution date over*
> *– the lesser of (A) the product of (i) approximately 89.40% and (ii) the aggregate principal balance of the mortgage loans as of the last day of the related Due Period (after giving effect to scheduled payments of principal due during the related Due Period, to the extent received or advanced, and unscheduled collections of principal received during the related Prepayment Period) and (B) the excess, if any, of the aggregate principal balance of the mortgage loans as of the last day of the related Due Period (after giving effect to scheduled payments of principal due during the related Due Period, to the extent received or advanced, and unscheduled collections of principal received during the related Prepayment Period) over approximately 0.50% of the aggregate principal balance of the Mortgage Loans as of the cut-off date.*

We will discuss the reasoning for the complexity of the entire Principal Distributions section at the end of this chapter. For now we should implement the Class M-1 Principal Distribution Amount by entering the following formula in cell BL10:

```
=MAX(MIN(BK10,(SUM(Balances!P14,Balances!T14,Balances!Z14,
    Balances!AF14,Balances!AL14,Balances!AR14,Balances!AX14)-IF
    (Balances!N15,0,SUM('Group 1 - Waterfall'!AO10,'Group 2 -
    Waterfall'!CC10))+Balances!BE14)-MIN(struc_M1PrinPct*('Group 1 -
    Waterfall'!T10+'Group 2 - Waterfall'!T10),('Group 1 - Waterfall'!T10+
    'Group 2 - Waterfall'!T10)-(struc_SrOrgPrinPct*(grp1_TotalBal+
    grp2_TotalBal)))),0)
```

This formula converts the excerpt defining the Class M-1 Principal Distribution Amount into Excel. It seems like a ridiculous formula, but it is lengthy because it must reference multiple cells on different sheets. A number of items must be

	BK	BL	BM
6	*Principal*		
7	Aggregate Principal Distribution Amount	Class M-1 Principal Distribution Amount	M-1 Distribution Paid
8	109,171,239	54,828,715	49,211,000
9			
10	-	-	-
11	-	-	-
12	(0)	-	(0)
13	-	-	-
14	-	-	-
15	-	-	-

FIGURE 5.12 The beginning of the mezzanine principal distribution section.

referenced in a way that prevents circular references. Copy and paste this formula over the range of cells BL10:BL509. Enter the text **Class M-1 Distribution Amount** in cell BL7.

3. Next, enter the text **M-1 Distribution Paid** in cell BM7. We will now pay cash to the M-1 certificate by entering the following formula in cell BM10:

=IF(Balances!N15,MIN(BK10,Balances!BE14),MIN(BL10,Balances!BE14))

Notice that the formula checks to see which deal state is active from the Balances sheet. If the deal is pre-Stepdown Date or if a Trigger Event is active, then anything that remains from the Senior certificates is applied to the M-1 tranche. If the other deal state is active, then the Class M-1 Principal Distribution Amount is paid. As always this is capped by the balance of the M-1 tranche. Copy and paste this formula over the range of cells BM10:BM509. The mezzanine principal section should begin as seen in Figure 5.12.

4. There will be repetition for the remaining Mezzanine Certificates, but we should go over the M-2 tranche to be clear on how the formulas should vary. Enter the text **Class M-2 Principal Distribution Amount** in cell BC7. Enter the following formula in cell BR10:

=MAX(MIN(BK10-BL10,(SUM(Balances!P14,Balances!T14,Balances! Z14,Balances!AF14,Balances!AL14,Balances!AR14,Balances!AX14)- IF(Balances!N15,0,SUM('Group 1 - Waterfall'!AO10,'Group 2 - Waterfall'! CC10))+Balances!BE14+Balances!BI14)-MIN(struc_M2PrinPct* ('Group 1 - Waterfall'!T10+'Group 2 - Waterfall'!T10),('Group 1 - Waterfall'!T10+'Group 2 - Waterfall'!T10)-(struc_SrOrgPrinPct* (grp1_TotalBal+grp2_TotalBal)))),0)

Copy and paste this formula over the range of cells BR10:BR509. This formula is different from the one in Step 3, not only because it is readjusted for the M-2 tranche, but it also subtracts any payments to the M-1 tranche. Read the Class M-2 Principal Distribution Amount definition on page S-87 for details.

5. Next, enter the text **M-2 Distribution Paid** in cell BS7. Enter the following formula in cell BS10 to see the principal payment variation for the M-2 tranche:

=IF(Balances!N15,MIN(BK10-BM10,Balances!BI14),MIN(BR10,Balances! BI14))

The pattern that emerges is to always deduct out the payments that have already been made to more senior classes of Mezzanine Certificates. Copy and paste this formula over the range of cells BS10:BS509.

6. Repeat Steps 4 and 5 to complete the M-3, M-4, and M-5 tranches, making sure to change cell references accordingly. Be careful to do this in the correct columns, because the skipped columns will be completed in Chapter 6. The correct columns are noted here:

BX: **Class M-3 Principal Distribution Amount**
BY: **M-3 Distribution Paid**
CD: **Class M-4 Principal Distribution Amount**
CE: **M-4 Principal Distribution Paid**
CJ: **Class M-5 Principal Distribution Amount**
CK: **M-5 Distribution Amount**

7. We should summarize how much cash remains after all the Mezzanine Certificate principal distributions are made. Enter the text **Undistributed Mezzanine Principal** in cell CP7 and the following formula in cell CP10:

=BK10-BM10-BS10-BY10-CE10-CK10

Copy and paste this formula over the range of cells CP10:CP509.

8. Finalize the Mezzanine Certificate principal distributions by integrating them with the Balances sheet. To do this, go to the Balances sheet and enter the following formula in cell BH15:

='Mezzanine - Waterfall'!AX10+'Mezzanine - Waterfall'!AY10

Copy and paste this formula over the range of cells BH15:BH514. I know the additional cell reference seems useless at this point, but it will be made relevant in Chapter 6. Repeat this step for each Mezzanine Certificate, making sure to reference the correct principal payment cells.

NUMBER GAMES OR RISK PARSING?

Now that we can see firsthand how complex the principal distribution waterfall can be, we have to ask ourselves, why? The prospectus supplement provides an immediate answer on page S-97, excerpted here:

> *The allocation of distributions in respect of principal to the Class A Certificates on each distribution date (a) prior to the Stepdown Date or (b) on which a Trigger Event is in effect, will have the effect of accelerating the amortization of the Class A Certificates while, in the absence of Realized Losses, increasing the respective percentage interest in the aggregate principal balance of the mortgage loans evidenced by the Subordinate Certificates. Increasing the respective percentage interest in the trust of the Subordinate Certificates relative to that of the Class A Certificates is intended to preserve the availability of the subordination provided by the Subordinate Certificates.*

This statement explains that prior to the Stepdown Date or when a Trigger Event is active the Senior certificates will be accelerated, meaning they will receive more principal proportionally than the Mezzanine Certificates. In most cases the Senior certificates will receive principal, whereas the Mezzanine Certificates will receive nothing. Conceptually, if the Senior certificates are paying down faster than the Mezzanine Certificates, then they are getting priority over the mortgage flows and can be thought of as a safer instrument.

When there is no problem with a Trigger Event and the Senior certificates are being accelerated because the current period is prior to the Stepdown Date, the reasoning for such mechanisms is to prepare for possible deterioration. The Stepdown Date is created to occur when there is a specific level of comfort with the balance between Senior certificate and Mezzanine Certificate balances, the latter often referred to as subordination amounts. If the deal is performing as expected, then the Stepdown Date is achieved and the payment structure allows more cash to flow to the Mezzanine Certificates. However, if there is trouble and the Trigger Event is activated, then the Senior certificates continue to accelerate.

In general, although the Principal Distributions section shows that funds can be released to the Mezzanine Certificates prior to the Stepdown Date, this is unlikely because the Senior certificates will be accelerating and taking most, if not all, the principal. We can see this when the model is complete, but the prospectus supplement discloses this risk to mezzanine investors on page S-19, which is partially excerpted here:

> *Unless the aggregate certificate principal balance of the Class A Certificates has been reduced to zero, the Mezzanine Certificates will not be entitled to any principal distributions until at least June 2009 or a later date as*

described under "Description of the Certificates—Principal Distributions"
in this prospectus supplement or during any period in which delinquencies
or realized losses on the mortgage loans exceed the levels set forth under
"Description of the Certificates—Principal Distributions" in this prospectus
supplement.

The design of such a system limits the risk to the senior investors and provides
the opportunity of return to the mezzanine investors, but any return is predicated on
the performance of the assets. The system is not risk proof and will fail to protect
investors if delinquencies and defaults exceed the expectations of the original design.
The hard-coded numbers seen in the prospectus at this point have been based on
expectations for delinquency and default and if there are significant deviations, then
investors are exposed to loss. Given their subordinated position, the Mezzanine Certificates are particularly sensitive to variations in the underlying asset performance.

The entire system of risk parsing can seem useless when an investor takes a loss.
There are two reasons that this could occur: (1) the assets are performing far worse
than expected or (2) the investor did not understand the structure they invested in
and have taken exposure in a tranche that is susceptible to loss even in expected
stress situations. This second point has been endemic because of an over reliance
on rating agency ratings. Hopefully as the market tries to recover from the massive
mortgage exposure losses of 2007 and 2008, underwriters will not write products
that have the potential for loss beyond historical norms, structurers will be able to
project loss more accurately, and investors will understand payment structures in
more detail.

CHAPTER 6

Credit Enhancement Mechanisms to Mitigate Loss

The changing priority of principal payments given different deal states is one mechanism that is used to mitigate loss and can be thought of as a form of credit enhancement. However, there are other mechanisms built into Wall Street deals that serve to explicitly mitigate loss. The two most important concepts are excess spread and overcollateralization. Both of these concepts play an important role in the example model, which will be evidenced by the results of implementing the Model Builder sections.

In general, excess spread is the basic concept that transactions are set up with assets that generate more yield than fees and liability costs. This means there is an excess amount of cash in a transaction. This is not really a foreign concept considering any bank that keeps a transaction on their balance sheet encounters this phenomenon. No doubt the bank is funding its assets for less than what the assets are yielding. These excess amounts may be used to add to loss reserves, create capital for more products, or be paid out to shareholders. In a structured transaction, the excess spread is used to cover loss, reimburse shortfalls, or is paid out to the deal's equity holders.

There are some important differences between excess spread in a structured transaction and a bank owning assets that generate more return than liabilities. The primary difference is the behavior of a pool of obligors. A bank will have diversified assets that are dynamically exiting and entering the balance sheet. In a nonrevolving, structured transaction, there is a discrete set of borrowers who have specific credit profiles. It is not surprising that higher interest rate obligors will tend to default and prepay more so than lower or more average yielding obligors. Obligors with high rates tend to be of poorer credit quality. As pools age, the obligors with poorer credit tend to be the ones to default. With regard to prepayment, obligors with higher rates are more incentivized to prepay their loan in favorable interest rate environments. Both of these occurrences cause the overall asset yield to decrease over time and the excess spread to decrease. The prospectus supplement warns of this on page S-17, which is excerpted here:

Prepayments and liquidations of mortgage loans with relatively higher mortgage rates will cause excess interest to be reduced to a greater degree than will prepayments and liquidations of mortgage loans with relatively lower mortgage rates.

Overcollateralization is the other major form of credit enhancement and is created when there is more asset value than liabilities. This is not immediately clear from reading the prospectus because the total of the tranches appears to equal the beginning asset principal amount. However, the C/E tranche stands for credit enhancement, and exists in the transaction for the benefit of the other tranches. This C/E tranche is designed to grow and contract as the transaction progresses in time. It's difficult to conceive of, but the C/E tranche is not an actual funded tranche. It is a numerical representation of the difference between the assets and the liabilities. It is useful to implement it as a tranche because it makes calculations and balance tracking easier. The formal definition of overcollateralization in the prospectus supplement starts on page S-8 and is excerpted here:

Overcollateralization: As of the closing date, the aggregate principal balance of the mortgage loans as of the cut-off date will exceed the aggregate certificate principal balance of the Fixed Rate Certificates, the Class P Certificates and the Class X Certificates as of the closing date by approximately $4,525,582, and therefore the overcollateralization target amount will not be met.

Excess interest, if any, generated by the mortgage loans will be initially applied to distribute principal on the Fixed Rate Certificates, subject to the priorities described below and under "Description of the Certificates—Principal Distributions," until the required level of overcollateralization is reached. The required level of overcollateralization will initially be equal to approximately 1.10% of the aggregate principal balance of the mortgage loans as of the cut-off date. We cannot assure you that sufficient interest will be generated by the mortgage loans to create overcollateralization or thereafter to maintain or restore overcollateralization at the required level.

From this definition we see that the C/E tranche amount of $4,525,582 is in fact the overcollateralization. We also see that the overcollateralization can change over time and is dependent on excess interest to assist in funding increases. To work through how excess spread and overcollateralization interact, we will start Model Builder 6.1. The focus of this Model Builder will be excess spread and overcollateralization, but we will also discuss and implement more subtle mechanisms of credit enhancement along the way.

MODEL BUILDER 6.1: EXCESS SPREAD, OVERCOLLATERALIZATION, AND CREDIT ENHANCEMENT

1. Excess spread is first noticeable after we pay all the required fees and liability interest. Therefore, the logical place to begin is at the end of the interest waterfall on the Mezzanine – Waterfall sheet. Go to this sheet and enter the following formula in cell AX10:

=G10-K10-P10-U10-Z10-AE10

Copy and paste this formula over the range of cells AX10:AX509. This formula takes the interest amount at the start of the mezzanine waterfall and subtracts out the current period's mezzanine interest distributions. Enter the text **XS Remaining Pre Sr. Prin Use** in cell AX7.

2. The formula just entered in cell AX10 seems like the excess spread, but for us to keep with the prospectus supplement we should look at how it is defined. On page S-98, we find the following statement that continues the flow of funds:

> *With respect to any Distribution Date, any Net Monthly Excess Cashflow will be paid in the following amounts and order of priority . . .*

The follow up question is, "What is the definition of Net Monthly Excess Cashflow?" Turn to page S-92 and we find the following definition:

> *"Net Monthly Excess Cashflow": The Net Monthly Excess Cashflow for any distribution date will be equal to the sum of (a) any Overcollateralization Reduction Amount and (b) the excess of:*
>
> *– the Available Distribution Amount for such distribution date over*
> *– the sum for such distribution date of the aggregate of (a) the Senior Interest Distribution Amounts distributable to the holders of the Class A Certificates, (b) the Interest Distribution Amounts distributable to the holders of the Mezzanine Certificates and (c) the Principal Remittance Amount.*

This definition should be implemented in the example model. Do this by going to the Balances sheet and entering the following formula in cell CU15:

=('Group 1 - Waterfall'!L10+'Group 1 - Waterfall'!M10+'Group 1 - Waterfall'!N10+'Group 1 - Waterfall'!O10+'Group 1 - Waterfall'!P10+'Group 1 - Waterfall'!R10)+('Group 2 - Waterfall'!L10+'Group 2 - Waterfall'!M10+'Group 2 - Waterfall'!N10+'Group 2 - Waterfall'!O10+'Group 2 - Waterfall'!P10+'Group 2 - Waterfall'!R10)-('Group 1 - Waterfall'!V10+'Group 2 - Waterfall'!V10)-('Group 1 -

Waterfall'!AB10+'Group 1 - Waterfall'!AD10+'Group 1 -
Waterfall'!AL10)-('Group 2 - Waterfall'!AB10+'Group 2 -
Waterfall'!AD10+'Group 2 - Waterfall'!AJ10+'Group 2 -
Waterfall'!AL10+'Group 2 - Waterfall'!AR10+'Group 2 -
Waterfall'!AT10+'Group 2 - Waterfall'!AZ10+'Group 2 -
Waterfall'!BB10+'Group 2 - Waterfall'!BH10+'Group 2 -
Waterfall'!BJ10+'Group 2 - Waterfall'!BP10+'Group 2 -
Waterfall'!BR10+'Group 2 - Waterfall'!BZ10)-('Mezzanine -
Waterfall'!K10+'Mezzanine - Waterfall'!S10+'Mezzanine -
Waterfall'!AA10+'Mezzanine - Waterfall'!AI10+'Mezzanine -
Waterfall'!AQ10)

Do not be discouraged by the size of this formula; it's simple repetitive arithmetic. The reason it is created this way is to avoid circular references. The formula replicates the Net Monthly Excess Cash Flow. Copy and paste this formula over the range of cells CU15:CU514. Also, enter the text, **Net Monthly Excess Cash Flow** in cell CU12.

Very careful readers will question why the values in the column on the Mezzanine – Worksheet, labeled "XS Remaining Pre Sr Prin Use" are the same as the Net Monthly Excess Cash Flow. Specifically, the excess spread does not seem to remove principal as suggested by the prospectus supplement. This is because the principal component of the Available Distribution Amount is equal to the Principal Remittance Amount, so the two cancel each other out. All that is left are additional funds from interest. We created the formula to be very literal in our translation of the prospectus definition and to check our calculations. We will soon see how this amount is converted to principal.

3. We can now move forward with the Net Monthly Excess Cash Flow instructions from page S-98, which continue with the following excerpt:

> *(i) to the holders of the class or classes of Fixed Rate Certificates then entitled to receive distributions in respect of principal, in an amount equal to the Overcollateralization increase Amount, distributable as part of the Group I Principal Distribution Amount and Group II Principal Distribution Amount . . .*

Remember that we left unfinished formulas on the Fixed Rate Certificates sheets. The Principal Distribution Amounts were the sections that we left unfinished. This first subsection requires the Net Monthly Excess Cash Flow to be directed to the Fixed Rate Certificates up to the Overcollateralization Increase Amount. We will soon define the Overcollateralization Increase Amount, but earlier we discussed the concept. The reasoning behind this mechanic is to first direct excess spread to the Senior certificates so their balance is reduced vis-à-vis the Mezzanine Certificates.

Jump to page S-93 to understand the definition of the Overcollateralization Increase Amount, which is excerpted here:

> *"Overcollateralization Increase Amount": The Overcollateralization Increase Amount with respect to any distribution date will equal the lesser of (a) the Net Monthly Excess Cashflow for such distribution date and (b) the amount, if any, by which the Overcollateralization Target Amount exceeds the Overcollateralized Amount on such distribution date (calculated for this purpose only after assuming that 100% of the Principal Remittance Amount on such distribution date has been distributed).*

The concept that this definition tries to address is that if the current overcollateralization is less than the target overcollateralization, then the periodic excess spread should be used to increase the overcollateralization to the target level. Reading through this definition now brings up a whole host of new definitions that we will have to systematically deconstruct. Right now we should understand that there is a minimum amount of overcollateralization that needs to be achieved and if it is not met, then funds need to be directed in such a way that the overcollateralization is increased. We will implement this formula as soon as we define and understand the terms Overcollateralization Target Amount and Overcollateralized Amount used in the previous excerpt.

The Overcollateralization Target is defined on the same page (S-93) and excerpted here:

> *"Overcollateralization Target Amount": The Overcollateralization Target Amount with respect to any distribution date, (i) prior to the Stepdown Date, an amount equal to 1.10% of the aggregate principal balance of the Mortgage Loans as of the cut-off date, (ii) on or after the Stepdown Date, provided a Trigger Event is not in effect, the greater of (x) 2.20% of the then current aggregate outstanding principal balance of the Mortgage Loans as of the last day of the related Due Period (after giving effect to scheduled payments of principal due during the related Due Period, to the extent received or advanced, and unscheduled collections of principal received during the related Prepayment Period) and (y) 0.50% of the aggregate principal balance of the mortgage loans as of the cut-off date or (iii) on or after the Stepdown Date and if a Trigger Event is in effect, the Overcollateralization Target Amount for the immediately preceding distribution date. On and after any Distribution Date following the reduction of the aggregate Certificate Principal Balance of the Fixed Rate Certificates to zero, the Overcollateralization Target Amount shall be zero. Notwithstanding the foregoing, the percentages set forth above are subject to a variance of plus or minus 5%.*

OC Target Pct	1.10%
OC Target Pct Stepdown	2.20%

FIGURE 6.1 The overcollateralization amounts follow a strict set of rules based on assumptions entered on the Inputs sheet.

This definition sets the minimum amount for overcollateralization and is a good place to start implementing formulas because it does not rely on other overcollateralization definitions. To implement this formula, there are a couple of inputs we need to set up. Go to the Inputs sheet and enter the following text and values in the corresponding cell references:

D21: **OC Target Pct**
D22: **OC Target Pct Stepdown**
E21: **1.10%**
E22: **2.20%**

Name cell E21 **struc_OCTargPct** and **E22 struc_OCTargPctStp**. This section of the Inputs sheet should look like Figure 6.1.

4. With the necessary inputs complete, go to the Balances sheet and enter the following text in the corresponding cell references to label the upcoming overcollateralization section:

CO11: **Overcollateralization Amounts**
CO12: **OC Target Amount**
CP12: **OC Amount**
CQ12: **OC Amount (for Inc/Red Calc)**
CR12: **OC Increase Amount**
CS12: **OC Reduction Amount**

5. Still on the Balances sheet, we begin with the OC Target Amount, which was defined in Step 3. Enter the following formula in cell CO15:

=IF(SUM(P14,T14,Z14,AF14,AL14,AR14,AX14)<=0.001,0,IF
(K15,MAX(struc_OCTargPctStp*D15,$D$14*struc_SrOrgPrinPct),
$D$14*struc_OCTargPct))

The beginning of this formula checks to see if the senior tranches are paid off. If they are, then overcollateralization is not necessary. After the initial IF statement the formula then checks to see if the Stepdown state is active. Reading the Overcollateralization Target Amount definition, you see that the Stepdown state check is necessary because there are two different targeted overcollateralization amounts depending on whether the Stepdown Date has been achieved. If the Stepdown Date has been achieved, then the overcollateralization amount is the maximum of the overcollateralization target percentage for Stepdown (2.20%) multiplied by the aggregate mortgage balance at the end of the period and the aggregate mortgage balance at the beginning of the period multiplied by the senior original principal distribution percentage. If the Stepdown Date has not been achieved, then it is the aggregate mortgage balance multiplied by the standard overcollateralization target percentage. Copy and paste this formula over the range of cells CO15:CO514.

6. Once we know how much overcollateralization the transaction is targeting, the next logical step is how much overcollateralization the transaction currently has. Although we were provided an indication of the overcollateralization definition from page S-8 of the prospectus supplement, the formal definition is located on page S-93:

> *"Overcollateralized Amount": The Overcollateralized Amount with respect to any distribution date will equal the excess, if any, of (a) the aggregate principal balance of the mortgage loans as of the last day of the related Due Period (after giving effect to scheduled payments of principal due during the related Due Period, to the extent received or advanced, and unscheduled collections of principal received during the related Prepayment Period) over (b) the aggregate Certificate Principal Balance of the Fixed Rate Certificates, the Class P Certificates and the Class X Certificates (after taking into account the distributions of the Principal Remittance Amount on the related distribution date).*

The Overcollateralized Amount definition uses the familiar word *excess* to imply that the Overcollateralized Amount is the difference between the end of period mortgage collateral balance and the sum of the end of period liability balances. This is translated into the following formula in cell CP14:

=MAX(D14-SUM(P14,T14,Z14,AF14,AL14,AR14,AX14,BE14,BI14,BM14, BQ14,BU14),0)

Copy and paste this formula over the range of cells CP14:CP514. A basic internal validation for the model is the result of this formula in the closing period (cell CP14). It should return the value 4,525,782. This is equivalent to the CE certificate starting balance as defined on page S-8.

7. We next need to create a similar formula, but for calculation purposes only. It is important to complete this calculation because of the nuanced definition of the Overcollaterized Amount and the overcollateralization total that is used for the Overcollateralization Increase and Reduction Amounts. In Step 6, we used a formula that returns the Overcollateralized Amount after giving effect to all reductions. Given that we structured the formula slightly different from the actual definition (by using the end of period balances), this amount would include any adjustments from the Overcollateralization Increase or Reduction Amounts.

Because of this, for calculation purposes, we should enter the following formula in cell CQ15:

=MAX(D15-SUM(P14,T14,Z14,AF14,AL14,AR14,AX14,BE14,BI14,BM14, BQ14,BU14,-('Group 1 - Waterfall'!N10+'Group 1 - Waterfall'!R10+'Group 2 - Waterfall'!N10+'Group 2 - Waterfall'!R10)),0)

Copy and paste this formula over the range of cells CQ15:CQ514. The question arises, "Why even have the original calculations for the Overcollateralized Amount?" It was implemented because it is a good check to see that the amount in column CQ is the overcollateralization pre-increase or reduction. Therefore, when we implement the increase or reduction, we should be able to reconcile differences.

8. By knowing the target amounts and the actual amounts of overcollateralization, we are now ready to calculate the increase and reduction. Beginning with the increase, which was defined in Step 3, enter the following formula in cell CR15:

=MAX(MIN(CS15+((G15+H15)-SUM(R15,X15,AD15,AJ15,AP15,AV15, BC15,BG15,BK15,BO15,BS15,BW15,'Group 1 - Waterfall'!N10,'Group 1 - Waterfall'!O10,'Group 1 - Waterfall'!P10,'Group 1 - Waterfall'!R10,'Group 1 - Waterfall'!V10,'Group 2 - Waterfall'!N10,'Group 2 - Waterfall'!O10,'Group 2 - Waterfall'!P10,'Group 2 - Waterfall'!R10,'Group 2 - Waterfall'!V10)),CO15-CQ15),0)

Copy and paste this formula over the range of cells CR15:CR514. Notice that to avoid circular references we must reference collateral cash flows and fees directly from the Waterfall sheets.

9. The Overcollateralization Reduction Amount is defined on page S-93 and excerpted here:

> *"Overcollateralization Reduction Amount": The Overcollateralization Reduction Amount with respect to any distribution date will equal the lesser of (a) the Principal Remittance Amount on such distribution date and (b) the excess, if any, of (i) the Overcollateralized Amount for such distribution date (calculated for this purpose only after assuming that 100% of the Principal Remittance Amount on such distribution date has been distributed) over (ii) the Overcollateralization Target Amount for such distribution date.*

It is much easier to translate this definition into a formula than it is the Overcollateralization Increase Amount. Enter the following formula in cell CS15:

=MAX(MIN(('Group 1 - Waterfall'!AL10+'Group 2 - Waterfall'!BZ10),CQ15-CO15),0)

CI	CO	CP	CQ	CR	CS
11	*Overcollateralization Amounts*				
12	OC Target Amount	OC Amount	OC Amount (for Inc/Red Calc)	OC Increase Amount	OC Reduction Amount
13				7,918,372	12,405,436
14		4,525,782			
15	12,444,155	5,128,371	4,525,782	602,589	-
16	12,444,155	5,726,747	5,128,371	598,376	-
17	12,444,155	6,319,456	5,726,747	592,709	-
18	12,444,155	6,905,056	6,319,456	585,600	-
19	12,444,155	7,482,124	6,905,056	577,068	-
20	12,444,155	8,049,269	7,482,124	567,145	-
21	12,444,155	8,605,141	8,049,269	555,873	-

FIGURE 6.2 The overcollateralization amounts are tracked on the Balances sheet to make sure risk is properly being mitigated.

Copy and paste this formula over the range of cells CS15:CS514. At this point the overcollateralization section should look like Figure 6.2.

10. The entire purpose of the overcollateralization calculations is to be able to calculate how much needs to be taken out of monthly excess spread and directed to principal pay-down. In the previous chapter, we left a few of the senior principal distribution formulas unfinished. Go back to the Group 1 – Waterfall sheet and delete the current formula in cell AN10. Enter the following formula in cell AN10 instead:

=MAX(N10+O10+P10+R10+((AM10*Balances!CR15)-
    (AM10*Balances!CS15)),0)

Copy and paste this formula over the range of cells AN10:AN509. Notice that this formula adds amounts to the principal distribution if there is an Overcollateralization Increase Amount (based on the pro rata share mechanism) and subtracts amounts if there is an Overcollateralization Reduction Amount.

The same should be done on the Group 2 – Waterfall sheet. Delete the current formula in cell CB10 and replace it with the following formula:

=MAX(N10+O10+P10+R10+((CA10*Balances!CR15)-
    (Balances!CS15*'Group 2 - Waterfall'!CA10)),0)

Copy and paste this formula over the range of cells CB10:CB509.

11. Another area that was left blank was a calculation involving the excess for each loan group. On the Group I – Waterfall sheet, in cell AK7, enter the text **Group I Excess**. Enter the following formula in cell AK10:

=MIN('Mezzanine - Waterfall'!AX10*AM10,AM10*Balances!CR15)

Copy and paste this formula over the range of cells AK10:AK509.

This process should also be completed for the Group 2 – Waterfall sheet. Enter the text **Group II Excess** in cell BY7 and then enter the following formula in cell BY10:

=MIN('Mezzanine - Waterfall'!AX10*CA10,CA10*Balances!CR15)

Copy and paste this formula over the range of cells BY10:BY509.

12. We need to make sure we are tracking the use of the Monthly Excess Spread. Go back to the Mezzanine – Waterfall sheet and enter the following labels in the corresponding cells:

AY7: **(i) OC Increase Due**
AZ7: **(i) OC Increase Paid**

Enter the following formula in cell AY10:

=Balances!CR15

Copy and paste this formula over the range of cells AY10:AY509. Also enter the following formula in cell AZ10:

=MIN(AI10,AJ10)

Copy and paste this formula over the range of cells AZ10:AZ509. The combination of these steps pays the Overcollateralization Amount so that it is no longer counted for further uses of the Monthly Excess Spread.

13. As we get closer to the end of the waterfall, we should continue to implement internal validations. Enter the following labels in the corresponding cells:

BA7: **XS Remaining Post Sr Prin Use**
BB7: **Concurrent Check**

The first part of this section serves to move the excess spread through the waterfall after applying it to the senior principal. Do this by entering the following formula in cell BA10:

=AI10-('Group 1 - Waterfall'!AK10+'Group 2 - Waterfall'!BY10)

Copy and paste this formula over the range of cells BA10:BA509. This formula takes the excess spread and subtracts out each loan groups' excess spread allocation for senior principal. The formula is done this way so that another check can be implemented to make sure the right amount of cash is being passed through. Enter the following formula in cell BB10 as an internal validation to the previous formula:

=AI10-AK10

	AX	AY	AZ	BA	BB
5					
6	**Monthly Excess Spread Distributions**				
7	XS Remaining Pre Sr. Prin Use	(i) OC Increase Due	(i) OC Increase Paid	XS Remaining Post Sr. Prin Use	Concurrent Check
8	22,395,865	7,918,372	7,918,372	14,477,493	14,477,493
9					
10	602,589	602,589	602,589	-	-
11	598,376	598,376	598,376	0	0
12	592,709	592,709	592,709	-	-
13	585,600	585,600	585,600	-	-
14	577,068	577,068	577,068	-	-
15	567,145	567,145	567,145	0	0

FIGURE 6.3 Because excess spread is first visible after paying mezzanine interest, the Mezzanine-Waterfall sheet tracks allocations of the excess.

Copy and paste this formula over the range of cells BB10:BB509. The Mezzanine – Waterfall sheet should start to develop as seen in Figure 6.3.

14. The next step is to continue with the flow of funds for the excess spread. Step (ii) on Page S-99 directs this cash to pay the interest carry forward amounts for the Mezzanine Certificates, as excerpted here:

> *(ii) sequentially, to the holders of the Class M-1 Certificates, the Class M-2 Certificates, the Class M-3 Certificates, the Class M-4 Certificates and the Class M-5 Certificates, in that order, in each case up to the related Interest Carry Forward Amount related to such certificates for such distribution date . . .*

We implemented the formulas to calculate the interest carry forward amounts earlier, so all that we have to do is pay the amounts out of the excess spread. Earlier we also capped the interest carry forward amounts to column AL, which is the balance of excess spread funds after increasing the overcollateralization amount. All we need to do now is calculate how much was used and deduct that amount from the remaining excess spread. Do this by entering the following formula in cell BC10:

=SUM(M10,R10,W10,AB10,AG10)

Copy and paste this formula over the range of cells BC10:BC509. Also, enter the text **(ii) Interest Carry Forward Paid** in cell BC7 as a label.

15. After calculating the Interest Carry Forward Paid, we should move the cash along the excess spread allocations by determining how much is remaining. This

	BC	BD
5		
6		
7	**(ii) Interest Carry Forward Paid**	XS Remaining Post Interest Carry Forward
8	-	14,477,493
9		
10	-	-
11	-	0
12	-	-
13	-	-
14	-	-
15	-	0

FIGURE 6.4 The second allocation of excess spread is toward mezzanine interest carry forward amounts.

is easy because we have the money prior to the Interest Carry Forward Paid. All we need to do is subtract what was paid from what was remaining in cell BD10 by entering the following formula:

=AL10-AN10

Copy and paste this formula over the range of cells BD10:BD509. Label cell BD7 by entering the text **XS Remaining Post Interest Carry Forward**. The second allocation of excess spread should develop the Mezzanine – Waterfall sheet as seen in Figure 6.4.

16. Moving on to the third allotment of excess spread, we read the following instructions on page S-99:

> *(iii) sequentially, to the holders of the Class M-1 Certificates, the Class M-2 Certificates, the Class M-3 Certificates, the Class M-4 Certificates and the Class M-5 Certificates, in that order, in each case up to the related Allocated Realized Loss Amount for such class of certificates for such distribution date . . .*

Section (iii) is one of the more interesting uses of excess spread, particularly for Mezzanine investors. According to this language the Mezzanine Certificate holders are allowed to receive funds from excess spread to reimburse themselves for principal write-downs caused by loss earlier. If for some reason a deal takes loss to the Mezzanine Certificates and then later the deal performs better, the excess spread that flows through the structure can be used to "write up" or reimburse the Mezzanine Certificates for any losses that they have been allocated thus far.

From a modeling perspective, this will occur when a forward-loaded loss timing assumption is assumed that decreases rapidly over time. Losses and write-down will occur quickly and then funds will be available for reimbursement later.

What's particularly interesting about this phenomenon is that it is poorly understood by users of some third-party modeling software. Most third-party modeling software does not go into the detail of displaying all allocations of excess spread. Rather this particular phenomenon would show up as a negative loss in those systems, often confusing users.

To model out section (iii), we need to implement the Mezzanine Certificate loss allocation by turning to the definition of the Allocated Realized Loss Amount, which is on page S-86, but thoroughly described on page S-100 as excerpted here:

Allocation of Losses

Any Realized Losses on the mortgage loans will be allocated on any distribution date first, to Net Monthly Excess Cashflow, second, to the Class CE Certificates, until the Certificate Principal Balance of the Class CE Certificates has been reduced to zero and third, to each class of Mezzanine Certificates in reverse numerical order until the certificate principal balance of each such class has been reduced to zero. The pooling and servicing agreement will not permit the allocation of Realized Losses to the Class A Certificates, the Class P Certificates or the Class X Certificates. Investors in the Class A Certificates should note, however, that although Realized Losses cannot be allocated to these certificates, under certain loss scenarios there may not be enough interest and principal received or advanced on the mortgage loans to distribute to the Class A Certificates all interest and principal amounts to which they are then entitled.

Once Realized Losses have been allocated to the Mezzanine Certificates, such amounts with respect to such certificates will no longer accrue interest and such amounts will not be reinstated thereafter (except in the case of Subsequent Recoveries). However, Allocated Realized Loss Amounts may be distributed to the holders of the Mezzanine Certificates from Net Monthly Excess Cashflow, according to the priorities set forth under "—Overcollateralization Provisions" above.

Any allocation of a Realized Loss to a certificate will be made by reducing the Certificate Principal Balance of that certificate by the amount so allocated as of the distribution date in the month following the calendar month in which the Realized Loss was incurred.

The Allocation of Losses is an extremely important part of the transaction that we should look at in detail. First, we read that the Net Monthly Excess Cash

Flow is meant to absorb the losses, which we see by the increase of overcollateralization in case deterioration occurs. If the excess spread cannot maintain the overcollateralization, then it is effectively reduced by the losses until no credit enhancement exists. With both of those gone, losses are allocated to the Mezzanine tranches by reducing their balance. Notice that it states in reverse numerical order, meaning that the principal of the M-5 tranche would be reduced by loss to zero first, then the M-4 tranche, and so on. Mezzanine investors must realize that the loss allocation is a real principal reduction, as explained in the third paragraph and reinforced by the second paragraph, where it is made clear that a reduced certificate will no longer accrue interest on the reduced amount.

To start this process, we must first track the realized losses. Go to the Balances sheet and enter the following formula in cell CV15:

=‘Group 1 - Waterfall’!K10+‘Group 2 - Waterfall’!K10

Copy and paste this formula over the range of cells CV15:CV514. This formula takes the loss amounts from each loan group and adds them up. Enter the text **Realized Losses** in cell CV12.

Still on the Balances sheet, there is one more item we should add. Enter the text **Losses Not Covered By Excess Cash Flow** in cell CW12. This column will calculate the losses that cannot be covered by excess spread. Do it by entering the following formula in cell CW15:

=MAX(0,CV15-CU15)

Copy and paste this formula over the range of cells CW15:CW514. The end of the Balances sheet should look like Figure 6.5.

C1	CU	CV	CW
10			
11	*Excess Spread & Loss*		
12	Net Monthly Excess Cash Flow	Realized Losses	Losses Not Covered by Excess Cash Flow
13	22,395,865	-	-
14			
15	602,589	-	-
16	598,376	-	-
17	592,709	-	-
18	585,600	-	-
19	577,068	-	-

FIGURE 6.5   The last part of the Balances sheet tracks loss and loss not covered by excess spread.

17. According to the loss allocation terminology from the prospectus supplement, the next allocation of losses is to the CE tranche. Recall that we left off with undistributed Mezzanine principal at the end of the Mezzanine – Waterfall sheet (column CP). We need to do two steps to calculate the loss allocation to the C/E tranche. The first is to calculate how much a C/E certificate holder would get paid from the remaining cash. Go to the Mezzanine – Waterfall sheet and enter the following formula in cell CQ10:

=MIN(CP10,Balances!BY14)

Copy and paste this formula over the range of cells CQ10:CQ509. Enter the text **C/E Principal Distribution Paid** in cell CQ7. This pays residual cash up to the C/E starting amount.

We then need to cover losses from the C/E amount. This is done by entering the following formula in cell CR10:

=MIN(Balances!BY14-CQ10,Balances!CW15)

Copy and paste this formula over the range of cells CR10:CR509. Also, enter the text **C/E Realized Loss Write Down** in cell CR7.

18. The next loss allocation is to the Mezzanine tranches. Stay on the Mezzanine – Waterfall sheet and enter the following text in the corresponding cells:

CL7: **M-5 Realized Loss Write-Down**
CM7: **M-5 Cumulative Write-Down (pre-XS Rec.)**
CN7: **M-5 Write-Off Recovery From Excess**
CO7: **M-5 Write-Off Recovery Balance**

The first calculation we will start on is the realized loss write-down. In cell CL10 enter the following formula:

=MIN(Balances!BU14-CK10,Balances!CW15-'Mezzanine - Waterfall'!CR10)

Copy and paste this formula over the range of cells CL10:CL509. This formula assigns loss to the M-5 tranche, after assigning loss to the C/E tranche, but like the previous C/E write-down formula it also caps the loss at the tranche's balance, less current principal distribution. Note that if there is a loss filtering through the waterfall to the Mezzanine Certificates, there most likely will not be a principal distribution, but we should build in the capability for all possibilities.

We should also track the cumulative write-down. Enter the following formula in cell CM10:

=CL10+CM9

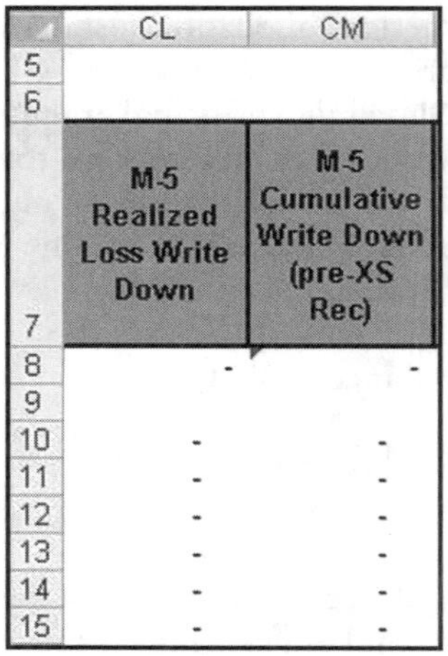

FIGURE 6.6 The write-down portion of the M-5 tranche resulting from loss.

This formula should be copied and pasted over the range of cells CM10:CM509. This section of the M-5 tranche should look like Figure 6.6.

19. Step 18 will have to be repeated for each Mezzanine tranche. There are some alterations in the two formulas that we have to implement for each tranche, so we will work through the M-4 tranche as an example. First enter the necessary text in the corresponding cells to create labels:

CF7: **M-4 Realized Loss Write-Down**
CG7: **M-4 Cumulative Write-Down (pre-XS Rec.)**
CH7: **M-4 Write-Off Recovery From Excess**
CI7: **M-4 Write-Off Recovery Balance**

In cell CF10 enter the following formula:

=MIN(Balances!BQ14-CE10,Balances!CW15-CR10-CL10)

The pattern that emerges is twofold: first, a tranche can never be written down by more than the tranche balance for the period and second, the loss amount that is assigned to a tranche is in reverse. For the cell CF10 formula, copy and paste it over the range of cells CF10:CF509.

Remember to complete the cumulative write down by entering the following formula in cell CG10:

=CF10+CG9

Copy and paste this formula over the range of cells CG10:CG509. Now repeat these steps for the M-3, M-2, and M-1 tranches. Also recall from Chapter 5 that the principal payment on the Balances sheet for the Mezzanine Certificates included the realized loss write-down columns. This is the direct link to loss reducing the Mezzanine Certificate balances.

20. Once we know the write-down of the Mezzanine tranches we are ready to track the *write-up* or recovery from excess spread. As section (iii) states, the loss recovery is applied in sequential order, but starting from the M-1 tranche down. This is different than the reverse order we just implemented for the assignment of loss. The logic makes sense though—it is more in line with seniority to have loss assigned first to the most junior tranches and recoveries first to the more senior tranches.

To implement this concept, enter the following formula on the Mezzanine – Waterfall sheet in cell BP10:

=MIN(BD10,BO10-SUM($BP$9:BP9))

This formula looks to the amount of excess spread available up to section (iii) and pays up to the total amount written down. Notice though that the total amount written down is reduced by amounts previously recovered. We never want to recover more than what was originally lost. Copy and paste this formula over the range of cells BP10:BP509.

We should also track the cumulative write-downs after taking into effect recoveries. This is done in cell BQ10 with the following formula:

=BO10-SUM($BP$10:BP10)

Copy and paste this formula over the range of cells BQ10:BQ509. The write-up from recovered funds is shown in Figure 6.7.

21. The recovered amounts should then be summarized back on the Mezzanine – Waterfall sheet, where we have been tracking the uses of excess spread. Enter the following formula in cell BE10 to complete this functionality:

=SUM(BP10,BV10,CB10,CH10,CN10)

Copy and paste this formula over the range of cells BE10:BE509. Also, label cell BE7 by entering the text **(iii) XS Allocated to Loss Recovery**.

We should also carry over the cash and sum up what cash remains and is available for section (iv). Enter the following formula in cell BF10:

=BD10-BE10

Copy and paste this formula over the range of cells BF10:BF509. Label cell BF10 **XS Remaining Post Allocated Loss Recovery**. Look at Figure 6.8 for details on how this section should look.

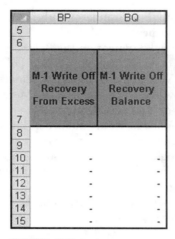

	BP	BQ
5		
6		
7	M-1 Write Off Recovery From Excess	M-1 Write Off Recovery Balance
8	-	
9		
10	-	-
11	-	-
12	-	-
13	-	-
14	-	-
15	-	-

FIGURE 6.7 The opposite flow of funds can occur when money is available to reimburse Mezzanine Certificates for written-down principal.

	BE	BF
5		
6		
7	(iii) XS Allocated to Loss Recovery	XS Remaining Post Allocated Loss Recovery
8	-	14,477,493
9		
10	-	-
11	-	0
12	-	-
13	-	-
14	-	-
15	-	0

FIGURE 6.8 Excess spread can be used to reimburse Mezzanine Certificates.

22. The next section we will implement is section (iv) of the excess spread distributions. Label the appropriate areas by entering the following text in the corresponding cells:

BG7: **(iv) Net WAC Carryover**
BH7: **XS Remaining Post Net WAC Carryover**

Prior to implementing any calculation we should recall from Chapter 4 that we would come back to Net WAC Carryover and explain the concept in this chapter. First let's review the section (iv) excess spread distribution from page S-99:

> *(iv) to the Net WAC Rate Carryover Reserve Account, the aggregate of any Net WAC Rate Carryover Amounts for the Fixed Rate Certificates ...*

From this statement it becomes clear that we must understand the definition of both the Net WAC Rate Carryover Reserve Account and the Net WAC Rate Carryover Amounts. Both definitions are found on page S-93. The Net WAC Rate Carryover Reserve Account is defined here:

> *"Net WAC Rate Carryover Reserve Account": The reserve account established by the trust administrator from which payments in respect of Net WAC Rate Carryover Amounts on the Fixed Rate Certificates will be made.*

This does not need to be directly modeled, because section (iv) directs cash to this account. Essentially the column that sums up the excess spread available up to section (iv) is this amount. The important definition is what constitutes a Net WAC Rate Carryover Amount, which is excerpted here:

> *"Net WAC Rate Carryover Amount": For any class of Fixed Rate Certificates and any distribution date, an amount equal to the sum of (i) the excess, if any, of (x) the amount of interest such class of certificates would have accrued for such distribution date had the related pass-through rate been the related Formula Rate, over (y) the amount of interest such class of certificates accrued for such distribution date at the related Net WAC Pass-Through Rate and (ii) the unpaid portion of any Net WAC Rate Carryover Amount for such class from the prior distribution date together with interest accrued on such unpaid portion for the most recently ended Interest Accrual Period at the related Formula Rate applicable for such class for such Interest Accrual Period.*

To implement this concept we must calculate the Net WAC Rate Carryover Amount for each of the fixed rate certificates. We will first do this on the Group

1 – Waterfall sheet for the A-1 tranche. On the Group 1 – Waterfall sheet in cell AE10 enter the following formula:

=MAX(IF(Balances!$F14,liab1_FxdRateClnUp,liab1_FxdRate)-
   X10,0)*OFFSET($B10,0,MATCH(liab1_DayCtSys,grp1_DayCountSys,0))
   *Balances!P14

This formula first checks to see if the clean-up call is activated. The Net WAC pass-through rate is subtracted from the appropriate fixed rate depending on the clean-up call state. A MAX function is used because most of the time the difference should be negative. However, when it is positive, the rate is multiplied by the day-count factor and by the beginning of period balance. Copy and paste this formula over the range of cells AE10:AE509. Also, enter the text **A-1 Current Net WAC Carryover Amount (Required)** in cell AE7.

23. We still have more work to do to finish off the Net WAC Rate Carryover Amount. We have calculated the periodic carryover amount, but need to track the Net WAC Rate Carryover Amount on a cumulative basis and charge interest on those amounts. This is done for the A-1 tranche in column AF. In cell AF10 enter the following formula:

=AE10+(AF9+IF(Balances!$F14,liab1_FxdRateClnUp,liab1_FxdRate)*
   (OFFSET($B10,0,MATCH(liab1_DayCtSys,grp1_DayCountSys,0))*
   (AF9-AG9)))-AG9

Copy and paste this formula over the range of cells AF10:AF509. This formula adds the current Net WAC Rate Carryover Amount to the cumulative running balance. Notice that capitalized interest is only charged on the cumulative amount, based on the current Formula Rate. Any of the Net WAC Rate Carryover Amount that can be covered by excess spread is subtracted from the cumulative amount. Label this column by entering **A-1 Cumulative Net WAC Carryover Amount (pre-XS Rec)** in cell AF7.

24. The previous two columns are akin to calculating what is due and the running balance of what is owed. The final step to implementing the Net WAC Carryover Amount is calculating amounts to be reimbursed from excess spread. Complete this for the A-1 tranche by entering the following formula in cell AG10:

=IF(SUM(Balances!$P14,Balances!$T14,Balances!$Z14,Balances!$AF14,
   Balances!$AL14,Balances!$AR14,Balances!$AX14)<0.0001,0,MIN
   (AF10,'Mezzanine - Waterfall'!$BF10*(Balances!$P14/SUM
   (Balances!$P14,Balances!$T14,Balances!$Z14,Balances!$
   AF14,Balances!$AL14,Balances!$AR14,Balances!$AX14))))

This formula takes the lesser of what is needed, the cumulative shortfall plus accrued interest, and what is available, the A-1 tranche's pro-rata share of the

	AE	AF	AG
5			
6	*Dark Blue Indicates Post Principal Events*		
7	**A-1 Current Net WAC Carryover Amount (Required)**	**A-1 Cumulative Net WAC Carryover Amount (pre-XS Rec)**	**A-1 Net WAC Carryover Covered By XS**
8	289,527		289,527
9			
10	-	-	-
11	-	-	-
12	-	-	-
13	-	-	-
14	-	-	-
15	-	-	-

FIGURE 6.9 The Net WAC Carryover Amount is incorporated into the A-1 tranche calculations.

excess spread remaining through section (iii) of the excess spread distributions. Copy and paste this formula over the range of cells AG10:AG509. Also, enter the text **A-1 Net WAC Carryover Covered By XS** in cell AG7. Figure 6.9 shows the extra fields necessary for the A-1 tranche.

25. Careful prospectus supplement readers will question how it is known that the Net WAC Rate Carryover Amount should be distributed on a pro rata basis for the Class A certificates. For this we have to turn to page S-99 of the prospectus supplement, past the excess spread distribution section. There we find the following excerpt:

> ...*the trust administrator will withdraw from the Net WAC Rate Carryover Reserve Account, to the extent of the amount then on deposit therein, the aggregate of any Net WAC Rate Carryover Amounts for the Fixed Rate Certificates for such distribution date and will distribute such amounts to the holders of such classes of certificates in the following amounts and order of priority:*
>
> *(i) concurrently, to the Class A Certificates, on a pro rata basis based on the Certificate Principal Balance for each such class prior to any distributions of principal on such distribution date and then on a pro rata basis based on any remaining Net WAC Rate Carryover Amount for each such class; and (ii) sequentially, to the Class M-1, Class M-2, Class M-3, Class M-4 and Class M-5 Certificates.*

Because we know that each Class A certificate should be allocated its Net WAC Rate Carryover Amount on a pro rata basis, we should replicate Steps 22 to 24 for each Class A certificate. Remember to make the appropriate changes to cell references during the replication.

26. For the Mezzanine Certificates, we can go ahead and repeat Steps 22 and 23, but not Step 24. This is very important as the Mezzanine Certificates pay their Net WAC Carryover Amount sequentially. As an example of the proper formula, on the Mezzanine – Waterfall sheet enter the following formula in cell P10:

=MIN(O10,BF10-'Group 1 - Waterfall'!AG10-'Group 2 -
    Waterfall'!AG10-'Group 2 - Waterfall'!AO10-'Group 2 -
    Waterfall'!AW10-'Group 2 - Waterfall'!BE10-'Group 2 -
    Waterfall'!BM10-'Group 2 - Waterfall'!BU10)

This formula pays the M-1 tranche's Net WAC Rate Carryover Amount from the excess spread after the Class A certificates have received any necessary Net WAC Rate Carryover distributions. Copy and paste this formula over the range of cells P10:P509. Also, in cell P7 enter the text **M-1 Net WAC Carryover Covered By XS**.

27. Repeat Steps 22, 23, and 26 for the M-2, M-3, M-4, and M-5 certificates. To aid with the location of these sections the following labels should be entered in the corresponding cell references on the Mezzanine – Waterfall sheet (replace x with the appropriate tranche number):

M-x Current Net WAC Carryover Amount (Required): V7, AD7, AL7, AT7
M-x Cumulative Net WAC Carryover Amount (pre-XS Rec): W7, AE7, AM7, AU7
M-x Net WAC Carryover Covered By XS: X7, AF7, AN7, AV7

The appropriate formula variations from Steps 22, 23, and 26 should be entered starting in row 10 of each of these columns and copied through to row 509.

28. With all the Net WAC Rate Carryover Amounts calculated, we can come back to the excess spread summary section and add up the total amount used. On the Mezzanine – Waterfall sheet in cell BG10 enter the following formula:

=SUM('Group 1 - Waterfall'!AG10,'Group 2 -
    Waterfall'!AG10,'Group 2 - Waterfall'!AO10,'Group 2 -
    Waterfall'!AW10,'Group 2 - Waterfall'!BE10,'Group 2 -
    Waterfall'!BM10,'Group 2 - Waterfall'!BU10,P10,X10,AF10,AN10,AV10)

Copy and paste this formula over the range of cells BG10:BG509.

29. To move the cash along enter the following formula in cell BH10:

=BF10-BG10

Copy and paste this formula over the range of cells BH10:BH509. Figure 6.10 shows this section.

	BG	BH
5		
6		
7	**(iv) Net WAC Carryover**	**XS Remaining Post Net WAC Carryover**
8	290,844	14,186,649
9		
10	-	-
11	-	0
12	-	-
13	-	-
14	-	-
15	-	0

FIGURE 6.10 Cash is moved along through the excess spread allocations.

30. We have one more step to complete the waterfall. Technically there are two steps as defined on page S-99 and excerpted here:

    (v) to the holders of the Class CE Certificates as provided in the pooling and servicing agreement; and
    (vi) to the holders of the Residual Certificates, any remaining amounts; provided that if such distribution date is the distribution date immediately following the expiration of the latest prepayment charge term or any distribution date thereafter, then any such remaining amounts will be distributed first, to the holders of the Class P Certificates, until the Certificate Principal Balance thereof has been reduced to zero; and second, to the holders of the Residual Certificates.

    The reason this is considered one step is because it is a release to the residual holders. Because we are not modeling the Class P certificates, we can end the waterfall at Step 5. Enter the following formula in cell BI10:

    =BH10

    A bit ridiculous as it is just the previous column, but still the formula aids you in distinguishing amounts. Copy and paste this formula over the range of cells BI10:BI509. Also, enter the text, (v) **Released to CE/Residual Class** in cell BI7.

At this point, with the waterfall complete, some serious congratulations are in order. You have progressed through an incredibly complex waterfall where cash weaves in and out of the hands of multiple parties, each taking their allocated share along the way. The system has been detailed in legal vernacular and transferred to an electronic medium. This is the essence of reverse engineering a Wall Street transaction.

Now before we start patting ourselves on the back, jumping out of our chairs among the cubicles, and telling our managers about the model, we should take time to make sure we are correct. In the next chapter, we will learn how to internally validate the model and produce a couple of sheets that verify whether we are reverse engineering the deal accurately.

CHAPTER 7

Auditing the Model

Whenever a person hears the word "audit," their heart begins to race and a sense of dread sets in. There is probably good reason, because when it comes to auditing a model, the audit determines if the efforts getting to this point have been justified. The previous statement is a bit of an exaggeration—even if the audit proves that something is wrong, it usually means fixing part of what has been completed thus far, rather than a complete loss of work up to this point.

Auditing a model that has been based on a public document such as a prospectus supplement, is made easier by the documentation, which often contains results from the original transaction creator. As we will see in this chapter, the example prospectus supplement that we have been working with has a detailed section to assist in model auditing. The section is a series of decrement tables that show each tranche's pay-down over time, under various scenarios. Prospectus supplements, in general, often have similar data detailing the performance of the transaction given various stresses to key assumptions. Some produce decrement tables as we see in the example, whereas others offer yield and duration tables.

These output sections can be used directly by a reverse engineer to check whether their model produces the same results as those in the documentation. Also, if a model audit is being conducted, two parties can *tie* (in financial modeling lingo to *tie* a model is to verify that the numbers being checked are the same between both models) a model to a certain degree of accuracy with each other and the prospectus. Usually this is done with a respected auditor who can issue a letter attesting to the degree of accuracy of verification.

In addition, the model should be internally validated with a few key metrics. Reverse engineers not only want to check that their model ties to the documentation, but that it is also structurally sound. It would be a grave error to create a model that "makes up" cash. Checks should be implemented to test whether the cash flowing into the transaction is all accounted for. Also, a system should be set up to make it clear to the model user that there is a problem, such as tranches not paying down or assets with zero remaining terms, and so on.

Finally, you may want to expand on the analysis and use the results for other decisions. In the example model, although we will audit the model using the decrement tables, we will also create an Analytics sheet to measure other key measures.

MODEL BUILDER 7.1

1. The first section that we want to check is whether the model we created is correct or not. We will do this by checking if the results of our model tie to those of scenarios in the prospectus. Scenario decrement tables are located in the current prospectus supplement starting on page S-74. The decrement tables are organized by four different prepayment scenarios as shown in Figure 7.1.

   The tables are then organized by providing each tranche's annual current balance as a percent of the tranche's original balance. We have a sheet called Balances in the example model, but we should create a separate output sheet that organizes that data in the same format as the prospectus supplement's decrement tables so that we can quickly compare the two. Start this by inserting a new worksheet in the example model and naming it **Output**.

2. The top of the Output sheet will contain information relevant to the transaction as a whole and the scenario under analysis. Much of this is creating labels and referencing existing cells. Enter the following text or formula references in the following cells on the Output sheet:

   A1:   =gbl_ProjnName
   A3:   S3 (merged): **INPUTS & ASSUMPTIONS**
   A4:   **Current Balance**
   A5:   **Interest Rates**
   A6:   **Maximum Periods**
   A7:   **Total Number of Loans**
   A8:   **Servicer Advances**
   C4:   =Inputs!I13+Inputs!I14
   C5:   =assets_FxdFlt
   C6:   =gbl_TotalPeriods
   C7:   =gbl_LoanID1+gbl_LoanID2
   C8:   =gbl_ServicerAdv
   E4:   **Loss Stress**
   E5:   **Prepayment Multiple**
   E6:   **Current Prepay Scenario**

Prepayment Scenarios[1]			
I	II	III	IV
50%	100%	150%	200%

FIGURE 7.1 There are four different prepayment scenarios based on the prospectus supplement's base prepayment curve.

F4: =Inputs!E11
F5: =Inputs!E12
F6: =struc_CurPpayScen
H4: **Cut-Off Date**
H5: **Closing Date**
H6: **First Payment Date**
H7: **Day-Count System**
H8: **Pmt Frequency**
I4: =gbl_OrigDate
I5: =gbl_ClosingDate
I6: =gbl_FirstPayDate
I7: =gbl_DayCountSys
I8: =gbl_PMTFreq
K4: **Servicing Fees**
K5: **PMI Fee**
K6: **WA Combined Fees**
K7: **Stepdown Hard Date**
K8: **Stepdown Sr Enh Pct**
L4: =fees_ServicingFee
L5: =struc_WAPMIFee
L6: =struc_WACombFees
L7: =struc_StepDnDate
L8: =struc_StepDnSrPct
A11: S11 (merged): **COLLATERAL & LIABILITY INFORMATION AND DEC TABLES**

3. The major part of the Output sheet should be the decrements. Prior to the tranche percentages we need to provide some labels and basic information. Enter the following text and cell references:

A13: **Class**
A14: **Current Balance**
A15: **Yield**
C13: =Balances!D11
E13: =Balances!P11
F13: =Balances!T11
H13: =Balances!Z11
I13: =Balances!AF11
K13: =Balances!AL11
L13: =Balances!AR11
N13: =Balances!AX11
O13: =Balances!BE11
P13: =Balances!BI11
Q13: =Balances!BM11

R13: =Balances!BQ11
S13: =Balances!BU11
E14: =Balances!P14
F14: =Balances!T14
H14: =Balances!Z14
I14: =Balances!AF14
K14: =Balances!AL14
L14: =Balances!AR14
N14: =Balances!AX14
O14: =Balances!BE14
P14: =Balances!BI14
Q14: =Balances!BM14
R14: =Balances!BQ14
S14: =Balances!BU14

Note that some columns are skipped to adhere to the format seen in the example model. Cell formatting is entirely up to you, but the format seen in the example model is suggested. Also, whereas we have created space for each tranche's yield, we have not created the sheet yet that contains this. We will come back to fill in the yields after we create that sheet.

4. The primary part of the Output sheet uses the OFFSET function to find each tranche's correct annual balance and then divides that balance by the tranche's original balance. To implement this, enter the following formula in cell E18:

=OFFSET(Balances!$P$14,A18*12,0)/$E$14

Copy and paste this formula over the range of cells E18:E48. Repeat this step for each tranche, changing the column references so they reference each tranche's appropriate balances. Make sure that the A column does not change—this is set to multiply each period by 12 to provide the correct row reference to retrieve the annual balances.

5. At this point, you can check the example model's percentages of original balance against the percentages in the prospectus supplement. Unfortunately the prospectus supplement only provides whole percentages with no decimal places, limiting the precision of the tie-out. The example model ties with every percentage in the prospectus supplement, with the exception of five numbers being off by 1 percentage point or less. Two of the 1 percentage point differences are for the A-2F tranche, which has a unique pay-down caused by the lockout feature. This feature works based on percentages and if the original deal structurer rounded to a precision that is different from the example model then small differences can be seen. Overall the degree of difference is very small and the example model has reverse engineered the transaction. Figure 7.2 shows the complete Output sheet.

Project Name

INPUTS & ASSUMPTIONS

Current Balance	1,131,286,782	Cut-Off Date	5/1/2006	
Interest Rates	Fixed	Closing Date	5/25/2006	
Maximum Periods	500	First Payment Date	6/25/2006	
Total Number of Loans	110	Day-Count System	30 / 360	
Servicer Advances	No	Pmt Frequency	Monthly	

Loss Stress	1.0x	
Prepayment Multipl	1.0x	
Current Prepay $cce	150.00%	

Servicing Fees	0.38%
PMI Fee	0.30%
WA Combined Fees	0.82%
Stepdown Hard Date	6/25/2009
Stepdown Sr Enh Pct	19.30%

COLLATERAL & LIABILITY INFORMATION AND DEC TABLES

Class	Collateral	A-1	A-2A	A-2B	A-2C	A-2D	A-2E	A-2F	M-1	M-2	M-3	M-4	M-5
Current Balance	1,131,286,782	484,445,000	203,118,000	65,311,000	83,228,000	86,053,000	53,316,000	54,559,000	43,211,000	22,626,000	8,484,000	10,741,000	5,657,000
Yield	9.33%	7.15%	6.82%	6.20%	6.45%	6.61%	6.23%	6.71%	7.01%	7.02%	7.03%	0.00%	0.00%
Year													
0	100%	100%	100%	100%	100%	100%	100%	100%	100%	100%	100%	100%	100%
1	73%	70%	18%	100%	100%	100%	100%	100%	100%	100%	100%	100%	100%
2	47%	42%	0%	0%	33%	100%	100%	100%	100%	100%	100%	100%	100%
3	31%	23%	0%	0%	0%	22%	90%	83%	40%	40%	40%	40%	100%
4	20%	18%	0%	0%	0%	0%	42%	73%	26%	26%	26%	17%	27%
5	13%	11%	0%	0%	0%	0%	23%	52%	17%	17%	6%	0%	0%
6	8%	7%	0%	0%	0%	0%	15%	33%	11%	3%	0%	0%	0%
7	5%	5%	0%	0%	0%	0%	15%	16%	4%	1%	0%	0%	0%
8	3%	3%	0%	0%	0%	0%	10%	5%	0%	0%	0%	0%	0%
9	2%	2%	0%	0%	0%	0%	5%	0%	0%	0%	0%	0%	0%
10	1%	1%	0%	0%	0%	0%	1%	0%	0%	0%	0%	0%	0%
11	1%	0%	0%	0%	0%	0%	0%	0%	0%	0%	0%	0%	0%
12	0%	0%	0%	0%	0%	0%	0%	0%	0%	0%	0%	0%	0%
13	0%	0%	0%	0%	0%	0%	0%	0%	0%	0%	0%	0%	0%
14	0%	0%	0%	0%	0%	0%	0%	0%	0%	0%	0%	0%	0%
15	0%	0%	0%	0%	0%	0%	0%	0%	0%	0%	0%	0%	0%
16	0%	0%	0%	0%	0%	0%	0%	0%	0%	0%	0%	0%	0%
17	0%	0%	0%	0%	0%	0%	0%	0%	0%	0%	0%	0%	0%
18	0%	0%	0%	0%	0%	0%	0%	0%	0%	0%	0%	0%	0%
19	0%	0%	0%	0%	0%	0%	0%	0%	0%	0%	0%	0%	0%
20	0%	0%	0%	0%	0%	0%	0%	0%	0%	0%	0%	0%	0%
21	0%	0%	0%	0%	0%	0%	0%	0%	0%	0%	0%	0%	0%
22	0%	0%	0%	0%	0%	0%	0%	0%	0%	0%	0%	0%	0%
23	0%	0%	0%	0%	0%	0%	0%	0%	0%	0%	0%	0%	0%
24	0%	0%	0%	0%	0%	0%	0%	0%	0%	0%	0%	0%	0%
25	0%	0%	0%	0%	0%	0%	0%	0%	0%	0%	0%	0%	0%
26	0%	0%	0%	0%	0%	0%	0%	0%	0%	0%	0%	0%	0%
27	0%	0%	0%	0%	0%	0%	0%	0%	0%	0%	0%	0%	0%

FIGURE 7.2 The Output sheet is the main tool used to verify the model and quickly describe results.

6. The next step is to create internal validations to makes sure the model runs correctly as we change variables or input different data. The major internal validation is to make sure that all the cash we introduce into the structure is accounted for in the waterfall. We need to do this for both loan groups. Go to the Group 1 – Waterfall sheet and enter the following text in the corresponding cell references:

AV7: **Cash In**
AW7: **Cash Out**
AX7: **Difference**

Next enter the following formulas in the corresponding cell references:

AV10: **=(L10+M10+N10+O10+P10+R10+AK10)**
AW10: **=V10+AB10+AH10+AP10+AS10+AT10**
AX10: **=AV10-AW10**
AV8:   **=SUM(AV10:AV509)**
AW8:   **=SUM(AW10:AW509)**
AX8:   **=SUM(AX10:AX509)**

Copy and paste the formulas entered in AV10, AW10, and AX10 within their respective columns, down to row 509. The Group 1 cash check is shown in Figure 7.3.

	AV	AW	AX
5			
6	*Cash In vs. Cash Out*		
7	Cash In	Cash Out	Difference
8	642,903,670	642,903,670	-
9			
10	9,863,727	9,863,727	-
11	11,050,239	11,050,239	-
12	12,213,258	12,213,258	-
13	13,344,543	13,344,543	-
14	14,435,734	14,435,734	-
15	15,478,054	15,478,054	-

FIGURE 7.3 By independently adding up all the cash that should flow into the model and subtracting the cash that should flow out of the model, we can see if we made up or lost cash.

7. We now need to repeat Step 6 for the second loan group. Enter the following text in the corresponding cell references:

CX7: **Cash In**
CY7: **Cash Out**
CZ7: **Difference**

Next enter the following formulas:

CX10: =L10+M10+N10+O10+P10+R10+BY10
CY10: =V10+AB10+AJ10+AR10+AZ10+BH10+BP10+BV10+CD10+
       CH10+CJ10+CL10+CN10+CP10+CR10+CU10+CV10
CZ10: =CX10-CY10
CX8: =SUM(CX10:CX509)
CY8: =SUM(CY10:CY509)
CZ8: =SUM(CZ10:CZ509)

As with the first loan group, make sure to copy and paste the formulas in cell CX10, cell CY10, and cell CZ10 in their respective columns, down to row 509.

8. Although these internal validations are good to have on the waterfall sheets, it would be preferable to have a section on the Inputs sheet to see if there are problems immediately after running a scenario.

   Go to the Inputs sheet and enter the following text in the corresponding cells:

G11: **Group 1: Cash In = Cash Out**
G12: **Group 2: Cash In = Cash Out**

Next enter the following formulas:

I11: =IF('Group 1 - Waterfall'!AX8<0.01,"OK","ERROR")
I12: =IF('Group 2 - Waterfall'!CZ8<0.01,"OK","ERROR")

9. Another excellent validation is whether the assets paid down correctly. The following formulas check the payout amounts and whether or not there is an asset balance at the end of legal maturity. Enter the following text in the corresponding cells:

G13: **Group 1 Pay-down**
G14: **Group 2 Pay-down**
G15: **Balance at Legal Final**

Also, enter the following formulas:

I13: =('Group 1 - Waterfall'!H8+'Group 1 - Waterfall'!N8
    + 'Group 1 - Waterfall'!R8)

I14: ='Group 2 - Waterfall'!H8+'Group 2 - Waterfall'!N8
+ 'Group 2 - Waterfall'!R8

I15: ='Group 1 - Waterfall'!G369+'Group 2 - Waterfall'!G369

10. The final set of validations is focused on the data tape. One of the most frustrating parts of working with large pools of loans or representative lines is the occasional error on the data tape that prevents the asset amortization code from running correctly. Typical problems include loans with very small remaining terms or balances. Enter the following formulas in their corresponding cell references to check for these types of errors:

K11: =MIN('Group 1 - Assets'!F1:OFFSET('Group 1 - Assets'!F1,
gbl_LoanID1,0),'Group 2 - Assets'!F1:OFFSET('Group 2 - Assets'!F1,
gbl_LoanID2,0))

K12: =MAX('Group 1 - Assets'!F1:OFFSET('Group 1 - Assets'!F1,
gbl_LoanID1,0),'Group 2 - Assets'!F1:OFFSET('Group 2 - Assets'!F1,
gbl_LoanID2,0))

K13: =MIN('Group 1 - Assets'!D1:OFFSET('Group 1 - Assets'!D1,
gbl_LoanID1,0),'Group 2 - Assets'!D1:OFFSET('Group 2 - Assets'!D1,
gbl_LoanID2,0))

K14: =MAX('Group 1 - Assets'!D1:OFFSET('Group 1 - Assets'!D1,
gbl_LoanID1,0),'Group 2 - Assets'!D1:OFFSET('Group 2 - Assets'!D1,
gbl_LoanID2,0))

K15: =IF(OR(K11<1,K13<1),"ERROR", "OK")

Also create labels for each of these previous entries by entering the following text in the corresponding cell references:

J11: **Data Tape Rem Term Min**
J12: **Data Tape Rem Term Max**
J13: **Data Tape Balance Min**
J14: **Data Tape Balance Max**
J15: **Data Tape Error**

Figure 7.4 depicts the internal validation section of the Inputs sheet.

	F	G	H	I	J	K	L
9							
10		TESTS					
11		Group 1: Cash In = Cash Out		OK	Data Tape Rem Term Min	173	
12		Group 2: Cash In = Cash Out		OK	Data Tape Rem Term Max	359	
13		Group 1 Paydown		532,064,773	Data Tape Balance Min	16,107	
14		Group 2 Paydown		599,222,009	Data Tape Balance Max	122,389,585	
15		Balance at Legal Final		0	Data Tape Error	OK	
16							

FIGURE 7.4 Internal validations on the Inputs sheet are a quick way to see if the model is operating properly.

11. The final section we should create is an Analytics sheet, where we can perform time-related calculations such as yield and duration. Insert a new worksheet and name it **Analytics**. First, set up labels for the multiple fields that we will fill in by entering the following text:

A1: **Analytics**	E7: **Accrued Interest**
A17: **Period**	E8: **Dollar Price**
B17: **Date**	E9: **Yield (Monthly)**
C17: **Day Factor**	E10: **BEY (Annual)**
E5: **Initial Principal**	E11: **PV vs. Price**
E6: **Price**	E12: **Duration**

12. With basic labels, the next section is to add the tranche references. Enter the following text and references in the appropriate cell references:

F17: **Assets**	M17: **=Balances!AX11**
G17: **=Balances!P11**	N17: **=Balances!BE11**
H17: **=Balances!T11**	O17: **=Balances!BI11**
I17: **=Balances!Z11**	P17: **=Balances!BM11**
J17: **=Balances!AF11**	Q17: **=Balances!BQ11**
K17: **=Balances!AL11**	R17: **=Balances!BU11**
L17: **=Balances!AR11**	

We should also reference these tranche names. In cell F4, enter the following formula:

=F17

Copy and paste this formula over the range of cells F4:R4.

13. To get the correct timing, we need to implement the following formulas in their corresponding cell references:

A19: **='Group 1 - Waterfall'!A9**
B19: **='Group 1 - Waterfall'!B9**
C20: **='Group 1 - Waterfall'!C10**

Copy and paste each of these formulas over the cell ranges in parentheses: A19 (A19:A519), B19 (B19:B519), C20 (C20:C519).

14. The purpose of this framework is to get the periodic cash flows for the assets and each tranche of debt. We will reference the appropriate cells to get the cash flow,

but we also want to be able to discount the cash flow at the estimated monthly yield. Enter the following formula in cell F19:

=('Group 1 - Waterfall'!N10+'Group 1 - Waterfall'!L10+'Group 1 - Waterfall'!M10+'Group 1 - Waterfall'!N10+'Group 1 - Waterfall'!O10+'Group 1 - Waterfall'!P10+'Group 1 - Waterfall'!R10+'Group 2 - Waterfall'!N10+'Group 2 - Waterfall'!L10+'Group 2 - Waterfall'!M10+'Group 2 - Waterfall'!N10+'Group 2 - Waterfall'!O10+'Group 2 - Waterfall'!P10+'Group 2 - Waterfall'!R10)/(1+F$9)^$A19

The reason we are discounting by the estimated yield is because the system we are setting up will be ready to be optimized, so we can solve for the actual yield. The definition of the yield is the rate at which the sum of the present values of a series of cash flows is discounted back so it is equal to the original price. If we solve for this equality by changing the monthly yield, we will eventually get the actual yield of the cash flows. Copy and paste this formula over the range of cells F19:F519.

15. Step 13 should be repeated for each tranche of debt, making sure to change the references so it sums all the cash flow paid to the tranche. Note that in this section, we capture all the flows to the tranches. This can be more than just what is represented on the Balances sheet. For instance, the Mezzanine Certificates include additional flows from columns such as the Net WAC Rate Carryover and Interest Carry Forward. Another nuance of this process is that by using the periods in column A, we assume equal time periods between each period, including the first period. If there is an uneven amount of time between the transaction close and the first payment date, this formula should be adjusted.

16. The next step is to create summary information above the discounted cash flows. Enter the following formulas in their corresponding cell references:

F5: ='Group 1 - Waterfall'!G10+ 'Group 2 - Waterfall'!G10	M5: =Balances!AX14
G5: =Balances!P14	N5: =Balances!BE14
H5: =Balances!T14	O5: =Balances!BI14
I5: =Balances!Z14	P5: =Balances!BM14
J5: =Balances!AF14	Q5: =Balances!BQ14
K5: =Balances!AL14	R5: =Balances!BU14
L5: =Balances!AL14	

17. Row 6 is reserved for entering any pricing information for the tranches. For now we will assume 100%. Enter the value **100%** in the range of cells F6:R6.

18. Row 7 is where any accrued interest should be entered. For now we will assume 0 accrued interest for each tranche. Enter the value 0 in each cell in the range of cells F7:R7.
19. Given a price and accrued interest, we can now calculate a new dollar price for the tranche. Enter the following formula in cell F8:

=F5*F6+F7

Copy and paste this formula over the range of cells F8:R8.
20. Row 9 is for the monthly yield. For now enter 0% in each cell in the range of cells F9:R9. This cell will change as we iterate to find the correct yield.
21. The next row down converts the monthly yield to an annual yield based on the bond equivalent yield (BEY) calculation. Enter the following formula in cell F10:

=2*((1+F9)^6-1)

Copy and paste this formula over the range of cells F10:R10. Alternatively, you could also multiply the monthly yield by 12 to get a normal annual yield.
22. In row 11, we will compare the sum of the present values of the cash flows to the original price. This tells us if we need to optimize the monthly yield calculation. Enter the following formula in cell F11:

=SUM(F19:F519)-F8

Copy and paste this formula over the range of cells F11:R11.
23. The final metric is the duration of the asset or tranche. Enter the following formula in cell F12:

=IF(SUM(F19:F519)=0,0,SUMPRODUCT(F19:F519,
    $A$19:$A$519)/(SUM(F19:F519)*12))

Be careful when using duration if the security is floating rate—duration is not very useful for variable rate securities. Copy and paste this formula over the range of cells F12:R12. Figure 7.5 shows how the Analytics sheet should look.
24. In its current state the analytics sheet can be used, but it is inefficient. A user would have to perform a goal seek on the yield by setting the PV vs. Price row to zero and changing the yield for each column. We can automate this by creating a subroutine. Go to the VBE and insert a new module. Name this module **Sensitivities**. Enter the following code in this module:

```
Sub SolveYield()

Const YieldChange As String = "rng_YieldChange"
Const Target As String = "rng_YieldTarget"
Dim TargetRange As Range
```

	A	B	C	D	E	F	G	H
1	**Analytics**							
2								
3								
4						Assets	A-1	A-2A
5					Initial Principal	1,131,286,782	484,445,000	203,118,000
6					Price	100%	100%	100%
7					Accrued Interest	-	-	-
8					Dollar Price	1,131,286,782	484,445,000	203,118,000
9					Yield (Monthly)	0.76%	0.59%	0.56%
10					BEY (Annual)	9.33%	7.15%	6.82%
11					PV vs Price	(0)	(0)	0
12					Duration	2.09	1.98	0.61
13								
14								
15								
16								
17	Period	Date	Day Factor			Assets	A-1	A-2A
18								
19	0	05/25/06				21,567,788	9,166,228	8,606,593
20	1	06/25/06	0.083			23,905,725	10,295,705	9,894,527
21	2	07/25/06	0.083			26,155,695	11,389,455	11,142,217
22	3	08/25/06	0.083			28,301,837	12,439,884	12,340,768
23	4	09/25/06	0.083			30,328,669	13,439,454	13,481,456
24	5	10/25/06	0.083			32,218,655	14,380,405	14,553,570

FIGURE 7.5 The Analytics sheet performs calculations that are useful to both investors and structurers.

```
Dim YieldRange As Range
Dim i As Integer

i = 1

For i = 1 To Range(Target).Cells.Count
    Set TargetRange = Range(Target).Cells(1, i)
    Set YieldRange = Range(YieldChange).Cells(1, i)
        TargetRange.GoalSeek Goal:=0, ChangingCell:=YieldRange
Next i

End Sub
```

This subroutine loops through each yield, optimizes the difference between the present value of the cash flows and the original price, and then moves on to the next tranche. To assist with using this macro, go to the Inputs sheet and create a form button next to the Calculate Asset button. Name this button **Calculate Analytics** and assign it the **SolveYield** macro.

At this point the model is now complete. We have the ability to change assumptions, create cash flow, run the cash through a very complex waterfall, check to see if the results are in line with the original structurer's results, and now calculate other important metrics regarding the deal. It is very important to implement a decent analytics and output framework. If the calculations are unusable, the most complex and sophisticated models can go unused.

CHAPTER 8

Conclusion of Example Transaction and Final Thoughts on Reverse Engineering

The prospectus supplement has been read, the model built and verified, so now what? A few concepts that are part of the example transaction require discussion and we have some general thoughts on reverse engineering to go over. With regard to transaction concepts, the example model that was selected provided enough breadth of concepts to encompass the language and formulas found in many types of mortgage-related deals, structured transaction, and even general corporate transactions. Particularly in this deal, there are items that we could have gone into detail about, but chose not to given the applicability to an audience of readers.

MORTGAGE INSURANCE AND SERVICER ADVANCES

One of the more obvious sections is analyzing the impact of mortgage insurance on the transaction. Mortgage insurance is provided by the PMI Mortgage Insurance Co. (PMI) and is detailed starting on page S-100 of the prospectus supplement. If we wanted to go further with the mortgage analysis, we could have taken the PMI Coverage Percentages and Claim Amount definitions found on page S-103 and integrated them into the analysis.

The result of such an implementation would help with those running loss sensitivities, as a certain percentage will be absorbed by the mortgage insurance. One of the justifications for not reverse engineering the mortgage insurance is that it adds a third-party source of credit risk to the modeling results. The payment of the mortgage insurance is predicated upon the creditworthiness of the PMI Mortgage Insurance Co. If they suffer a severe impact resulting from a downturn of the real estate market there is a chance that they will not be able to pay the claims against the policies. Therefore, any model that took the PMI policy into the results of the analysis could be overestimating results.

A similar thought process arises for servicer advances. Servicer advances are also third-party credit risks. However, in reality, servicers play an important role in smoothing the cash flows of transactions, but as seen by the 2007/2008 credit crisis, these servicers can encounter highly stressful scenarios where they may look closely at each loan they are advancing upon. If the advances become too high because of system-wide delinquency increases, the servicers themselves could be brought to dangerous levels of exposure as they may or may not get reimbursed depending on further deterioration in the market. Combined with this are regulations that are constantly being enacted or proposed to help regulate this process.

REVERSE ENGINEERING IN THE CURRENT AND FUTURE MARKET

This book uses a mortgage transaction as an example of how to reverse engineer a deal, but the process needs to be thought of in more general terms. A rigorous reverse engineering seems excruciatingly detailed, but it is for a good purpose—modern Wall Street transactions are becoming ever more complicated with fewer professionals thoroughly understanding the underlying mechanics. This is evident as recent events in the credit markets have called into question previous practices of solely relying on rating agencies or third parties to gauge the quality of a transaction. Investors themselves need to understand the nuances of each transaction prior to committing funds.

In discussions with professionals regarding the topic of whose responsibility it is to thoroughly analyze a transaction, I was somewhat surprised by one buy-side professional who thought it was not the investor's responsibility. His belief was that other parties should simplify the transaction so the investor can make a quick purchase decision. Given the products that investors have been trading on Wall Street, I have to disagree completely with that thought and suggest that the investor share the burden of thoroughly understanding the detailed processes and mechanics of a complex transaction.

Whether this information is garnered by hiring a third party to go through the full reversal process or training internal staff, full comprehension of possible performance is the only way a company can truly add appropriate risks to their books. This painstaking process is also one way to help avoid situations such as the 2007/2008 credit crisis. Some investment professionals were selecting securities based solely on ratings and yield. If there were two securities rated *A* and one offered 5 basis points (bps) more yield, often an investor would simply choose the higher yielding security. We have found that this asset selection methodology does not work.

Going forth, Wall Street will continue to produce innovative and complex transactions. Staff at those banks needs to verify that their models are correct, understand what their competition is doing, and investors need to be able to pick apart the transactions that are being offered to them. Fully reverse engineering these transactions is the best way to accomplish all these tasks. With a fully reversed model built, one can understand how cash moves in a deal and how investment in any level of the transaction should perform.

Appendix

The following instructions are optional implementations to the model. They can assist in speeding up the development of reverse engineering transactions or even just generally building models.

AUTOMATIC RANGE NAMING

Earlier, in Chapter 4, we created a Liability sheet and entered in all the pertinent information for the transaction's liabilities. In the example model, there were seventeen unique liabilities with multiple characteristics that required naming. This can be done by hand, but it is very time consuming.

If we examine the naming convention set up in the example model, we see that we created a standard name for each type of liability and then attached an ID number for the liability to the end of the name. For example, the name of D6 on the Liabilities sheet is liab1_Adv_Rate. In this case, the standard name is liab$x$_Adv_Rate, where x is replaced by the liability number. Each liability will have an advance rate cell, which is distinguished by the liabilities number. So we need two pieces of information to create names for the liabilities: a liability input name and a liability number.

Although it might seem like column C is a good candidate for the liability input name, the names have spaces, which Excel does not allow as part of a named cell or range of cells. We will create alternate input names that do not include spaces. In the range of cells B4:B14, enter the following text in the corresponding cell. Note that we are *not* naming these cells, but entering the text as the value for the cells:

B4: ID
B5: Name
B6: Adv_Rate
B7: Balance
B8: Price
B9: Int_Type
B10: DayCtSys
B11: FxdRate
B12: FxdRateClnUp
B13: Index
B14: Margin

The area should look like Figure A.1.

	A	B	C
1	***Liabilities***		
2			
3			**Tranches**
4		ID	**ID**
5		Name	**Name**
6		Adv_Rate	**Advance Rate**
7		Balance	**Initial Certificate Principal Balance**
8		Price	**Price**
9		Int_Type	**Interest Type**
10		DayCtSys	**Day Count System**
11		FxdRate	**Fixed Rate**
12		FxdRateClnUp	**Fixed Rate Post-Clean Up Pct**
13		Index	**Index**
14		Margin	**Margin**

FIGURE A.1 Column B is a hidden column that contains the text values, which will be read into parts of named cells through a VBA subroutine.

Prior to naming all the items, there are a few cells that we will have to name to assist in the process. On the Liabilities sheet, name the following cell and ranges:

C4: **strt_liabTable**
B4: B15: **rng_liabFields**
D4: U4: **rng_liabIDs**

With those cells named, we can implement the subroutine to automate the naming of each item. Go to the VBE and insert a new module. Name this module `Misc`. Enter the following code:

```
Sub AddNames()

Dim i As Integer, k As Integer, TrancheCt As Integer,
 FieldCt As Integer
Dim LiabFields As Variant

TrancheCt = Range("rng_liabIDs").Count
LiabFields = Range("rng_liabFields")
FieldCt = Range("rng_liabFields").Count

For i = 0 To (FieldCt - 2)
    For k = 1 To (TrancheCt - 1)
        Range("strt_liabTable").Offset(i, k).Name = "liab"
```

```
        & k & "_" & LiabFields(i + 1, 1)
    Next k
Next i

End Sub
```

Go back to the Liabilities sheet and create a button or image. Assign the AddNames subroutine to this button or image. Finally, column B, where the liabilities names for the Excel name are stored, can be hidden for formatting purposes.

About the CD-ROM

INTRODUCTION

This appendix provides you with information on the contents of the CD that accompanies this book. For the latest and greatest information, please refer to the ReadMe file located at the root of the CD.

SYSTEM REQUIREMENTS

- A computer with a processor running at 120 Mhz or faster.
- At least 32 MB of total RAM installed on your computer; for best performance, we recommend at least 64 MB.
- A CD-ROM drive.
- Microsoft Excel 2003 or higher.
- Microsoft Excel Add-In: Analysis ToolPak.
- Microsoft Excel Add-In: Analysis ToolPak—VBA.

NOTE: Many popular spreadsheet programs are capable of reading Microsoft Excel files. However, users should be aware that a slight amount of formatting might be lost when using a program other than Microsoft Excel. This also applies to PDF programs.

USING THE CD WITH WINDOWS

To install the items from the CD to your hard drive, follow these steps:

1. Insert the CD into your computer's CD-ROM drive.
2. The CD-ROM interface will appear. The interface provides a simple point-and-click way to explore the contents of the CD.

If the opening screen of the CD-ROM does not appear automatically, follow these steps to access the CD:

3. Click the Start button on the left end of the taskbar and then choose Run from the menu that pops up.

4. In the dialog box that appears, type *d:***start.exe**. (If your CD-ROM drive is not drive *d*, fill in the appropriate letter in place of *d*.) This brings up the CD Interface described in the preceding set of steps.

WHAT'S ON THE CD

The following sections provide a summary of the software and other materials you'll find on the CD.

Content

Prospectus   A pdf version of the example prospectus used throughout the book. While the prospectus can be downloaded from the SEC Edgar web site, it is important to use this version as the page numbers correspond to references throughout the text. Note that the HTML version of the prospectus on the SEC Edgar web site does not have page numbers.

Model.xls   The final and complete model that is built by following the Model Builder exercises throughout the book.

Applications

The following applications are on the CD:

Adobe Reader is a freeware application for viewing files in the Adobe Portable Document format.

Shareware programs are fully functional, trial versions of copyrighted programs. If you like particular programs, register with their authors for a nominal fee and receive licenses, enhanced versions, and technical support.

Freeware programs are copyrighted games, applications, and utilities that are free for personal use. Unlike shareware, these programs do not require a fee or provide technical support.

GNU software is governed by its own license, which is included inside the folder of the GNU product. See the GNU license for more details.

Trial, demo, or evaluation versions are usually limited either by time or functionality (such as being unable to save projects). Some trial versions are very sensitive to system date changes. If you alter your computer's date, the programs will "time out" and no longer be functional.

CUSTOMER CARE

If you have trouble with the CD-ROM, please call the Wiley Product Technical Support phone number at 1-800-762-2974. Outside the United States, call 1-317-572-3994. You can also contact Wiley Product Technical Support at **http://support.wiley .com**. John Wiley & Sons will provide technical support only for installation and other general quality control items. For technical support on the applications themselves, consult the program's vendor or author.

To place additional orders or to request information about other Wiley products, please call 1–877–762-2974.

For more information regarding the CD-ROM
About the CD-ROM section on page 19.

WILEY

John Wiley & Sons, Inc.